CHILDHOOD

IN

ANGLO-SAXON ENGLAND

CHILDHOOD

IN

ANGLO-SAXON ENGLAND

SALLY CRAWFORD

SUTTON PUBLISHING

First published in the United Kingdom in 1999 by
Sutton Publishing Limited · Phoenix Mill
Thrupp · Stroud · Gloucestershire · GL5 2BU

British Library Cataloguing in Publication Data

A catalogue record for this book is available from the British Library

ISBN 0 7509 1918 3

 ALAN SUTTON™ and SUTTON™ are the
trade marks of Sutton Publishing Limited

Typeset in 11/12pt Ehrhardt.
Typesetting and origination by
Sutton Publishing Limited.
Printed in Great Britain by
Bookcraft, Midsomer Norton, Somerset.

Contents

List of Illustrations and Tables

Picture Credits and Acknowledgements

I am very grateful to the following owners of images for allowing their illustrations to be reproduced here:

S.C. Hawkes, numbers 1, 16, 18, 26, 33, 50; the British Library, 2, 3, 21, 22, 23, 24, 30, 32, 34, 35, 41, 42, 43, 44, 45, 46, 47, 48, 49; A. Howrie, 4; English Heritage, 5; Norfolk Museums Service, 6; D. Brothwell, 7, 8; Bodleian Library, 20, 27, 28, 29, 39; Oxford Archaeological Unit, 51.

I owe a debt of thanks for the academic support, advice and encouragement given by colleagues at St Hilda's College, Oxford, The Queen's College, Oxford, Corpus Christi College, Oxford, and the Department of Ancient History and Archaeology at the University of Birmingham, with particular thanks to Graham Norrie. This book has been a long time in the making, and would never have begun without the support of Sonia Hawkes and the great help and guidance of John Blair. Teresa Clay has given valuable encouragement and constructive advice throughout, and my very grateful thanks to all the friends who have listened patiently and have always been optimistic. Special thanks are due to Ellen and David Crawford for endurance, and to Dr Anthony Randall, without whom this book would never have reached its conclusion.

Any book on Anglo-Saxon childhood is overdue: this is not necessarily the book the subject needed, but I hope this one will fill the gap until a better one is written.

Introduction

The study of the history of childhood has, in recent decades, moved forward in leaps and bounds, so that we now have detailed and intensive study of the Roman family, and the family in medieval Europe.[1] One area that has been overlooked, however, is childhood in Anglo-Saxon England. Never has the term 'Dark Ages' been more relevant than to the study of the early medieval child. Philipe Ariès, the founder of the study of the history of childhood, reflected in 1960 that 'in medieval society the idea of childhood did not exist'.[2] Recent work by childhood historians has revised this assertion and has updated many of the suggestions about attitudes towards children in pre-modern history, but while our understanding of the child in past times in general has developed with the discipline, the Anglo-Saxon child remains caught up in outdated prejudices and ignorant speculations.

In the nineteenth century, the Victorian scholar John Thrupp painted a grim picture of Anglo-Saxon childhood: 'At first, the child could be exposed as soon as born: when reared, he could be sold into slavery: he was liable to be punished for his father's crimes, and to be sold in payment of his debt. At the time of the Norman conquest all these barbarous liabilities had ceased: and although the child was still regarded as occupying a position of extreme subjection or dependence, he had ceased to be a chattel or a slave.'[3] A century later, Anita Schorsch demonstrated that no change in the perception of childhood had touched the medieval period: 'Medieval communities dealt with their children as they dealt with their animals . . . Both shared the floor, the worms, the dirt, and every manner of disease that being a dog or a child in this period invited and implied. In perhaps one way alone children were uniquely different from the animals with whom they wallowed: children were treated as if they were expendable.'[4]

In 1983, Neil Postman felt able to describe the Dark Ages as a time when 'childhood disappears'.[5] Recent work has done much to rectify the image of children and childcare from the eleventh century onwards, but the early Anglo-Saxon period still appears to be difficult territory for childhood historians.[6] Overviews of the history of childhood persistently rush from the late Roman period to the eleventh century with only an embarrassed glance at pre-Conquest England. John Boswell, in his magisterial survey of the abandonment of children in western Europe from late antiquity to the Renaissance, offered twenty-nine pages on 'western Europe in the Early Middle Ages' of which only three or four paragraphs are about Anglo-Saxon England, while Charles Somerville, in

The Rise and Fall of Childhood devoted only a handful of pages to European childhood from AD 500 to 1000, explaining that: 'the period between the fall of Rome and the year 1000 is the most obscure in all of western history. We can say little about the lives of children, aside from obvious inferences from the authoritarian family pattern common at that time.'[7]

In practice, the evidence for the Anglo-Saxon period, while not abundant, is sufficiently informative for me to feel able to devote a whole book to the subject of Anglo-Saxon childhood. The aim of this book is to redress the balance in childhood studies, and to present, as far as is possible given the existing evidence, a picture of childhood and family in the Anglo-Saxon period. This period covers the arrival of the Anglo-Saxons in England in the fifth century to the Norman Conquest in the eleventh century. The evidence for the child from the Anglo-Saxon period is presented through a variety of forms of discourse, both archaeological and documentary, but these varying forms do not complement each other and cannot present a holistic view of the child – rather, we can snatch at presentations and representations of a set of social personae, or aspects of different childhoods, associated with children through the period. The evidence for the earlier period until the arrival of Christianity is drawn largely from archaeological sources, in the form of excavated cemeteries and settlements, but later documentary sources also offer insights into pre-Christian Anglo-Saxon society. From the seventh century onwards Anglo-Saxon society is more clearly recorded in documentary sources such as lawcodes, wills, charters, poetry and the accounts of the lives of the saints, but the archaeological evidence, particularly from the cemeteries, also has a part to play in building a picture of later Anglo-Saxon childhood.

The beginning of the Anglo-Saxon period in England is usually placed somewhere in the fifth century, when the Romano-British culture, with its villas, towns and roads, faded into archaeological obscurity, and a new group, migrating from the coasts of what are now Holland, Germany and Scandinavia, began to make its presence felt in eastern England. The culture of these Germanic settlers, with their distinctive artefacts, cemeteries and settlements, spread rapidly westwards, and soon dominated lowland Britain. The settlers brought a new language, and a way of life that was rural, familial and pagan. The archaeological evidence indicates that the earliest Anglo-Saxons lived in relatively small, dispersed hamlets or farmsteads, with no great constraints on land use. Fences are rarely visible on these sites, and when their timber-built halls began to deteriorate, they were simply abandoned, and new ones were built elsewhere. Little is known about the religion of these people, but their burial ritual included grave goods, and the rich variety of artefacts recovered from their graves by archaeologists may give some insight into the social structures of these communities.

The kin group was at the heart of early Anglo-Saxon society, and was responsible for the safety, protection and good conduct of its members. To be without family or kin was a desperate plight, as Old English poems such as *The Wanderer* and *The Seafarer* testify.

At the end of the pagan period, there were significant political, cultural and economic upheavals in Anglo-Saxon England. Christianity was introduced to Anglo-Saxon society by the late sixth century, and with it, Mediterranean or

An imported glass palm cup found in grave 132 of a girl aged about five in the early Anglo-Saxon inhumation cemetery at Finglesham, Kent.

Roman ideas on age thresholds and appropriate treatment of juveniles almost certainly had an impact on the old Germanic social structures. With Christianity came formal schooling. Education, a great factor in extending the period of perceived childhood, was apparently introduced widely and may not have been confined only to the small upper-class section of society. A general move from rural to urban life is identifiable towards the end of this period, putting different strains and influences on family structure and attitudes towards offspring. Old family groups and kinship ties may have been weakened, as the fragmented political units of early Anglo-Saxon society, probably originally based around kinship groups, were gradually merged, and Anglo-Saxons gained wider, supra-familial, regional and even national identities. Where once the family was looked to for fulfilment of responsibilities and obligations, now responsibility devolved from the kin to the Church and 'state', to whom loyalty was now owed and from whom care was expected. These factors had a reconstructable effect on attitudes towards children. Later written sources, immediately post-dating Christianity, nonetheless have something to say about the earlier society the Church tried to reconstruct, both in terms of allowable marriage bonds and in terms of new extensions to the family in the form of god-parents.

The study of earlier Anglo-Saxon children and their families is valuable not only in its own right as a fascinating area of research, but also for its wider implications. A great deal of myth and misunderstanding surrounds research into family life in past societies, in particular the question of social attitudes towards children. Any endeavour to clarify our understanding of even one society from the past may help all such studies of childhood. More specifically, the scrutiny of

Anglo-Saxon childhood should complement recent interest in the reconstruction of society at this time. It is difficult to investigate thoroughly any facet of adult life in the Anglo-Saxon world when the researcher does not know the parameters within which she or he is working: an analysis of adult burial ritual, for instance, is going to be severely hampered if the age at which the ritual distinguishes adults from juveniles is unknown.

In the documentary sources, we can see that Christianity, with its ideals of human society drawn from a Mediterranean model, was sometimes at odds with the traditional Germanic society. Much of the literature from the Christian period deals with 'correct' socialisation, but to what extent did the strictures of the Church – about the rearing of children, the proper formation of family relationships, the education of children and the socialisation of children – have an impact on actual Anglo-Saxon practice? One of the aims of this book will be to try to reconstruct, as far as possible, the 'shape' of the Anglo-Saxon family and the place of the child within the family, including any experience of fosterage or of extended families.

An overall synthesis of the archaeological evidence and the comparative evidence of anthropological and literary sources may provide answers to simple questions that as yet have received no detailed response. First, it should be possible to establish at what age Anglo-Saxons considered that a child became an adult, and whether there were any rites of passage in the child's progression to adult status. Second, it should also be possible to establish whether this juvenile/adult age was firmly fixed, or whether it varied according to social occasion, as modern child/adult limits do. As an artificial barrier, it would not be surprising if the perceived age of transition from juvenility to adulthood was subject to variation.

Anglo-Saxon vocabulary recognised the stages of childhood (*cildhad*) and youth (*gugoðhad*). There were also various words for describing the condition of being a child.[8] Other sources of evidence indicate that the Anglo-Saxons distinguished between adults and children. A simple comparison of burial ritual suggests that child burials were not identical to those of adults in that, as a group, they were buried with significantly fewer grave goods than adults were. At the cemetery of Portway, Hampshire, the excavator noted that, with only three exceptions, the burials without grave goods were of children.[9] Documentary evidence from the Anglo-Saxon period reinforces the idea that juveniles were a recognised group apart from adults. Twenty-five of the surviving lawcodes from the Anglo-Saxon period deal specifically with the problems of children and their protection.[10] Seven of these lawcodes also deal with the problem of the juvenile age limit, and one code of Æthelstan is purely concerned with the problem of defining the age at which a child was able to take responsibility for its actions. For the lawmakers, from the late sixth-century Æthelbert of Kent to those of the Norman Conquest, the age limit hovered between ten years and twelve, with one brief and uncharacteristic leap to fifteen in the legislation of King Æthelstan. The question of appropriate age thresholds between the adult and juvenile worlds was one that exercised this section of Anglo-Saxon society at least.

The biological arguments for placing children in a special category are almost too obvious to need stating, and even though there must be caveats about the relationship between physical growth and social transition, in the light of some modern researches and excavation reports to be discussed later, the arguments need to be outlined here. In biological terms, children are quite simply not adults. Children are different; their perceptions are different, as are their requirements. They are dependants, learners and developers in different proportions through their earliest years. They are not, mentally or physically, part of the adult world, particularly in their first five to ten years of life. It has long been held by child psychologists that in any given society, the physical and mental development of the normal child follows the same pattern from year to year: although no two individuals are exactly alike, all normal children tend to follow a general sequence of growth characteristic of the species and of a cultural group. Every child has a unique pattern of growth but that pattern is a variant of a basic sequence.

This concept is of crucial importance in my examination of childhood based on difficult and incomplete evidence. Within certain parameters, the age at which a child in any society will be able to take on a full adult role will vary according to diet, the complexity of the society, the responsibilities that must be borne in adult life, and so on, but the fact remains that children are different because they are immature – because that is part of being a child. Other social categories, such as priests or slaves, are not biologically predetermined – a slave does not have to be a slave except that society makes him so; there is nothing about him, physically, that decrees he should be a slave as opposed to a freeman – and indeed in Anglo-Saxon society people could and did move from slavery to freedom and back again. In other words, we may take the fact that not all societies have slaves or priests as an argument for not assuming that there are slaves or priests in a given population until their presence is proven, but all societies have children who are, inevitably, different to adults, and therefore need to be treated as such. The only circumstance under which children can be ignored as a separate group in, for example, a cemetery population, is if it can be shown absolutely clearly that they were not accorded differential treatment in the burial ritual.

Given that children are *not* adults, it follows that the society of which they form a part must have to differentiate between the treatment of juveniles and adults. How a society manifests these differences may vary because, notwithstanding the biological changes that occur during it, childhood is essentially a social construct – the childhood you experience is dependent not on biological growth, which would mean that all children everywhere and at all times were treated in exactly the same way, but rather is a product of a particular social setting.[11] Today, for example, children are given some adult attributes from an early age. After weaning, they tend to eat the same foods as adults (though some foods such as fish fingers or spaghetti shapes are considered more appropriate for children than for adults), and wear clothes that imitate adult fashions. There are also, however, compulsory forms of differentiation. Children have to go to school, they may pay half price for some services such as public transport and amusements (although the age limit on this varies from place to place) and are conventionally excluded from certain topics of conversation that are not considered by adults to be good for them. All adult life, not just the lives of parents, is affected by this special treatment afforded to children. A trivial example is that, because certain aspects of adult society are ideally considered taboo for children, adults in the UK have restricted viewing on terrestrial television up to the nine o'clock 'watershed'. We also have recognised ages at which children may become formally initiated into the adult world, although these age limits are not consistent. At sixteen they may marry, at eighteen they may vote, and at twenty-one they may have a large party to celebrate complete membership of adult society. In other societies, different customs prevail. The Kayapo tribe of central Brazil considers children to be extensions of their parents until they are weaned, and until that time, they wear their hair long and have red ear-lobe plugs, like adults.[12]

Finally, of course, it should be recognised that 'the child is father to the man', and that the study of Anglo-Saxon children is important because much adult social behaviour is shaped by childhood experience. However, as James Schultz remarked, the modern assumption that upbringing or nurture may have an impact on the behaviour of the adult does not apply in all societies at all times.[13] According to Schultz's study of medieval High German literature, there was no perceived link between childhood and adulthood. Skills learnt in childhood by literary figures bore no relationship to their skills in adulthood, and their nature – what they were genetically programmed to be – was far more significant. Thus Parzival, who was kept ignorant of knighthood until he was a youth, at his first contact with the courtly world of the military knight becomes an adept fighter, capable of overthrowing experienced warriors. Parzival's noble blood determined his skills, not his childhood and training. This literary construct of the High German Middle Ages is taken further by Schultz: he suggests that adult behaviour determines the childhood of the heroes, rather than the other way around. Thus a saint will have a saintly childhood – no saint could do otherwise. Effectively, in medieval High German literature, it does not matter how traumatic or dislocated a childhood may have been – abandonment, fosterage and orphanage are a commonplace for such children – there will be no impact on the character or behaviour of the adult. If such literature has any bearing on a society's actual views about childhood, then it is worth noting that the Anglo-Saxon perspective is ambiguous. The saintly Cuthbert behaved like a 'normal' child until he was miraculously warned that his destiny was to be a holy man. The saint Guthlac was clearly and emphatically conditioned by his childhood (nurture): it was because he had listened to heroic tales in his childhood that he determined to become a warrior in his later years. The hagiographer emphasised that Guthlac's innate good nature came through even when he was leading a band of warriors, because he tended to give away a proportion of his booty to the poor, like an earlier version of Robin Hood. Ultimately, Guthlac's destiny caught up with him (as indicated by the miracles at his birth) and he became a monk. The lack of a link between nurture and adult behaviour is suggested by the Old English poem *The Fates of Man* which effectively argued that, no matter how carefully and lovingly parents reared their children, in the end, when the child left home, the parents could not control the destiny of their offspring. This fatalistic prognostication may argue against nurture having a part to play, but such comments do strike a chord with many modern parents. It is a simple and true enough observation that parents do their best to bring up their children well, and often their own personal hopes for their adolescents are at odds with reality. Not all Anglo-Saxon parents had to ask themselves where they went wrong – the biographer Asser remarked that King Alfred's children, brought up within the royal court and carefully educated, were a credit to their father.[14] Furthermore, the literary Anglo-Saxons of the later period were fully aware of the Biblical teaching that 'he who spares the rod spoils the child', a maxim encapsulating the belief that there was a clear correlation between nurture and adult behaviour: what happened in childhood would have a direct impact on the child's mature character.

The whole question of the place of children in any society is a vexed one. Children occupy an anomalous, subliminal position. They are both within the boundaries of 'normal' society, learning how to occupy their place in it, but they are also outsiders, a group apart, with their own particular requirements and rules. Because of this, evidence demonstrating adult attitudes towards children tends to be conflicting and baffling, but children as a distinctive group to whom distinctive rules apply, are worthy of separate and intensive study if the full complexity of earlier Anglo-Saxon society is to be more clearly comprehended.

A brief introduction to the study of childhood and family structure is provided in the first chapter of this book, because a grasp of the general discussions about the theory of childhood is essential for any informed and meaningful interpretation of the archaeological and documentary evidence; and the theoretical

A nobleman and his wife distribute alms to poor women and children. The nobleman's wife carries children in her arms, and behind her stands a nurse with a child. (British Library, Harley 603, f. 57v)

debates, well known to historians of childhood, are almost undiscussed within Anglo-Saxon studies. This chapter is followed by a discussion of the archaeological and documentary sources relevant to the study of Anglo-Saxon childhood.

The two significant types of archaeological material that have any bearing on the study of childhood are the excavated Anglo-Saxon cemeteries and the settlement sites. Of these two, the evidence from the cemeteries is by far the most important, offering valuable information, not only about the physical remains of the Anglo-Saxons (diet, pathology, life expectancy), but also about the social behaviour of the burying populations. The pagan Anglo-Saxons buried their dead with a variety of grave goods, and the types of grave goods associated with children, as well as their relationship to other burials in the communal cemeteries give clues about age-related mortuary ritual, and offer tantalising suggestions about the ritual importance of juveniles at various ages within the burial community.

The last thirty years has seen increasing sophistication in methods of interpreting burial archaeology, and current anthropological thinking on the interpretation of mortuary symbolism will be discussed in Chapter 2. Much of the archaeological evidence used in this book will be drawn from a database consisting of information from thirteen fifth- to seventh-century cemetery sites. Since documentary sources also exist which do appear to have some bearing on pre-Christian Anglo-Saxon society, these sources have also been dragooned into service. The use of later sources to elucidate earlier society is not without major pitfalls, and these will be examined in due course. The various sources – poetry, hagiography, medical texts, lawcodes, charters and wills – require a clear context if we are to be sure that they have any bearing on earlier Anglo-Saxon society, so their usefulness as evidence will be given careful scrutiny. It is always tempting for archaeologists to draw on sources that seem to fit their current theories while conveniently ignoring those that do not and completely overlooking the possibility that the plundered texts may not have any real relevance at all, but it would be equally misguided to ignore the documentary sources just because they are treacherous friends.

Since schooling and literacy did not emerge until the arrival of Christianity, the literature inevitably deals with the later Anglo-Saxon period. This is not to say that there is no link between the two periods: the early centuries of Anglo-Saxon occupation formed the foundations for the later society – the pagan period was not totally divorced from the Christian, any more than our own modern society owes nothing to the societies that preceded it. In the same way, much of the literature draws on oral traditions that extend back into the pagan past. Archaeological and historical evidence essentially provide two rather blurred windows looking onto Anglo-Saxon childhood, the one yielding an insight into the more physical aspects of juvenile life and death, the other being invaluable in providing evidence for the 'ideal' and psychological attitudes of adults towards offspring.

What I mean by 'childhood' is what Anglo-Saxons conceived children to be, and what I am studying is the treatment and environment of, the responsibilities given to, and the attitudes shown towards, children by Anglo-Saxon adults. Children offer no histories of themselves in this period; almost all the sources give us only the Anglo-Saxon adult's perception of the child and the child's world.

CHAPTER 1

Anglo-Saxon Childhood and the Social History of Children

An assessment of the place of children within a society must go beyond simple statements of archaeological fact or of historical deduction to say something about what the evidence actually means in terms of social structure. Under these circumstances, it is fundamental that the Anglo-Saxonist must place the evidence in the context of the wider discipline of childhood studies. This would enable interpretations of the burial ritual and other evidence from the period to be based on existing knowledge of what models of social patterning are comparable to those exhibited in the early Anglo-Saxon period, and what attitudes towards children such models would predicate. A background knowledge of current models of family structure, and the arguments for or against a 'concept of childhood' will be indispensable to an analysis of the evidence from the Anglo-Saxon period, and will be a constant backdrop to the questions and solutions postulated in this book. Since so little work has been done on childhood by Anglo-Saxonists, I am going to take this opportunity to outline some of the major lines of debate in the field of childhood history.

As the science of demography improves, so the ability to assess documentation and archaeological evidence gains in depth, and our awareness of the life of 'everyman' within the wider context of society increases. Childhood, for long an obscure and forgotten aspect of social history, has become an increasingly popular area of study. Van Gennep, in *The Rites of Passage* (1932), raised interest in the idea that age could be relevant to our understanding of past societies. The importance of childhood in particular as an index to culture and behaviour was given impetus by the historian Phillipe Ariès in his influential publication *Centuries of Childhood* (1960). Within this study, Ariès set out an original thesis that still has some currency today. He regarded attitudes towards childhood as being progressive, deriving their evolutionary power from contemporary economic and social advancement. He felt that treatment of children improved through history, as societies became more affluent and civilised. He maintained that the crucial *concept* of childhood – the idea that children occupy a special place within society and should be treated not as miniature and incomplete adults but *as children* – did not arise until the mid-seventeenth century, when children were technically accepted as a separate group, characterised by weakness and imbecility. He saw the modern concept of childhood, with its associated emphasis on the family unit, as having emerged in the mid-eighteenth century, as a function of society's need to impose conformity and classifications on its members. People in the medieval period, Ariès claimed, simply did not demarcate childhood from adulthood. There were no 'rites of passage' or threshold ages, and no concept of transition from one status (child) to another (adult). Ariès's own summary neatly expressed the contrast he saw between medieval attitudes and later attitudes. In the former, the child was given no differential treatment; it was integrated into society as quickly as its development allowed. Family ties were loose and sentimental attachment to children was lacking. In the modern period, children are, in theory, deeply loved from birth by their parents, the period of childhood has clearly defined boundaries, and the family unit is private and apart from the rest of society:

> In medieval society the idea of childhood did not exist; this is not to suggest that children were neglected, forsaken or despised. The idea of childhood is not to be confused with affection for children; it corresponds to an awareness of the particular nature of childhood, that particular nature which distinguishes the child from the adult, even the young adult. In medieval society, this awareness was lacking. This is why, as soon as the child could live without the constant solicitude of his mother . . . he belonged to adult society. The infant who was too fragile as yet to take part in the life of adults simply 'did not exist'.[1]

It is important to note that Ariès explicitly stated that the fact that children 'did not exist' should not be equated with neglect or abuse, nor did he, in his work, give a detailed psychological analysis of why these vulnerable infants 'did not exist'.

Critics have observed that the flaw in Ariès's work lies in his source material. His generalised conclusions about childhood were models derived from an élite French literate culture and court society. However, if Ariès's theories are generally correct, then it follows that we should find no indication that children 'existed' in ritual or social terms in the Anglo-Saxon archaeological and documentary sources.

Ariès's belief that there was no concept of childhood in medieval society has been upheld most forcefully by Lawrence Stone. He, like Ariès, agreed that the emergence of a system of education was mainly responsible for the emergence of a concept of childhood. Stone went further than Ariès, though, in seeing the supposition that infants 'do not count', taken with the possibility that there was very little emotional contact between parents and children, as explicable by the mortality rate of the period, and the mortality rate as being a product of that lack of care. The high mortality rate would have ensured a complementary high birth rate. In a vicious cycle, women would have produced many offspring, too numerous to care for properly. Most of these offspring would die anyway, partly because their very numbers would have ensured that only the strongest and luckiest would survive, but this same proliferation of children would mean that in spite of high losses, a few at least of these children would live long enough to inherit the family property. The large number of children meant that they were mostly neglected, and that no child received intensive parental care. According to Stone's view of the past, it was psychologically necessary for parents not to care very much about their children, and not to build up any strong emotional feeling about them until children were past the risky period of infancy and stood a higher chance of survival. Only when children were old enough, when they were less weak and vulnerable, could parents afford to become attached to them. The corollary of this is that, since adults kept themselves from having strong emotional bonds with children, they could and did exploit and abuse juveniles. Stone made a further link between parental attitudes and social status. For the eighteenth century, for example, he places at one end of the social scale the 'Higher Court Aristocracy' who were negligent towards their offspring, the care of whom was given to nurses and teachers. The 'Upper Classes' cared for their children themselves, but believed in physical punishment. The professional and landed classes demonstrated 'permissiveness' and an affectionate mode of rearing their children. Lower artisans wanted their children to have a sound education, but treated them harshly, while the poor were indifferent, exploitative and brutal towards their children. Again, such a theory has implications for the interpretation of Anglo-Saxon childhood. Under the circumstances outlined by Stone, we should be able to find evidence for malnutrition among children and high levels of child mortality in the cemeteries.[2]

However, Stone's thesis that attitudes towards children were dependent on social status and the lack of a 'concept of childhood' was a licence for brutality and exploitation has been criticised. The most vehement of challengers has been Linda Pollock, who protested that 'Stone's dramatic and dogmatic synthesis has not one shred of sound logic and convincing evidence to support it'.[3] Stone's views have, though, been influential. Among those who have adhered to the 'early society equals brutality to children' theory is Lloyd de Mause, founder and editor of the *History of Childhood Quarterly*, who argued for a more psychological dimension to explain the apparently traumatic childhoods inflicted on children in past times: 'Ariès' central thesis is the opposite of mine: he argues that while the traditional child was happy because he was free to mix with many classes and ages, a special condition known as childhood was 'invented' in the early modern period, resulting in a tyrannical concept of family.'[4] De Mause agreed that infants 'did not count' in the medieval period, but he argued for what he designated 'generational pressure', rather than social and economic pressure, as the source of development in attitudes towards children – a generational pressure born of anxiety. With each generation, he argued, the birth of the child created anxieties in the parent based on fear of inadequacy and fear of challenge. In its turn, the child, when it grew and became a parent, would attempt to overthrow or improve on the parental model. The resulting pressures would lead inexorably to change, and to the present enlightened state of parenting. De Mause took modern ideals of parenting as the yardstick by which the efforts of all past societies were measured and which had, if the theory was to hold water, to be demonstrated to come up to the modern mark. De Mause charted the improvement in attitudes towards childhood by the following 'Periodisation of Modes of Parent-Child Relations':

1. Infanticidal Mode (antiquity to 4th century AD)
2. Abandonment Mode (4th to 13th centuries AD)
3. Ambivalent Mode (14th to 17th centuries)
4. Intrusive Mode (18th century)
5. Socialisation Mode (19th to mid-20th century)
6. Helping Mode (mid-20th century to present)

This 'Periodisation' charts the progress of man from antiquity, when children were apparently treated as chattels, to be kept or destroyed like any farm animal, without compunction, through increasing awareness of the child as a human being in the seventeenth century, to be sentimentalised and toyed with, through the 'intrusive mode', when the child, full of stains and pollution of sin, was 'used as a "toilet" for adult projections', to the modern period, when the well-adjusted family, recognising the child's 'rights' as a human being (even, in the USA, to the extent of being allowed to 'divorce' its parents), which permits the child's wants to tyrannise the household.[5]

De Mause's comments on the period that he designates as operating the 'abandonment mode' are particularly relevant to this book, in that he outlines a now popular view of the medieval period that must be tackled at some point with reference to the Anglo-Saxons: 'Once parents began to accept the child as having a soul, the only way they could escape the dangers of their own projections was by abandonment, whether to the wet nurse, to the monastery or nunnery, to foster families, to the homes of other nobles as servants or hostages, or by severe emotional abandonment at home.'[6] To accept this model for the Anglo-Saxon period, we would expect certain indicators in our sources. We would expect, for example, a confusion of family allegiances in the burial ritual of children (if indeed the Anglo-Saxon burial ritual does reflect family groups), and we would expect some confusion of loyalties between families and other carers in the literature.

De Mause has made a valuable contribution to the controversy surrounding our understanding of childhood in the past, but his premise that western culture provides the optimum social environment for bringing up children, and that childrearing in past times failed to achieve this assumed standard, is unsubstantiated. In particular, De Mause relied for his understanding of Anglo-Saxon childhood on the work of J. Thrupp, whose 1862 book on *The Anglo-Saxon Home*, already cited earlier in this chapter, is hardly the best source for an uncritical and informed discussion of the Anglo-Saxon period. It is from Thrupp that he derives his descriptions of Anglo-Saxons beating their children, killing them and neglecting them. Some of his assertions, such as the insistence that no medieval art depicts parents and children in cordial contact is demonstrably incorrect – the late Anglo-Saxon *Harley Psalter* is full of scenes of parents holding their children's hands, cuddling them and caressing them. The *Harley Psalter* dates to the early eleventh century, and is an Anglo-Saxon copy of the Carolingian

A group of women and their children: the women are seen holding the hands of the children. (British Library, Harley 603, f. 7v)

Utrecht Psalter – an example of both Continental and insular artists accepting the possibility that women may be seen cuddling and holding their offspring in an apparently affectionate manner. De Mause painted a picture of unremitting parental selfishness and brutality, behaviour which is apparently unrelated to economic or social considerations.

Extreme though it may appear, other historians have supported this viewpoint. Edward Shorter argued that good mothering was the invention of modernisation and that the traditional family was a mechanism for transmitting property and position from generation to generation. In the same vein, Richard Lyman asserted that children were often beaten, sold and abandoned during the early medieval period, though he, like Ariès, saw economic motives as the root of this 'abandonment mode' behaviour.[7]

To add to the problems of tracking down the 'newly invented' child in the past is the issue of a gendered history of childhood. Shulamith Firestone accepted the proposition that 'childhood' was an invention of the seventeenth century, when children's toys developed, and children's behaviour was recognised by adults as showing 'otherness' and 'difference'. However, she pointed out that this was a gendered approach, and that for girls, 'childhood' did not apply. She argued that the female child went from swaddling clothes straight into adult female dress, did not go to school, acted like a 'little lady' and was married off to an older man by puberty. In a patriarchal society where men controlled the discourse and the power of recording the present was invested in males, not only were children – the traditional province and interest of women – marginal to the records of society, but female children dropped out of history and into oblivion.[8] Certainly for Anglo-Saxon society, the male dominance over the surviving records – both written and archaeological – means that male childhood is articulated more clearly than female childhood.

The prevailing assumption in the 1970s, then, was that it was only relatively recently that children had been seen as anything more than a burden, and therefore all actions of parents were to be understood in terms of what seemed most convenient to themselves, rather than in terms of what parents believed to be good for the child itself. However, it is a relief to be able to note that not all historians of childhood agree with this picture of an unremittingly violent and callous attitude towards offspring in the medieval period. There are historians who would prefer to propose that caring for children is not a modern invention, but that the average mother, and possibly father too, in any period, would put the welfare of the child first. The expression of this care varied according to prevailing economic and political conditions, and according to the current understanding of what was good for a child. So, for example, while modern thinking suggests that a child should be kept at home for as long as possible, in the belief that this is best for it, an Anglo-Saxon parent may have sent the child away, motivated by exactly the same belief. Indeed, it may be that modern ideas of how to bring up a child 'well' would actually be harmful to that child in another society, and it should be noted that the assumption that modern methods of childrearing are the best for our own society, let alone for past societies, has yet to be proven.

Among those who have argued for more sympathy towards the role of parents in earlier societies is Mary Martin McLaughlin, who proposed that children may always have been regarded as individuals, in spite of the oft-quoted notion that large families and high infant mortality rates would have made parents incapable of recognising the difference between one of their offspring and another. It followed, according to McLaughlin, that if the child's unique character was recognised by the parents, then the treatment of these children would have been differentiated according to the parents' perception of what would be good for that particular child. Parents would not have treated their children with the callousness engendered by anonymity.[9]

Other 'apologists' for past parenthood have reiterated this point. Linda Pollock in particular has been a fierce supporter of the theory of the caring parent. If parents today care, she stated, then the onus is on historians to prove that parents have not always cared, rather than simply assuming that our ancestors were inevitably unfeeling: 'It may be that I am placing too much emphasis on continuity in childrearing practices, but I am of the opinion that changes should be investigated against this background of continuity. There may indeed be subtle changes in childcare through the centuries – changes that so far lie hidden because of the prevailing interest to discover and argue for dramatic transformations.'[10]

Pollock moved childhood studies forward by attempting to analyse in detail the sources of information used by historians, and also in eschewing the sensational or simply bizarre episodes in the past that have given rise to equally sensational and bizarre theories. She tested and exploded many of the myths of childhood, demonstrating that childhood abuse does not occur in a normal parent–child relationship, but only when there is something lacking in that relationship.[11] She defended the contentious issue of swaddling by describing it as an indicator of care rather than of neglect, and questioned the usual use (or abuse) of mortality figures as an indication of inevitable neglect by suggesting that in fact the mortality figures have been greatly exaggerated. In her estimation, the mortality rate in England rarely exceeded 150 deaths in 1,000 births. She pointed out that, with 80 to 85 per cent of all children surviving birth for at least a few years, it would have been very difficult for mothers to avoid becoming attached to their children.[12]

Pollock's emphasis was on what remains constant in adult attitudes to children and childrearing through the centuries, rather than the more dramatic changes, defended by the assertion that it is the constants in human society that deserve study as well as the changes in interaction.[13] The Anglo-Saxon archaeological evidence provides a perfect opportunity to examine the 'normal' in one aspect of social behaviour – mortuary ritual – rather than the abnormal, because in the analysis of the data from cemeteries it is the general patterns of behaviour that become apparent rather than the odd individual cases.

One approach that can hardly be covered in the Anglo-Saxon period is the attempt (pioneered by the Opies in 1959) to examine childhood from the point of view of children themselves. This viewpoint sees children very firmly in the context of a special, distinct segment of society, having its own language, customs and attitudes, operating outside, although alongside, the boundaries of adult society. This approach is based on the belief that children and adults do not have the same perception of the society in which they live.[14] It is unfortunately not possible, given the nature of the evidence surviving from this period, that such an approach based on the psychology of children could be adopted as a method of looking into Anglo-Saxon childhood.

The range and variety of scholarly publications on the subject of the history of childhood indicates that the study is still an arena for conflict. Our interest in it is not merely sentimental, nor are studies of childhood in the past merely descriptive. Childhood, and adult attitudes towards that state, are emotive areas and difficult to define, not least because we are uncertain in our own society about the best method of bringing up a child. In effect, if we cannot decide on the 'right' way to rear a child today, historians of childhood in the past are in no position to offer judgemental reflections of ancient societies, although many of them apparently seek to do so! Thus childhood studies have posed a problem for historians. It is all too easy to discover either an attitude towards past processes of rearing children that fits a concept of what is 'right' or 'wrong' according to modern ideas, or to find a history of the past that reflects well on modern western societies' more 'enlightened' approaches to children.

What is evident is that 'childhood' is a *social* construct rather than a natural one. A. James and A. Prout, in what has been seen as a ground-breaking work in the development of childhood sociology, laid out a set of key features for reconstructing childhood, the first two of which are worth reproducing here in full:

1. Childhood is understood as a social construction. As such it provides an interpretative frame for contextualising the early years of human life. Childhood, as distinct from biological immaturity, is neither a natural nor a universal feature of human groups but appears as a specific structural and cultural component of many societies.
2. Childhood is a variable of social analysis. It can never be entirely divorced from other variables such as class, gender or ethnicity. Comparative and cross-cultural analysis reveals a variety of childhoods rather than a single or universal phenomenon.[15]

Given that childhood is a sociological phenomenon, Christopher Jenks has taken the relationship between the reconstruction of childhood and the variable of adulthood further, arguing that childhood can always and only be understood in reference to adult society, stating that the 'child . . . cannot be imagined except in relation to a conception of the adult' because to categorise childhood – to define the cultural and social place of a child in anthropological terms – is to seek to explain the unfamiliar, the child, in comparison to the familiar, the adult.[16] However, if a child can only be given shape and form through comparison with the adult, then the important corollary is that 'it becomes impossible to generate a well-defined sense of the adult, and indeed adult society, without first positing the child'. Childhood in this sense holds a mirror up to society as a whole. This assertion is accepted knowledge within the world of childhood sociologists, to the point where David Archard presumed it was obvious: 'It seems self-evident that the character of adult society will derive from the ways in which its children are brought up, and that, in turn, the nature of childrearing will reflect the values and priorities of adult society.'[17] When we can see what a culture makes of its children, we have a clearer idea of how that culture images its adult self.

FAMILY STRUCTURE

The development and quality of life of a child is inextricably intertwined with the type of society in which that child lives. As the overview of literature on childhood suggests, it is impossible to study the question of treatment of children without also examining the interlocking problem of size and shape of family, for it seems that the size of family must either determine the treatment of the children within it, or else it must reflect the child's position in society. The problem is one of size and focal point. If the rearing and upbringing of children is the important function of the family, then the structure of that family will be built around offspring. If, however, the family unit has some other primary function – say, an economic group kept together by ties of kinship for the purpose of managing a farm, or a defensive unit to ensure mutual protection – then the child becomes of peripheral importance, and its treatment and position may be changed accordingly. Just as there exists a body of theory to help interpret the position of the child in early societies, so also there is a range of theory to help explain the likely family organisation for that child to have lived in, dependent upon environmental, geographical and political considerations. Of factors that may have influenced family structure in the Anglo-Saxon period, we have knowledge of their cemeteries, their settlements and the climate, although availability of land and the relationship between the Anglo-Saxons and the native British remains obscure. Into what framework might these building blocks be fitted?

Size appears to be the crucial factor in all discussions of the family as related to treatment of children. The debate revolves around whether a large, extended family group, involving two or three generations and several lineal kin (cousins, brothers and so on), is likely to be beneficial for a child, or whether a smaller group – a nuclear group of parents and children only, as prevails in modern western society – is likely to lavish more care and attention on offspring. Fertility, an important factor in demographic studies, must also be taken into account. Would a large nuclear family, with eight or nine children, have more caring and attentive parents than a small nuclear family, with only two or three? Mortality rates must also be taken into consideration; does a high mortality rate influence the size and structure of the family unit? If so, can such structures be identified in the earlier Anglo-Saxon period, and should it be accepted that a high infant mortality rate would necessarily harden the parents' feelings toward surviving offspring? What about a social structure with a high rate of fosterage and adoption, and again, would this indicate a lack of care of children?

The question of whether a large or small family is more conducive to child welfare is a vexed one. On the one hand, Ariès, Stone and others argued forcibly that 'large' equals 'uncaring'. The larger the family, whether it includes cousins, siblings, aunts or grandparents, the more likely it is for the child to be dragged straight into adult society with no interim period of 'childhood'. This is the loose, unstructured, non-private social unit that Ariès described as the background for the child in the early chapters of his *Centuries of Childhood*. It is only in the modern period, Ariès maintained, that the family closed ranks against the outside world to concentrate on its private life as a small unit bent on the rearing of its children. On the other hand, modern writers believe that modern nuclear families are harmful to a child during its 'crucial epoch of personality formation', and have suggested that the large families of earlier societies offered a richer environment than that of the lonely modern child.[18] Underlying both of these proposals, however, are the same essential assumptions: that families have changed over time from being large and complex to small and simple, and that the rise of the nuclear family is inevitably associated with the rise of individualism and with industrialisation. There may be disagreement over the emotional value of large families, but there is no question over the idea that families in the past – and this includes the Anglo-Saxon period – were normally large and extended.

This concept has powerful proponents. Sir Robert Filmer put this argument forward as early as the seventeenth century, and it has been upheld more recently by Ariès, Stone and Boswell.[19] It is not surprising to find, then, that the assumption of the extended form as a norm pervades the archaeologist's view too.

The work of W.A. van Es on the site of Wijster in Holland provides a clear example. The excavations at Wijster revealed the physical remains of the last Continental settlement phase of a group that then migrated to England, to become part of the Anglo-Saxon settlement. Van Es speculated on the population structure of this group by supposing a standard family as having a generational depth of three. He supposed two grandparents, two parents and four children. He admitted that this formula was drawn from his own assumptions about the shape of families in the past, and this framework has been borrowed by other archaeologists in calculating family size.[20]

Although the principle of large, three-generational families in primitive societies has received much popular credence, it has been suggested that such an assumption cannot be substantiated. Demographic studies of medieval populations by Peter Laslett revealed that the family was, in his words, 'always and invariably nuclear', and he further asserted that the wish to believe in the large and extended household as the ordinary institution of an earlier England and an earlier Europe, or as a standard feature of an earlier non-industrial world is '. . . a matter of ideology'.[21] Ideology aside, statistics derived from Anglo-Saxon cemeteries indicate that the extended family was simply not an option. Only about 10 per cent of the earlier Anglo-Saxon population at any one time was aged over forty-five. Some families, at some times, would have included grandparents, but this can hardly have been the norm. If an Anglo-Saxon household is to be made up of eight people, then it is to adult siblings or cousins that we must look to make up the number, not to grandparents.[22] However, the documentary sources for Anglo-Saxon England indicate that the focus of the Anglo-Saxon family was the nuclear grouping of parents and children. This is suggested by the lack of specific terms in Old English for more distant relatives, and by the wills, where the inheritors were usually widows or children, and the lawcodes, where *wergild* or compensation was payable only to close relatives.[23]

A further finding of Laslett's studies of the 1599 census at Ealing was that families are essentially fluid in structure. There may be an overall 'norm' (inevitably the smallest unit, the nuclear family), but to this simple structure other units will be joined over time. Most children will have experience of an extended family – grown-up children may stay at home, widows may keep their daughters on at home, a group of siblings may choose to stay together, and a child may remain under the influence of a parent, perhaps living under the same roof, even after the child has grown up and established its own family.

These examples concentrated on ties between the immediate family, and no attempt has been made to include the possibility of cousins or more distant kin, or to separate the 'family' from a 'household' which may involve servants, slaves or distant relatives and dependants. Laslett focussed solely on the former, but a child's experience of domestic life may be wider than immediate family, and this is likely to be true for some Anglo-Saxon children, given the references to slavery, concubinage, serfdom and fosterage in the literature. Jack Goody regarded the larger household as the most important unit to consider, and believed that the major change over time in community structure was not the emergence of the nuclear family from the extended family, but the shrinking of the household to

A reconstruction of an early Anglo-Saxon village at West Stow, Suffolk. Timber-framed halls and their associated outbuildings were scattered across the unplanned settlement.

the nuclear family as ties of kinship and bonds of responsibility deteriorated.[24] This hypothesis is directly relevant to the Anglo-Saxon period, where much emphasis is placed in the literature on the need for large kin groups and on the mutual responsibilities of kin for each other and householders for everyone under their roofs. It is also clear from the literature that the introduction of Christianity played an important role in weakening these broad ties of kinship and the obligations of members of a large kin group to each other.

A final point raised by demographers and relevant to the upbringing and care of children in the Anglo-Saxon period is that there may be a direct relationship between wealth and size of family. Studies of African, Indian and Tibetan groups have shown that the economically higher caste families have the larger households made up of immediate family and dependant kin. Richard Wall also noted that, on the basis of his studies of medieval populations in England, larger households occurred where there was less available land – where settlements could not expand, households were, perforce, large.[25] According to this theory, family sizes in the earlier period of settlement in Anglo-Saxon England should have been small. Place-name and archaeological evidence indicates that the early settlers rapidly dominated large areas of England. Furthermore, the earlier settlements such as Mucking in Essex and West Stow in Suffolk show little sign of order or organisation, and no hint of land boundaries and household fences. Only in the later phases of settlements at eighth-century sites such as Catholme, Staffordshire, and Cowdery's Down, near Basingstoke, are there indications of spatial organisation and

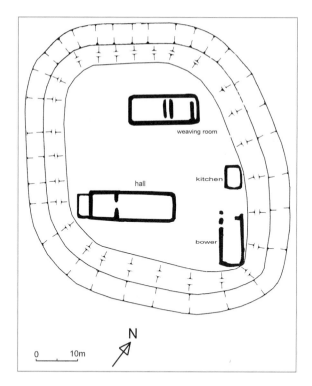

weaving room

hall

kitchen

bower

N

0   10m

Plan of the late Anglo-Saxon manor recovered by excavation at Goltho, Lincolnshire. The buildings are aligned within a restricted space.

boundaries, indicating some restrictions on the development of the settlement. In the eighth century, there are clear indications of limitations of land and property boundaries at planned settlements, proto-towns known as *wics* – houses were built in ordered rows, and at the *wic* sites of Ipswich and Hamwic (Southampton) there appear to have been embankments marking the limits of the controlled settlement. In this environment, perhaps, the larger household may have predominated if the population exceeded the available settlement space, although the populations at these trading emporia may have been seasonal. The Viking threat might also be taken into account from the ninth century onwards. The early fifth- and sixth-century settlements show no signs of having been defended, but by the ninth century, the dangers of living away from fortified settlements may well have encouraged adults to remain in the larger, safer, defended home rather than to move away, and enclosed manor sites such as Goltho in Lincolnshire may represent such a development.[26] In the late Anglo-Saxon period planned towns, or *burhs*, developed and multiplied, drawing a larger population into an urban environment. Excavations in Anglo-Saxon towns have indicated that, until the mid-tenth century, there was a low density of population, and the large, detached houses resembled farmsteads. But certainly, by the late tenth century, populations lived more densely in a truly urban environment. Excavations at York and Oxford, for example, have revealed closely built properties crowded on to street fronts, properties with cellars and even some suburban development.

What we do know about Anglo-Saxon inheritance patterns, on the basis of surviving wills, is that sons and daughters might expect to inherit an equal share of their parents' property. When King Alfred wrote a will favouring his sons over his daughters (specifically designed to ensure that his son Edward had the political power to succeed to the throne after Alfred's death), Alfred felt a need to explain and justify his decision. The surviving wills do, however, indicate that where a will had been made, property and goods would not pass automatically to the children. In a notorious case, the widow Enneawn publicly disinherited her son Edwin after he had sued her for a piece of land at a shire meeting.[27]

Richard Wall's emphasis on economic factors is important also for its implications that marriage was an economic strategy, rather than a social necessity. He considered that, among other factors, available wealth and ties of inheritance will influence family growth. Lineal inheritance, he postulated, will limit the ability of later-born siblings to leave the main household to establish their own homes. Economic factors will influence mortality and fertility rates: members of a well-fed household are likely to be more fertile and live longer, thus rich households will tend to have more members, and are more likely to be complex (with surviving grandparents) than nuclear. This again has implications for the Anglo-Saxon period, when there may have been poor nutrition. Poor families, on this basis, may have had few members and few living children, yet Ariès and Stone would see small families as ideal for the rearing of children. The idea of small, poor families in past times is clearly at odds with these suppositions. Ultimately, it must be accepted that different combinations of child mortality and fertility could give rise to the same pattern. The theories, such as there are, need to be considered in the context of the evidence.

One factor common to all the commentators I have discussed is that they have had little or nothing to say about the Anglo-Saxon period itself: their theories, if they start in an early period, deal with the literate classical civilisation and then leap forward to Anglo-Norman England. It is true that the evidence from fifth- to eleventh-century England is less easily accessible to social historians than the evidence from other periods, but nonetheless the evidence exists and is worth assessing, if only to give a broader basis for those attempting to build chronological models of the history of childhood. The Anglo-Saxon material tends to be, by its nature, anonymous and of general application. But a combination of archaeological and documentary data can allow us at least to frame the question 'Did the Anglo-Saxons have a concept of childhood?' In attempting to answer this question, it may also be possible to work out how Anglo-Saxon parents cared for their children, whether their treatment of children was an expression of affection in changing circumstances, or the result of changing attitudes, and what was the basis and shape of the 'family' in the Anglo-Saxon period.

CHAPTER 2

Archaeological Sources

The primary archaeological source material for information on early Anglo-Saxon population structure comes from the excavated cemeteries. The pagan Anglo-Saxons had two main forms of burial ritual: cremation, where the body of the deceased was burnt and the ashes placed in the ground, often in special burial pots, and inhumation, where the body was placed in a grave in the ground. Both rituals included the use of grave goods, that is, items such as knives, brooches and spears that were kept with the body as part of the burial ritual. Often these items – brooches, belt buckles, beads and wristclasps – must have been part of the clothing worn by the dead person, but other objects such as pots and bottles must have been deliberately placed with the deceased at the time of burial.

These two burial rituals were not used everywhere and at all times in Anglo-Saxon England. Cremations were carried out more in the east and north of the country – the Anglian areas – while inhumation predominated in the south. Mixed inhumations and burials occur in the middle, Thames Valley, region. Cremation may have been the more ancient ritual, but it began to be replaced in all areas by inhumation in the late sixth and seventh centuries. It is possible that the two rituals required different social structures, because cremation cemeteries tend to be far larger than inhumation cemeteries, and they have a smaller distribution. It seems likely that inhumation sites served small local communities of villages or hamlets, while cremation sites served much wider areas, perhaps even tribal regions. Cremation, although it is unspectacular from an archaeological point of view, needs far more elaborate preparation and technical skills than inhumation, and this may explain why a central cremation site was required to serve a large number of communities who did not have the resources to develop their own cremation cemetery.

There are many known cemetery sites in England, and many of these have been at least partially excavated. When Audrey Meaney published her invaluable catalogue of Anglo-Saxon cemeteries in 1964 she estimated that about 25,000 graves belonging to the early Anglo-Saxon period had been excavated, and many more have been investigated in the intervening years.[1]

Inevitably, the process of cremation means that much of the evidence required by archaeologists to interpret a past society has been destroyed, not least the body of the dead person itself. It is possible to reconstruct the sex and age of the cremated person on the basis of the surviving fragments of burnt bone, but only a small proportion of the cremated remains will be capable of this sort of analysis.

To complicate matters, it appears that the same spot may have been used for several cremation pyres, and the retrieval of bones by the Anglo-Saxons was not thorough in all cases, so that ashes from previous cremations may have been collected with the most recent pyre. The ashes within cremation urns frequently contain the remains of more than one individual; the extra fragments of other ashes may have been deliberate additions but are more likely to represent contamination. In addition, it has to be assumed that a significant proportion of the grave goods associated with the burial would have been destroyed by the fire. Molten remains of beads and brooches, for example, are found in cremation urns, but they only serve to emphasise how much material must have been lost. Items that were added to the cremated remains after the ashes of the dead person had been collected tend to be small items that would fit into a pot, such as bone combs, tweezers and knives. Miniature items were occasionally recorded as 'toys' in earlier site reports, but they have no particular connection with the burials of

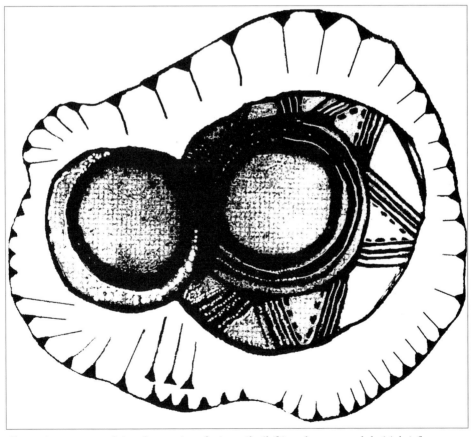

Cremation urns containing the remains of a juvenile (left) and a young adult (right) from Spong Hill, Norfolk.

children and clearly had a symbolic function in the adult burial ritual. The patterns and sizes of the urns used as a repository for the ashes may be a significant indicator of the status of the deceased, and much work on this aspect of the cremation burial ritual has been carried out by Julian Richards.[2] At the modern excavation of Spong Hill, Norfolk, it was possible to carry out a detailed analysis of the cremated human bone, but at many of the earlier excavations of cremation sites, the pots and artefacts, rather than their human occupants, were the object of antiquarian interest, to the extent that the contents were often dumped before the pots were taken away for study. Cremation sites, then, may yield some information about early Anglo-Saxon society, but their interpretation is much more difficult than inhumation sites, so inhumations are the major source of archaeological evidence for childhood in the earlier Anglo-Saxon period.

Even though the inhumation ritual predominated in the south, there are inhumation cemeteries in the north of the country, and it is possible to compare a range of inhumation populations across the country to study how Anglo-Saxon children fitted into the burial ritual, to assess the status and importance of the child within the burial ritual, to assess the existence of evidence for family sizes within the mortuary community, and to see what evidence there may be within the cemeteries for the health and diet of the Anglo-Saxon child.[3]

IDENTIFYING AGE AT DEATH OF SKELETAL REMAINS

While the ageing of adult skeletons is relatively problematic, it is possible to measure with some degree of accuracy the age at death if that death occurred before the individual reached biological maturity. Modern techniques for ageing skeletons have become much more refined in the last decade, with measurements based on microscopic analysis of tooth and bone growth offering the most accurate figures to date. However, these techniques have rarely been applied to Anglo-Saxon skeletal material, and for the most part the archaeologist is obliged to rely on the same crude methods that have been used for decades. Fortunately, juveniles can be aged to a reasonable degree of accuracy by standard methods of bone measurement and tooth development.[4] Often the skeletal remains may consist of no more than a few teeth, but provided the teeth survive, it is possible to age a skeleton with some confidence. In a study of juveniles, it is important to know just how specific the ageing error is likely to be (see below).

Pattern of Eruption of Deciduous and Permanent Teeth

Deciduous teeth

Central incisors	6–8 months
Lateral incisors	8–10 months
First molars	12–16 months
Canines	16–20 months
Second molars	20–30 months

Permanent teeth

First molars	6–7 years
Central incisors	6–8 years
Lateral incisors	7–9 years
Canines	9–12 years
First and second premolars	10–12 years
Second molars	11–13 years
Third molars	17–21+ years

Teeth become less useful as an indicator of age after the permanent teeth have finished erupting. Patterns of wear on the teeth may indicate the number of years since the teeth erupted, but it must be kept in mind that tooth attrition will be modified by local variations including the health and diet of the group or individual.[5] However, such patterns of wear are useful for ranking the age at death within a mortuary population, if it is assumed that diet was roughly the same for all members of the community.

There are other methods of gauging the age at death of an individual, which may be used if teeth have not survived. Juveniles have more bones than adults: as they mature, some bones fuse together. Ageing by the length of diaphyses and the state of epiphyseal fusion can be useful, although since epiphyseal fusion of the main parts of the skeleton does not begin until around thirteen years of age, this method is only helpful for corroborating evidence based on the later stages of tooth eruption.[6] The principle behind these methods of ageing is that the bones of the body, especially those in the skull, fuse after birth within a certain range of years for modern healthy skeletons. These dates of union are inevitably prone to variation according to genetic and dietary factors, and are not specific – epiphyses in the foot, for example, fuse over a period of ten years.[7]

An estimation of the age of adults at death can also be made, based on the changes of the pubic symphyseal face. This method of ageing is somewhat unreliable, but it can be used to give a general indication as to whether the skeleton is that of a young or an old adult. Measurement of bones can also give an approximate indication of age.

This rapid survey of ageing methods should suggest that estimated ages at death for juveniles could be regarded as fairly accurate, especially if the bone preservation is good enough to allow the rate of tooth development to be assessed. Even a skeleton in which all bones except teeth have disappeared is suitable for such assessment. The younger the age of the skeleton at death, the more accurate the estimate of age on the basis of dental development is likely to be.

In the complete absence of any skeletal remains, as may happen, for example, in the acidic sandy soils of Suffolk, a plausible guess at the age of an individual may be made by the size of the grave cut. This is not a perfect method by any means, but where there is a shortage of skeletal information, particularly in the case of infants, the size of the grave cut may be all there is to distinguish an infant from a

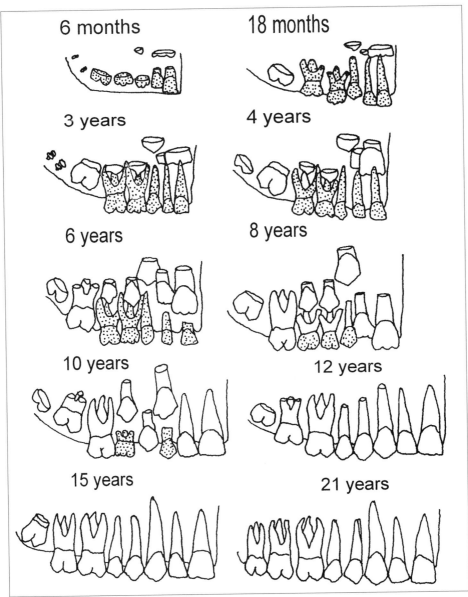

6 months

18 months

3 years

4 years

6 years

8 years

10 years

12 years

15 years

21 years

Diagrammatic representation of the stages in the development of juvenile teeth (after Brothwell 1981).

juvenile, and unless we are to argue the possibility of widespread dwarfism in Anglo-Saxon England, the grave dimensions can also be used to distinguish the biological child from the obvious adult. Identifying the sex of an immature skeleton is more problematic, and in general, Anglo-Saxon cemetery reports identify the sex by associated gender-related artefacts.[8]

METHODS OF INTERPRETING THE MORTUARY RITUAL

The problem of interpreting the symbols in the burial ritual is one that has taxed the ingenuity of many Anglo-Saxon archaeologists. There is a huge variety in Anglo-Saxon burials – it seems that no two burials are exactly alike. The size and shape of the grave, the presence or absence of grave furniture, the position of the body and the items buried with the dead all show considerable variation. The table below gives an indication of the range and grave goods that were found in just one cemetery, for example, and this is without taking into account the variation within the individual items. Was a brooch simply a brooch to the wearer, or did it matter if it was a saucer brooch rather than a cruciform brooch? Was the style of each burial determined by individual whim (in which case we cannot begin to interpret it in any meaningful way) or was there an overall set of social rules, or patterns of behaviour, to which the burials more or less conformed?

One method for interpreting society on the basis of its burial ritual is to assume that there is a direct correlation between the effort and energy put into the burial and the status of the person buried.[9] The 'cost' of the burial might be expressed in valuable grave goods, or in an elaborate ritual such as feasting

The Range of Grave Goods Found with Male Adults, Female Adults and Children Under Twelve Years of Age at Polhill, West Kent

Object	Child	Male Adult	Female Adult
Iron knife	8	31	12
Iron buckle	2	6	1
Latchlifter	1		4
Beads	3		7
Pot	1		
Belt fittings		3	1
Bronze buckle		10	1
Bag		2	2
Iron tool		2	1
Box		1	2
Finger ring			5
Chatelaine			4
Disc brooch			1
Pin			1
Comb			2
Seax		2	
Spear		12	
Shoe fittings		2	
Scabbard		1	

before, during or after the burial, or in the size and shape of the burial itself – a cremation will take more effort than a mound burial, and a mound burial will take more effort than a simple trench in the ground. The Anglo-Saxon documentary evidence reinforces this idea that the more important you were to your community, the more extravagant your burial was likely to be. There are several burials of kings in the Anglo-Saxon poem *Beowulf* which indicate that the funeral of a king would be in accordance with his rank and prowess as a warrior: before the hero Beowulf died, he asked his friends to bury him with treasure within a mound to show that he was the greatest and worthiest warrior of all men throughout the earth.

Current mortuary theory also asserts that each individual will have a number of social personae according to his status and role in society. An individual may be a father, a son and a tribal leader all at the same time, and the most important of these roles within that individual's society will tend to dominate over the lesser personae within the ritual. Are these interpretative theories relevant to children's burials? The grave goods found with adult males or females are assumed to 'belong' to that individual, correlating to their identity both socially and ritually. The same assumption is more difficult to make of child burials. Was a child given personal status within the burial ritual, or was the child's burial merely a reflection of parental or tribal status? The age of the child may have been completely irrelevant in the burial process, in which case there would be no grave goods associated particularly with children, as all children would have been ascribed the grave goods of their nearest relative. It is also possible that the grave ritual reflects not the status the children had achieved at the time of death, but what they might have become had they lived.

If the contention is that Anglo-Saxon children were recognised as children and were given special treatment according to their age, then it follows that the Anglo-Saxon mortuary ritual should substantiate this argument by verifying that children and adults were not given identical treatment in the mortuary ritual. Such differentiation, and the ritual age at which a 'child' became an 'adult', would have implications for our understanding of the role of children in Anglo-Saxon society. However, this contention poses a methodological problem – can we identify the signals in the burial ritual by which this separate group of children were identified? If the Anglo-Saxon burial ritual was age-related, and these rituals are archaeologically visible, they should be evident in the aspects of the burial (layout of the body, grave goods, grave furniture and so on) that have been visible to all excavators in the past fifty years or so, and analysis of such observations across a number of cemeteries will verify whether archaeologically identifiable age-determined mortuary patterns existed. In addition, no two pagan burial cemeteries are exactly identical in terms of preservation and content, and each excavation produces unique anecdotal evidence to add to the overall picture. At Snape in Suffolk, the unusual archaeological conditions allowed more organic material than usual to be identified. One burial of an adolescent would have been described as without grave goods in normal circumstances, but here the acidic soil had preserved a dark stain marking the outline of two drinking horns carefully placed at the feet of the corpse. Drinking horns are usually associated with the highest status burials, and this discovery is a salutary reminder that the archaeologist can only retrieve a small proportion of the total burial ritual.[10] Similarly, an unusual burial of a man, a child and a dog in one grave at Lovendon Hill does not appear to represent 'typical' Anglo–Saxon practice, in that the pattern has not been repeated elsewhere, but such odd examples may serve to flesh out a more detailed picture of Anglo–Saxon childhood where the sources are sparse.[11]

Whatever the analysis of the burial ritual may reveal about Anglo–Saxon attitudes towards their children, it must be remembered the burial ritual is indeed a ritual, rather than a direct reflection of the social structure of the society doing the burying. Rituals, by their nature, are self-perpetuating acts, and may fossilise behaviour or ideologies that are no longer current in the living society. Rituals may also lose their meaning – trees are brought into houses and decorated at Christmas, and few could offer any explanation for this behaviour except that it is 'traditional'. The original meaning of this act has long been forgotten: new meanings have been offered for the old ritual. Today, the Christmas tree – often a plastic facsimile – has meaning only as a ritual associated with the season, to be decorated each year because that is one of the practices forming part of the celebration. The empty ritual will perhaps be repeated annually long after our society (and possibly 'Christmas') has changed into something else. The rite of burial, marking one of the most profound ceremonies in the human experience, is particularly resistant to alteration. Clare Gittings studied the changing attitude towards death as a result of the post-medieval rise of individualism, and noted that feast and gift-giving traditions at funerals survived through the Reformation and into the modern period, remaining virtually unchanged in practice and significance. Even major political and social upheavals may not be enough to break strong customs designed to mitigate the impact of death and to reinforce the social bonds.[12] Any patterns associated with juveniles in the Anglo–Saxon burial ritual will only tell us about behaviour appropriate to funerals, and not necessarily about behaviour appropriate to living children.

TERMINOLOGY

One of the problems in uncovering the story of Anglo–Saxon children is the modern preconception about who or what a child ought to be, which clouds the interpretation, and understanding of the burial patterns. This is highlighted by the current archaeological practice by which there is no standard definition of 'child' in site reports, where each cemetery site report offers an apparently arbitrary 'juvenile' age range, frequently without any explanation or justification. In part this is because there is no existing study to identify what a child may have been in the Anglo–Saxon period.[13] Not all archaeological reports fail to engage with the problem of defining the child, but a wide and confusing range of terms and definitions are used in cemetery reports.[14] Those site reports which fail to discuss their methods of identifying children often confuse both the writer and reader. For example, the category of 'infant' varies from three years old at

Westgarth Gardens in Suffolk to twelve years at Raunds in Northamptonshire, while 'child' may vary from under thirteen years (Winnall II) to seventeen years (Raunds). There may be inconsistencies within a single site report: a nebulous category of 'adolescents' makes a sporadic appearance at Sewerby, Yorkshire, and Portway, Hampshire, – is this group the same as the 'subadult' group? At Portway, grave 48 is classed as 'subadult', aged eighteen to twenty-five, but appears as an adult within the tables of grave-good distribution. At Winnall, the grave catalogue classes a fifteen- to sixteen-year-old as 'adolescent', but in the demography tables, birth to fifteen years old is the first, juvenile category, presumably on the basis of biological development, although the reason for this category is not stated. Nowhere in these reports is there any explanation of how these categories are defined even though in each report it was felt necessary to distinguish 'child' from 'adult' for analytical purposes, and it is only by careful

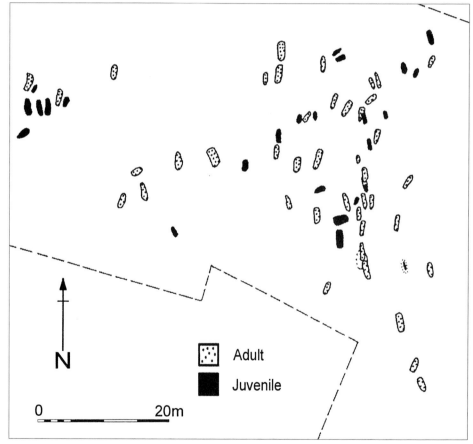

Distribution map of juveniles and adults at the cemetery of Portway, Hampshire, where 'juveniles' are classed as twelve or younger. Note the cluster of 'juvenile' burials in the north-west of the site.

scrutiny that it is possible to deduce what age ranges the writer was intending for any of these categories. Most archaeologists do not have the time to carry out such deductive searches. How, then, is the 'infant' population at Raunds to be compared with that at Westgarth Gardens? Terms such as 'juvenile', 'infant', 'adolescent' and 'subadult' are used with great fluidity and no firm attempt at definition.

The implications of this *laissez-faire* attitude are serious. Where such small samples are used, it is important that the age categories are clear. The movement of one or two individuals from one category to another can seriously distort such statistics as may be gleaned from individual cemetery analysis. Professor Evison compared the mortuary population at Buckland, Dover, with that at Polhill, West Kent, and found that the child/adult ratio was similar, but she used Brian Philp's figure of thirty juveniles at Polhill without taking into account the unstated fact

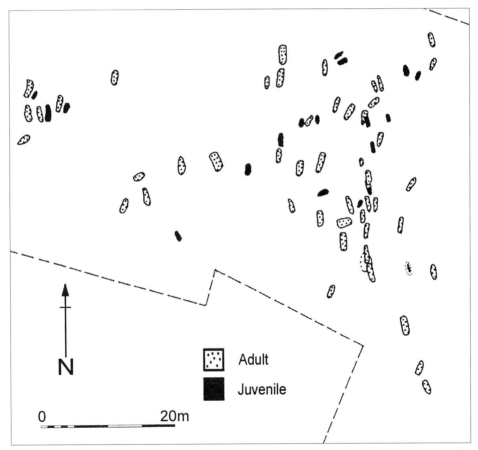

Distribution map of juveniles and adults at the cemetery of Portway, Hampshire, where 'juveniles' are classed as eighteen or younger. The cluster of 'juveniles' in the north-west of the site has disappeared, to be replaced by adult/juvenile pairs.

that, at Dover, individuals under eighteen are counted as juveniles for this purpose, while at Polhill the age limit was fifteen. If the Polhill age is raised to a comparable eighteen years, the number of 'children' increases to forty-one, and the consequent child/adult ratio shifts accordingly. The criteria for defining 'children' in the cemetery site reports needed to be carefully considered, or at least clearly stated, if such misleading effects are to be avoided.[15]

The vagueness of the adult/juvenile categories leads to further confusion when the excavator wishes to offer hypotheses about the social structure of the cemetery population, or age-related patterns that may be visible within it. Sex and age distribution maps, for instance, are a common feature of any excavation report, but what exactly do they tell us about age-related cemetery patterns? Age distribution maps may be quite misleading unless we know the terms on which they are created. The plans on the previous two pages demonstrate this point. The first shows an adult/juvenile distribution map for a typical cemetery, where the age limit for juveniles is twelve. In the second, the age limit is taken as eighteen. The two plans, naturally, give us different impressions about what was going on in the cemetery. Is the north-west group, for instance, a group of juveniles or a group of paired adult/juvenile burials? In the site report from which these plans were taken, using a third option, the (unstated) age limit of around fifteen is given in this distribution map, but which of these three versions is correct? The answer depends on what the maps are supposed to reveal. If they are there to demonstrate that adults are buried in one place and juveniles in another, then none of these maps is right unless we know what age determined an adult as opposed to a juvenile for those doing the burying.

STATISTICAL VALIDITY AND IDENTIFYING AGE THRESHOLDS

As can be seen in the table opposite, the percentage of burials of children aged fifteen and under in the earlier Anglo-Saxon inhumation cemeteries is not normal for a living population. It is well understood that a mortuary population is already a biased sample, being determined by cultural rather than biological determinants, and the general shortage of children in the sample may be a result of deliberate omission – dead children may have been disposed of in other ways.[16] The children in the burial sample, then, may represent a specially selected group. They may not be typical of the Anglo-Saxon child, or may have held some particular and special place in their society which gave them differential treatment at the time of death. This possibility aside, the fact that children are under-represented in the burials poses some problems for the archaeologist, not least one of maintaining some semblance of statistical validity in the analysis of the children's burials. There is no simple answer in archaeology to the question 'How many is enough?' Obviously, the more detailed the question asked of the data, the smaller the sample will be and the less likely the information is to be useful. Ideally, the data should contain every single excavated site, and while such a database may come into existence in due course, it is not yet available.[17]

Child Burials Within a Sample of Earlier Anglo-Saxon Cemeteries, Grouped by Age Band

Age band	Number of cases in age band	% of mortuary population	% of population surviving this age group
0	12	1.2	98.8
1–2	31	3.1	95.7
3–4	44	4.4	91.3
5–6	34	3.4	88.0
7–9	73	7.3	80.7
10–12	48	4.8	76
13–15	34	3.4	72.5
16–25	182	18.1	54.4
25+	547	54.4	0

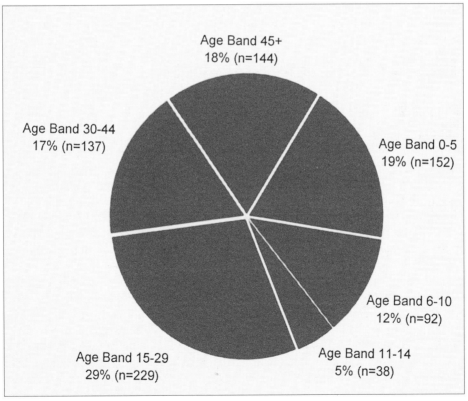

Age at death of a sample population from early Anglo-Saxon inhumation cemeteries.

Another consideration is to create appropriate categories for analysis so that the right questions are asked of the right data sets. Age grouping of juveniles must be done so that there are sufficient numbers in each group to provide meaningful results. One of the aims of this book is to assess whether children were treated differently to adults, and at what age the threshold between childhood and adulthood was crossed. In the database, the group of 'adults' must be compared to the group of 'children' to see if a difference in treatment existed in the burial ritual, but, given that we do not know how long Anglo-Saxon childhood was perceived to last, how are we to establish the proper groups? It would be unhelpful to draw the line between adult and juvenile at too young an age, say thirteen or fifteen, as some site analysts have been tempted to do, because this would presuppose that full adulthood was reached in the teens.[18] In fact, in some non-industrial modern groups, full adulthood may be reached at a much later age than westerners might expect, especially given life expectancy. The Loikop tribe of East Africa acknowledge membership of the senior warrior group between the ages of twenty-two and thirty, while the Ebric of Nigeria require a theoretical age of thirty-two for attaining adulthood, though the actual age of so-called 'adults' may be as low as twenty-four; and the tribes of the Hebrew Testament, according to the account in Numbers 1, counted men as adults and weapon-bearers only when they had attained the age of twenty.[19]

IDENTIFYING AGE MARKERS

Although there are rarely discussions of what criteria determine the labelling of 'children' and 'infants' in cemetery site reports, age markers – objects within the burial, or aspects of the burial, such as orientation of the body, presence or absence of grave furniture and layout of the body, which are associated with particular age groups – are commonly a focus of attention. In the assessment of symbols within the burial ritual, excavators frequently relate their findings to age distinctions. At Portway, Hampshire, the occupant of grave 60, an eleven- to twelve-year-old, is noted to have been buried with 'adult' grave features – a partially flint-lined grave with a wooden baulk. Two children aged five (grave 24) and eight or nine (grave 40) are observed to have had small spears, while another 'child', aged fifteen to sixteen, was buried with a normal-sized spearhead.[20] The excavator was looking for age-related goods, but was unable to find any convincing candidates. It may be that here, the excavators' own preconceptions about what constitutes an adult and what a juvenile may have prevented consideration that the evidence points to the age of eleven or twelve as being the threshold between childhood and adulthood. If this were so, the fact that two juveniles are buried with small spearheads and the third 'child' is not, instantly becomes rational: the third child, as his adult-sized spearhead indicates, is in fact, in the burial ritual, an adult. If the evidence is read with sensitivity, the ritual of burial is rational and meaningful. At the late fifth- to early seventh-century site of Empingham II, Rutland, it was noted in the report that children and subadults of both sexes were buried with fewer grave goods than adults, but there were three exceptions to this rule which demonstrated that 'a direct correlation between age and number of possessions cannot be upheld'.[21] The three exceptions in this case were aged thirteen to fifteen years (grave 85B), twelve to fourteen years (grave 24) and nine to ten years (grave 105) on the basis of tooth eruption. One might argue a case for the nine- to ten-year-old being marginally within the 'child' age band, but it may be that older 'children' actually qualified as 'adults' within the burial ritual. At Charlton Plantations in Wiltshire, burial 76 (of a juvenile aged twelve to fifteen) was noted as the 'only child burial . . . with any grave good', and attention was also drawn to the 'subadult' male in grave 78, aged fifteen to twenty at the time of death, buried with a spearhead. No 'child' aged under twelve was given a furnished burial at this site, if the male in grave 78 is assumed to be an 'adult' within the ritual.[22]

Where the ritual pattern seems vague and uninterpretable, it may be because we do not understand the rules on which the pattern is based. When a pattern emerges from one cemetery as clearly as at Portway, it is worth testing it against comparable cemeteries. The twelve-year age threshold emerging at Portway both makes sense of, and is corroborated by, findings at Sewerby, Empingham II and Charlton, where children over ten to twelve also seem to be classed as adults. If age divisions, whether based on anthropological or biological assumptions, are not applied too rigidly, then the divisions actually used by the populations may begin to emerge.[23] However difficult and obscure the Anglo-Saxon burial ritual may seem in other perspectives, it is nevertheless clear that the age of the deceased had an impact on the grave goods and form of burial of the individual, and an age threshold between ten and twelve years for transition from 'child' to 'adult' status within the burial ritual seems to be present within many pagan Anglo-Saxon inhumation cemeteries.

WHAT THE BURIAL RITUAL SAYS ABOUT THE CHILD'S PLACE IN ANGLO-SAXON SOCIETY

The first table overleaf shows the number of burials with and without grave goods from a sample Anglo-Saxon inhumation cemetery population, and the second table shows the number of grave goods included in the burial ritual by age groups. The pattern indicated by the tables is that, with increasing age, there is a likelihood that a dead person would be buried with more grave goods. Of those children who died at birth to five years in the cemeteries contributing to this data, over 50 per cent had no archaeologically identifiable grave goods at all, and just under 80 per cent of them were buried with either no grave goods or only a single item. These proportions gradually change with age, so that just over 60 per cent of those within the six to ten-year age group are buried with none or only one item, just under 50 per cent of those in the eleven to fifteen-year and the sixteen to twenty-year age group, and around 30 per cent of those in the older age groups. The pattern indicates gradual change, but the increasing lack of accuracy in ageing skeletons after puberty means that it is difficult to achieve a sharper picture, and in particular it is difficult to focus on what appears, from the documentary sources, to be the crucial transitional period between ten and fifteen years. Many skeletons within the teenage age range are classed by the bone

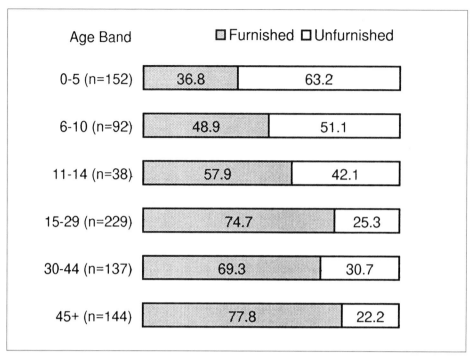

Furnished and unfurnished burials by age group within a sample Anglo-Saxon inhumation population.

Numbers of Artefacts in Furnished Inhumation Burials Within a Sample Anglo-Saxon Population

Age Band

Number of items	0–5 (n=152)	6–10 (n=92)	11–14 (n=38)	15–29 (n=229)	30–44 (n=137)	45+ (n=144)
1	55.4	33.3	27.3	21.6	14.7	17.0
2	21.4	22.2	18.2	18.1	16.8	19.6
3	12.5	17.8	4.5	11.1	20.0	17.0
4	1.8	4.4	13.6	8.2	9.5	15.2
5	3.6	6.7	4.5	7.6	10.5	10.7
6	1.8	6.7	0	7.0	5.3	2.7
7	0	0	13.6	5.3	6.3	5.4
8	1.8	4.4	4.5	4.1	6.3	3.6
9	0	2.2	4.5	4.1	3.2	3.6
10+	1.8	2.2	8.5	12.9	7.5	5.4

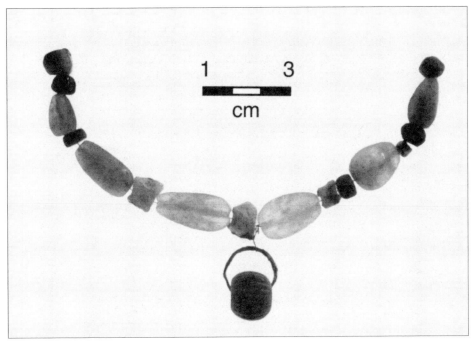

An amethyst necklace found with a child buried in grave 7 at Finglesham, Kent.

specialists as being between six and twelve years (a typical range at Buckland, Dover, for example) or thirteen and seventeen (for example at Morningthorpe, Norfolk, and Westgarth Gardens, Suffolk). It is a matter of fact that the most important threshold ages from an Anglo-Saxon perspective are, archaeologically, not particularly easy to identify with accuracy. What is noticeable, however, is that the burial ritual appears to have offered a certain amount of flexibility to the buriers. While over half of the children aged under five at the time of death were buried with no grave goods at all, and a further 22 per cent were buried with only one artefact, there were a few children who broke this rule, some quite significantly, such as the child in Polhill (grave 51) who was buried with beads and pendants, or the (probable) girl buried in Finglesham (grave 7) with gold necklace pendants, two pots, a chatelaine and a purse – an unusual and rich collection of artefacts more commonly associated with girls past puberty.

It is not possible to assess the relative 'cost' of grave goods – we cannot now know whether a knife was considered a greater or lesser loss to the wealth of a community than a brooch when they were deposited in the grave, but one way of identifying whether the cost of the burial changed with the age of the deceased is to look for evidence of materials which had to be imported into the community, such as gold, silver, garnet and amber. Such precious materials must have been in shorter supply than, say, wood, and some effort was required to transport these materials to communities within Anglo-Saxon England, so it is a reasonable starting place to infer that grave goods including such precious metals must have had some economic value.[24]

An assessment of Anglo-Saxon burials indicates that, until the age of about ten, only one burial in ten includes precious materials, and these usually take the form of gold pendants, reused Roman coins pierced for suspension, or amethyst and amber beads found on the necklaces of girls (given that, in the adult ritual, necklaces are gendered artefacts only associated with women). The child aged between one and two years at the time of death found in grave 113 at Lechlade, Gloucestershire had only two archaeologically recoverable grave goods – one alloy coin, and one gold coin minted in AD 348–60. The lack of grave goods might be taken as an indication of lack of status, but coins were valuable to the Anglo-Saxon community, and may additionally have held some amuletic value.[25]

For children who died over the age of eleven years, the likelihood of being buried with precious materials improves. Up to 35 per cent of burials between the ages of eleven and fifteen, and sixteen and twenty, were buried with such materials, although the number of precious metals and stones within the burials peaked within this age group. If you died at the relatively advanced age of over thirty-one, your burial ritual, while maintaining a high count of artefacts, would be given fewer precious metals, and anyone living into old age would be buried with fewer artefacts adorned with precious metals. The reason for an apparent decline in status of the elderly in the burial ritual may stem from the same basis as the Salian lawcode which placed the *wergild* of a young woman of free status and childbearing age at three times the value of a post-menopausal woman, and more if she were pregnant. According to the Visigothic laws, a young woman's *wergild* was only slightly less than that of an adult male of free status.[26] Women of childbearing age, and men in their youthful prime, may have been of the highest value to the community compared to the old or the very young.

Although children who died between birth and five years were likely to be buried with only a single item, there seems to have been no particular artefact deemed appropriate for such a burial. Compared to older children buried with a single artefact, the choice of object to give to the grave of the youngest children seems to have been wide-ranging. Knives or single beads were among the most popular items, but buckles, nails, wires, animal teeth, flint flakes and a bronze toilet instrument are all included in the range of items found with infants. In the database sample, children who died between birth and five years were buried with a range of seventeen items; eleven- to fifteen-year-olds, by comparison, received a range of only six items, nearly half of them being buried with a knife. In the adult range, if a burial contained a single artefact, that artefact was most likely to be a knife. What is also clear from a study of the inhumation cemetery evidence is that, while there were some artefacts and assemblages that were associated with the adult burial ritual – shields, swords, wristclasps and sets of pots or containers, for example, are exclusive to the older age groups – there are no artefacts found in the graves of infants and younger children which are not also found in the graves of adults: in other words, there are no artefacts dedicated to child burials.

The overriding impression given by the Anglo-Saxon cemetery evidence is that children had only a marginal place in the burial ritual, in that their social status

The Most Common Grave Goods Found with Burials Under the Age of Fifteen

Grave good	Age Band			
	0–5 (n=152)	6–10 (n=92)	11–14 (n=38)	Total (n=282)
Knife	14	27	13	43
Beads	18	11	2	31
Buckle	5	14	8	27
Brooch	2	13	11	26
Containe	13	4	6	23
Pin	7	8	6	21
Coin	4	2	12	18
Totals	63	79	58	189

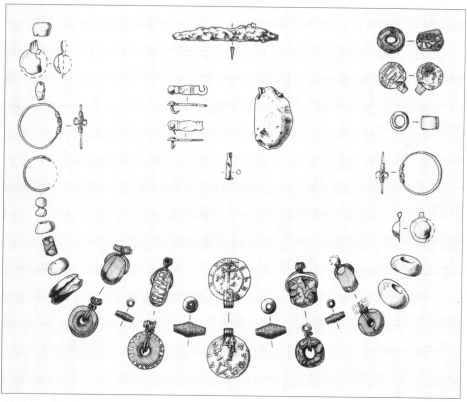

Necklace found with a child aged about five buried in grave 132 at Finglesham, Kent. Several of the beads may have been thought to have amuletic properties.

was expressed entirely in adult terms, and that status was low. At Wheatley, a child aged about five was buried with a broken (adult) brooch, and the 'subadult' at Finglesham, Kent (grave 210), was buried with an incomplete bracelet. At Lechlade in Gloucestershire, the excavator commented that disc brooches in particular showed a strong association with children and many of them were very worn.[27] The grave goods are unlikely to have been personal possessions for these children, and probably represent inherited or donated adult gifts to children either in life or in death. The presence of broken and worn grave goods in the burials of some children may indicate that they had only token or symbolic significance within ritual terms. For children, the ritual dominated over the personal, reducing the individual to a token place in the social order. The indiscriminate range of grave goods associated with the youngest burials emphasises that the burial ritual was not designed to accommodate children; being incidental to the ritual, their burials allowed greater flexibility in choice of token artefacts. By the age of eleven to fifteen, the deceased had come, in symbolic terms, within the sphere of the adult world and their burials reflect a more coherent and constrained application of the burial ritual.

CHAPTER 3
Documentary Sources

When the Anglo-Saxons were converted to Christianity from the late sixth century onwards, they were introduced to the concepts of writing and manuscript production. Despite the growth of literacy we have limited surviving records offering some information on what the Anglo-Saxons had to say about their own society, and what they thought of the pagan society of their immediate past. Archaeologists are wary of using documentary sources in conjunction with archaeology, for fear that the prejudice of the text will affect the interpretation of the archaeological record, but in the case of Anglo-Saxon society, what better place to look for anthropological parallels to the childhood indicated in the archaeological evidence than to texts dating from the Anglo-Saxon period? As Richard Bradley famously pointed out, 'it would be a mistake for Saxonists to shrink away from written evidence into a vague, amnesiac pre-history when the great virtue of their discipline is the very breadth of its data'.[1]

One of the major problems with the use of documentary evidence is that it is difficult to establish how far the literature reflects a 'real' Anglo-Saxon society, and how far the texts are wholesale borrowings from foreign models, imitating or enlarging on Roman Christian ideology. Anglo-Saxon documentary evidence falls into several major categories including hagiography (the lives of saints), poetry (secular and religious), wills and charters, lawcodes, chronicles and medical texts. Obviously, these different literary genres will produce particular difficulties of interpretation, and these will be discussed briefly in the sections to follow.

HAGIOGRAPHY

The Anglo-Saxon *Lives* of the saints provide rich and colourful sources of semi-historical insights into Anglo-Saxon society, and are one of the few literary forms to offer a history of children, occasionally describing the births and incidents associated with the upbringing of those destined to become saints. Furthermore, a number of the recorded miracles involve children and their carers. Many of the *Lives* were written in Old English, and were intended to educate and inform not just a monastic literary élite but also a wider audience. Once the Anglo-Saxons had begun the process of conversion to Christianity in the late sixth century, the new converts were eager to be able to demonstrate their holiness by being able to boast of local saints. The first saints were those who worked among the still pagan populations – men such as Guthlac, Wilfred and Cuthbert – and their *Lives* were eagerly written up shortly after their deaths, and were recounted to listeners who would possibly have had personal knowledge of these saintly heroes. The earliest *Lives*, then, were written at a period when pagan practices still persisted. The early audiences of the *Lives* and people represented by the latest burials in the seventh-century furnished cemeteries were contemporary. The *Lives* are also invaluable as a starting point for discussion of the influences of Mediterranean and Christian practice on the threshold ages in Anglo-Saxon society. They provide a certain link between the old illiterate pagan society and the later literate Christian society.

Of all surviving forms of documentary evidence, the *Lives* are at once the most exciting and the most elusive – within these almost biographical tales we seem to be offered glimpses, as through a keyhole, of 'real' Anglo-Saxon behaviour, for the best writers of these *Lives* attempted to create an aura of reality in their work, often by citing reliable and trustworthy sources. Such claims to truthfulness, research and careful collation often obscure the fact that hagiography represents an elaborate, formal and artificial genre, and the constrained, formulaic nature of hagiographical work must be recognised.

The *Lives* were written to edify and entertain the populace: they competed against secular folklore and epic sagas to lure the hesitator and heathen, and even the clerics themselves, away from pagan tastes in literature and belief, towards the Church with its martyrs and holy men. Hagiography has a long pedigree, and the writers of the *Lives* had no shortage of literary exemplars upon which to draw. The art form was already highly sophisticated by the time Bede came to write the *Life of St Cuthbert*, or Felix the *Life of St Guthlac*.[2] The *Lives* followed an approved template, so that when Guthlac is described as taming birds through his saintly patience, he is following the example of St Gregory the Great or the earlier St Anthony. Likewise, the narrative of St Aidan stilling the stormy waters in Bede's *Ecclesiastical History* follows the example of no less a figure than Christ himself. These were deliberate mimickings of saintly miracles, founded on the understanding that the sanctity of the Anglo-Saxon saint would receive authority because his deeds paralleled those of earlier, known saintly men and women. Hagiographers often gave the audience heavy hints to remind them of this very point by driving home the fact that their saint was 'like' another holy man. Thus, Cuthbert's childhood is 'like' that of Samuel while, more poignantly, the almost ridiculous death of the adult St Edmund (used for target practice by the Vikings until he was shot through with spears so that, as the hagiographer wrote, these looked like the bristles on a hedgehog) is given dignity by being described as 'like' that of St Sebastian.[3]

The most influential of these model *Lives*, ones which had certainly become familiar to the Anglo-Saxon Church in the early eighth century and probably before, were the Latin translation of St Athanasius's *Life of St Anthony*, by Evagrius, Jerome's *Life of St Paul the Hermit*, and the fifth-century *Life of St Martin* by Sulpicius Severus. The huge influence of these models means that no descriptive passage in an Anglo-Saxon *Life* can be assumed to be genuinely Anglo-Saxon in thought or content without first ascertaining whether or not the passage has been modelled on one of these earlier texts or on incidents in the

Bible. Similarly, hagiographers consciously borrowed events, sentences and even whole passages from other contemporary writers. Thus Felix seems to be using his own words to describe St Guthlac's childhood, but the later parts of the *Life* resemble Bede's *St Cuthbert* more and more closely until, in the words of translator Bertram Colgrave, the likenesses 'reach their climax in the death scene in which Felix borrows considerable sections from Bede's *Life* of that saint'.[4] Originality and historical accuracy were not the priority in this genre.

Given this literary and historical background, it would be unreasonable to claim any 'reality' or historical accuracy in the portrayals of the Anglo-Saxon saints. In order to conform to the rules of this genre, the *Lives* followed a set pattern, and their saints, in the same way as modern stereotyped heroes, had to fulfil the expectations: signs of wonder to accompany the birth (Guthlac, Æthelwold), model parents (Guthlac) or terrible parents (Anselm); and early signs of prodigality or holy favour had to be demonstrated (Cuthbert, Edith, Eadberga), perhaps followed by a period of youthful rebellion (Guthlac, Wilfred) to make the consequent conversion to Christianity yet more singular. After the conversion came the usual miracles, involving a selection of animals, men, women and children to be tamed, saved from drowning or fire, or healed.

It is also a characteristic of Anglo-Saxon saints that they were of royal or at least noble birth, without exception. The entry of nobility into monasteries in the Anglo-Saxon period emphasised the power associated with Christianity, and notable holiness conferred power. Only the upper echelons of society were selected to join convents. At the royal foundation of Wilton, where King Edward's daughter Edith was brought up, her hagiographer described her as being in good company: 'The community of virgins and brides of Christ was at that time drawn, as is customary, from the highest ranks of society – from the most illustrious daughters of the princes, thegns and magnates of the realm.'[5] It was from this pre-selected group that the saints were drawn. In her evaluation of the phenomenon of the royal saint, Susan Ridyard postulated that those who would be saints had to be influential in life before they became famous after death. A royal patron of a monastery could ensure prosperity for the community, while such a person, if sanctified after death, could ensure continuing patronage from the saint's royal kin. There is no reason to suppose that the *Lives* mirror everyday life. Indeed, what often singles the saints out is their reluctance to accept the privileges due to them, or else they are discovered demeaning themselves in an unacceptable manner. Thus Princess Eadberga as a young convent girl was beaten by a prioress for reading a book in private, until her royal identity was revealed, whereupon the prioress apologised – it had not been wise to beat the daughter of the king. In the event, Eadberga showed her virtuous nature by begging forgiveness and promising never to break the rule again.

A combination of the formal structure of the hagiography, the high status of the participants, and the layers of meaning in any action, means that information from the *Lives* about the childhood of a saint must obviously be treated with care. 'Layers of meaning' are particularly misleading. An apparently matter-of-fact statement may be a complicated vehicle for allegory. Bede described Cuthbert as receiving intelligence of his holy destiny at the age of eight; this is the age at which Bede himself was adopted by Benedict Biscop, and joined the monastery at Monkwearmouth, Jarrow, and at which boys were taken into monasteries according to the Roman custom. It may be that Cuthbert really received notice of his divine calling at this age, but it is a certainty that the hearers of the tale would have recognised the symbolism and significance of the number. At an age when a child would be physically given to a monastery, Cuthbert became a changed boy in spirit, a servant of God. This is not over-sophistication – the audience was alive to layers of meaning, and symbols and secret messages were habitually read into texts.

Given this background, it may well seem that nothing can possibly be gleaned about the status and treatment of children in the later Anglo-Saxon period from such obviously unreliable sources. Yet, if properly used, these sources may provide positive evidence to corroborate archaeological material, or to redefine Anglo-Saxon attitudes to childhood, particularly in relation to current theories on parental attitudes towards children in pre-industrial societies.[6] Hagiographers wrote within the limitations and strictures of the genre, but this is not to say that they could not improve on the exemplar, or apply the example to their own experience, or to that of their subjects.

Another salient factor in the discussion of the usefulness of this material is that, although an Anglo-Saxon might demand, and discover, layers of meaning in hagiographical literature, or take advantage of the narrative to draw Biblical parallels – Bede used the Cuthbert incident to illustrate the text 'when I was a child I thought as a child' – this does not preclude the possibility that one of the layers of meaning might be rooted in literal truth; the difficulty is to recognise it.[7] On his death, we are told that Cuthbert was wrapped in a rich garment, after a life of poverty and austerity, to signify that he was going to spiritual riches in the heavenly kingdom. This description was not merely a literary device: the burial vestments of Cuthbert exist to be seen today, moreover the Anglo-Saxon description of these garments reflects relatively accurately the number and type of Anglo-Saxon garments that survive on the body of Cuthbert.[8]

We know from other surviving literature that the Anglo-Saxons were ethnocentric in their treatment of source material, in the Apocrypha, such as the story of Judith which involved a purely Anglo-Saxon battle scene; it would not be wrong to take the description of the battle between the Hebrews and the Philistines as a good indication of how foot battles between the English and Vikings were carried out.[9] But, in the same translation, we find the Old English writer having to grapple with a concept he does not understand. The mosquito net in the original text is purely functional, but the Anglo-Saxon translator, perhaps unfamiliar with the purpose of such a device, and without any obvious native word to insert, endows the net with ambiguity and sinister overtones. It takes on a mystical significance entirely lacking in the original Latin. In the *Lives*, then, it is fair to suppose that any details will be at least familiar to the Anglo-Saxons. Details in the older texts that are alien to Anglo-Saxon culture will either be omitted, or Anglicised, or so confused that they should be readily identifiable as outside Anglo-Saxon experience.

This leads on to the question of what kind of veracity the readers of Anglo-Saxon *Lives* would have expected from their texts? The most important indication that the texts contain some truth is that many of the *Lives* were written by near contemporaries of the saints, or at least written within the living memory of those who had personally known the saint, and who would naturally be the most influential critics of the hagiographer's work. After the first flush of missionary work had subsided, clerics were desperate to prove that England was as civilised and holy as any other Christian land: 'Nor is England deprived of the Lord's saints, since such saints as this holy king lie buried in England, and the noble Cuthbert . . . also many other holy ones in England who have worked many miracles' was the claim made by Ælfric at the end of his *Life of King Edmund*.[10]

Churchmen were also desperate to attract funds to their establishments via the prestige of their own local saint. At this period of keen saint-seeking, the land had only been converted long enough to provide saints of fairly recent holiness. Under these circumstances, the hagiographer would certainly embellish a *Life*, for a popular *Life* would enhance the prestige of the religious establishment associated with the saint, but it could not afford to be wildly inaccurate, for those, as already suggested, most likely to read and criticise the first airing of the narrative would be members of the community in which the saint had lived and worked. While a cynic could claim that there may have been a certain amount of collusion among the friends of a saint to create a 'fitting' *Life*, there are, too, the protestations of the writers themselves to be taken into account. Anglo-Saxon prefaces are distinguished by their assertions of humility and professions of painstaking research and accuracy:

> I have not presumed to write down anything concerning so great a man without the most rigorous investigation of the facts, nor, at the end, to hand on what I had written to be copied for general use, without the scrupulous examination of credible witnesses. Nay rather, it was only after first diligently investigating the beginning, the progress, and the end of his most glorious life and activity, with the help of those who knew him, that I began at last to set about making notes.[11]

So claimed Bede for his *Life* of Cuthbert, and so, unfortunately, did Felix in almost precisely the same words in his preface to the *Life* of Guthlac. To be fair, it would be excessively suspicious to suppose that both men were engaged in a conscious deception; we must credit them for believing their works to have some measure of historical accuracy. If the saint had lived and died some time before the date of the *Life*, the hagiographer would go to extraordinary lengths to prove that his tale had the authority of first-hand evidence. Thus Ælfric in his preface to the *Life of King Edmund* indulged in a long rigmarole to prove the accuracy of his sources:

> A certain learned monk came south over the sea from St Benedict's monastery in the days of King Æthelred to Archbishop Dunstan, three years before he died, and this monk was called Abbo. Then they spoke until Dunstan talked of

St Edmund, just as Edmund's swordbearer told it to King Æthelstan, when Dunstan was a young man, and the swordbearer was a very old man. Then the monk put all the narrative into a book, and afterwards, when the book came to us a few years ago, then we translated it into English.[12]

Clearly, hagiographers cared that their tales should be taken as true stories, and felt the need to prove the reliability of their witnesses.

An understanding of the Anglo-Saxon concept of literary and historical truth is imperative. I would like to suggest that the 'reality' in these *Lives* is not necessarily, if ever, a literal one. For example, in the *Life of St Guthlac*, it is related that two weeping parents brought their child, Hwaetred, to the saint in a last desperate hope that the child could be cured. The child, in mad fits, had killed several people, and the parents were so distracted with grief that they would have almost preferred that their son died than the present dreadful situation have continued. Of course, Guthlac cured the mad boy and the family left rejoicing.[13] St Guthlac may never have healed a child called 'Hwaetred' and whether he did or not can never be proven. The very existence of Hwaetred could be called into doubt, but in more general terms, the fact that a boy is described as living with his parents is evidence that, in the earlier Anglo-Saxon period, the concept of caring parents maintaining a mentally unstable child at home – one who had killed several people no less – was not at odds with the Anglo-Saxon perception of their society. Somewhere in Mercia, around AD 730, it must have seemed plausible that someone like Hwaetred could be living at home under the protection of his parents. If such an incident were not in fact possible, then the audience would have been aware immediately that Felix's boast about his reliable sources was hollow, and arguably their faith in the powers of the saint might have been shaken – their 'willing suspension of disbelief' would have collapsed.

Writers of tales based on real life have an obligation to be true to the minutiae of day-to-day existence in order for the web of fiction to succeed, and it is on the minutiae of the *Lives* that we can draw for real evidence: on the details that are small enough to be necessarily accurate. This theory of 'reality' in the Anglo-Saxon *Lives* must be accepted if anything is to be deduced from them about juvenile upbringing at this time, but inevitably all statements in the *Lives* must be open to question unless there is corroborative detail elsewhere. The *Life* of Cuthbert recounts that he was brought up by a foster-mother, and spent some of his childhood as a shepherd. This appears to be a valid description of a Northumbrian boy's childhood, but Cuthbert is not the first saint in the genre to have passed his childhood with foster-parents, and the obvious Christian symbolism of the future bishop and shepherd of souls acting as a shepherd in childhood cannot be overlooked, any more than the implication that the child Cuthbert, without his own biological parents to look after him and apparently without any blood family, had already fulfilled the requirement of Christ: 'If anyone comes to me and does not hate his own father and mother and wife and children and brothers and sisters, yes, and even his own life, he cannot be my disciple' (Luke 14:26). The Christian demand that children should reject their parents was particularly acute at a time when those parents were likely to be pagan, and was a motif much explored in early medieval ecclesiastical literature, the clearest expression of which in an Anglo-Saxon context came when Bishop Wilfred sent his men to forcibly remove a child he had baptised from its pagan parents.[14]

The table below shows trends in the afflictions of those children who came to the saints to be healed, and these are the children who belong to a wider range of social categories. The list of guardians bringing the children for treatment to a number of saints, including Wilfred, Cuthbert, Guthlac and John of Beverley indicates who in the family was responsible for the child, or at least who was most interested in seeing the child cured.

Children Treated by Saints in the Anglo-Saxon Lives, Detailing their Status, Illnesses and Carers

Description	Status	Affliction	Carer
infant	villager	plague	mother
first-born infant		death	mother
three-year-old	lived at convent	pestilence	?
little boy	lived at monastery	distemper	?
neophyte	lived at monastery	ague	monks
juvenile	noble	madness/murderer	parents
juvenile		paralytic	some women
boy	noble	diseased knee	?
girl	noble	chronic pain in head and sides	?
boy	estate worker's son	demoniac	father
juvenile	mason's child	crushing fall	workmates
ten-year-old	noble	blindness	parents
juvenile	noble	lameness	father
juvenile	publican's daughter	sickness	father and kin
adolescent	lived at monastery	paralytic	monks

Is there a trend of younger children being brought in by their mothers? Is there a trend of noble children being brought in anonymously rather than obviously by their parents? What is clear from this table is that, while the saints themselves may be drawn from the upper echelons of society, they do deal with ordinary folk. In this respect, the Lives are not purely the preserve of a small and unrepresentative section of society. The interaction of the saints with their social inferiors extends the range and the historical value of these sources, and can show us something of the pathology of the Anglo-Saxon period. It is likely that only the most intractable of diseases would have been brought to the saint, probably after all other remedies had been tried. Tumours on the body, contagious diseases, broken bones and mental disorders, while not common, must have been feared by carers as part of the pattern of childhood illnesses.

The only Anglo-Saxon who did not enter the Church about whom we have any good details of childhood is King Alfred. His *Life* was written by his friend, Asser, Bishop of St Davids in Wales. The argument that Asser's *Life of King Alfred* was not contemporary, but a later medieval forgery, has been too thoroughly demolished, in spite of recent attempts to revive it, to merit discussion here. Asser's *Life* in many ways resembles a work of hagiography, in that his aims were to show Alfred as a model king. This included presenting Alfred as an extraordinary child. According to Asser, Alfred, the youngest of five brothers, was only five when he was sent to Rome in AD 853 by his father. In a famous passage, Asser recounted what happened next: 'King Æthelwulf sent his son Alfred to Rome in state, accompanied by a great number of both nobles and commoners. At this time the lord Pope Leo was ruling the apostolic see; he anointed the child Alfred as king, ordaining him properly, received him as an adoptive son and confirmed him.'[15] It is unlikely in the extreme that Alfred would have been 'anointed as king', but Asser wanted to suggest that Alfred had already been marked out for special favour, even as a child, and at a time when it must have seemed improbable that all of Alfred's older brothers would die before him without leaving a son old enough to succeed to the kingship.

Usefully, a letter written to King Æthelwulf by Pope Leo IV survives to give a different, but still interesting, picture of events: 'We have now graciously received your son Alfred, whom you were anxious to send at this time to the threshold of the Holy Apostles, and we have decorated him, as a spiritual son, with the dignity of the belt/sword, and the vestments of the consulate, as is customary with Roman consuls, because he gave himself into our hands.'[16] This provides corroborative evidence that Alfred *was* sent at this young age to the Pope, and that due honour was done, in Roman terms, to the young prince. King Alfred himself may have misinterpreted the significance of this event; Asser certainly did. According to Asser, King Alfred was sent to Rome a second time when he was two years older, this time in the company of his father: "[Æthelwulf] travelled to Rome that year in great state, taking his son Alfred with him, for a second time on the same journey, because he loved him more than his other sons; there he remained for a whole year. After this, he returned to his homeland, bringing with him Judith, daughter of Charles [the Bald], king of the Franks.'[17] Asser is the only source for Alfred's presence on this trip. The *Annals of St Bertin* mention Æthelwulf's journey, as does the *Liber Pontificalis*, but neither mention Alfred, so perhaps Asser is mistaken in his account. The marriage of Alfred's father, no longer a young man, to the Frankish princess who was aged only twelve, is recorded in other sources, however, and is our evidence for Alfred having lost his mother before he was seven. His father died when Alfred was nine.

THE LAWCODES

Like the *Lives*, the surviving Anglo-Saxon lawcodes have a bearing on our understanding of adult attitudes towards children provided that the evidence is treated with due care.[18] The earliest lawcodes are contemporary with the latest pagan burials – three seventh-century codes from Kent, and one seventh-century code from Wessex survive. Thereafter we have no codes until Alfred (reigned AD 871–99), but it seems probable that later codes draw heavily on earlier models now lost to us. The following brief summary of lawcodes is intended to outline the main intentions behind their issuing, and to suggest how these laws may be used to help extend our understanding and interpretation of earlier Anglo-Saxon attitudes towards children.

Of the many lawcodes that must have been issued to regulate the lives of the Anglo-Saxons, a small and disproportionate number survive. No laws from the once powerful kingdom of Mercia remain at all, while Northumbria and East Anglia are very poorly represented. Only Kent is fairly well recorded. Any study of the lawcodes must recognise from the outset that conclusions can only be directly related to small areas of the country, although they may have represented countrywide customs.

The basic ethical code behind the laws was probably the same throughout England. There is a strong sense of tradition running through the codes, and even where kings are not represented by their laws, later kings stress that their own laws are often no more than an extension or copy of those of their predecessors. Kentish laws, too, show striking similarities to Continental lawcodes, and there can be little doubt that Mercian and Northumbrian law, stemming from the same folk traditions and customs, would have been broadly the same as Kentish law; certainly the attitudes embodied in the existing codes must have been present in those we have lost.

It is questionable, though, how far the laws are an accurate reflection of attitudes that actually prevailed within society. English lawcodes were consciously modelled on the famous Roman laws: Bede says that the laws of Æthelbert were written 'according to the Roman example', but a cursory comparison of Roman to Anglo-Saxon law demonstrates that the borrowing stops at the style and format.[19] The Anglo-Saxon laws, written for the most part in the vernacular, show little sign of Roman influence in their content.

The fact that the laws were written in the vernacular is the clearest possible indication that they were an expression of Anglo-Saxon thought, not mere Roman copies for the sake of the intelligentsia. The laws were consciously issued as a statement of national identity, both in England and abroad. Laws were frequently issued at times of national insecurity, and may be regarded as an expression of a group's unity, history and standards. In the earliest laws in particular it can reasonably be asserted that the codes are an expression of how law-abiding people actually behaved, rather than how the lawmakers ideally wished them to behave. They are the codes by which the kings expected their people to live, rather than an ideal that was not attained.

Early Anglo-Saxon law was principally oral and customary, and initially the written law seems to have reflected the codes of behaviour common to the community, i.e. 'folk right', as asserted in the early lawcodes of the kings Hlothhere and Eadric of Kent: *riht is*: 'it is right that . . .'. The written law may have served as a supplement to the oral custom, giving more weight to those customs that were not sufficiently observed. Laws on the care of orphaned children in particular seem to fall into this category, as this law is restated throughout the Anglo-Saxon period with monotonous regularity, suggesting that kin would often ignore their legal duties towards orphans, given the opportunity.

A third element in Anglo-Saxon law is that of royal initiative. Here, the king might change an existing law, or issue a completely new one, and in this case, the law became an ideal to be attained, rather than an expression of custom. A striking example is Æthelstan's attempt in *c.* 935 to raise the age of criminal liability from twelve to fifteen years old:

> Now again the king has been addressing his councillors at Whittlebury, and has sent word to the archbishop by Theodred, that he thinks it cruel to put to death such young people and for such slight offences as he has learnt is the practice everywhere. He has declared now that both he himself and those with whom he has discussed the matter are of the opinion that no one should be slain who is under fifteen years old, unless he tries to defend himself or tries to run away and refuses to give himself up. Then, he shall be struck down whether his offence is great or small – whichever it may be. But if he will give himself up he shall be put in prison, as was declared at Grately; and he shall be liberated on the same conditions.

Æthelstan was at pains to state that this was his own idea, received with the approval of those whom he consulted. This change in law, however, was relatively short-lived; it was an age of legal maturity, rather than one integral to the traditional age of maturity. It is likely that among the people, the age at which a child reached theoretical adult status was still twelve years old.

There are further signs that in the later period, the law was no longer simply an expression of national behaviour, in harmony with folk custom, but became something more abstract. In a law of Canute it is apparent that the letter of the law was being taken and applied to infants in a ludicrously unjust way: 'It has been the custom up till now for grasping persons to treat a child which lay in the cradle, even though it had never tasted food, as though it were fully intelligent: but I strictly forbid such a thing henceforth.'

Finally, the king's own perception of himself as leader of the people, lawgiver and Christian could affect the content of the laws issued – weak and unenforceable laws such as one issued by Æthelred: 'And that widows and orphans should not always be unhappy but should readily be cheered', are more likely to have been written in the consciousness that a Christian king's duty was to protect widows and orphans than with any real expectation that action would be taken on the basis of this vague ruling. Similarly the disproportionately severe penalty for failure to baptise a child in a law of Ine King of Wessex: 'if it dies without being baptised, he shall pay as compensation all he possesses', is probably more a reflection of the desire of kings to be seen as Christian, and the fear that a wicked nation would incur the wrath of God, than of any importance attached to the life of an infant *per se*.

THE LEECHBOOKS

Documentary sources from the late Anglo-Saxon period testify to an industrious group of scholars intent on noting down medical treatments based on native English folk remedies and on translations of Greek and Latin source material. These vernacular books of medicine, known as Leechbooks, also give us some information about attitudes towards children in this period. The archaeological evidence for children's health in the form of the skeletal record from the cemeteries provides evidence about diseases of childhood that affect the bones, but can give precious little information on the many acute, osteologically invisible, ailments that Anglo-Saxon children may have suffered, such as infectious diseases, nor can the surviving skeletons yield much insight into how sick children were cared for, if they were cared for at all. Given these circumstances, it seems sensible to turn to the Anglo-Saxon Leechbooks for further details. Most of the Leechbooks – medical texts compiled for the use of skilled practitioners – were set out in their present form in the tenth century. The most well known of these texts is called *Bald's Leechbook*: it is the oldest medical text in English to survive in anything like its complete form. It borrows heavily from Latin texts, but the translator appears to be competent and knowledgeable about English diseases and herbs, because the recipes are selective, emphasising those that are relevant to the local population and often excluding diseases that occur only in a Mediterranean climate.[20] The existing medical texts also contain fragments from much older texts and from traditional pagan lore, indicating that the tradition of medical learning had been in existence for quite some time before the tenth century.[21]

The medical texts cover a wide range of adult diseases, some of which, such as spring fever and yellow fever – may be assumed to have affected children as badly or worse than adults. There are a few remedies dedicated to childhood illnesses, including teething problems and stomach aches, and these will be discussed later. The medical texts also provide information on conception and childbirth, as well as prognostications for a child's future in relation to the day of its birth. These fortune predictors offer advice according to the day of the month and the state of the moon. Inevitably, the prognostications contain the traditional broad promises and warnings peculiar to the genre: 'The thirteenth moon is dangerous for beginning things. Avoid arguing with your friends on this day. It will not be easy to track down a fugitive.' However, these astrological counsels offer insights, in their inevitable mundanity, into attitudes towards children and their possible prospects. Foremost, it is worthy of note that a typical prognostication indicated what might become of girls as well as boys; for the thirteenth moon, the parent is advised that: 'A child born on this day will be spirited, having a mark about his eyes: daring, rapacious, over-confident, self-centred: will not live long. A girl will have a mark on the back of her neck or on her thigh: over-confident, spirited, will indulge her body with many men: she will die young.'[22]

Advice for the day embraced when to begin or end a range of Anglo-Saxon activities, including putting children to school (the fourteenth and seventeenth moons), and the destined careers for children include trading (for boys on the fourteenth moon) and being a doctor (for boys and girls on the twenty-second moon). The prognostications are late Old English glosses of Latin texts; they may have been copied as curiosities, but their existence in Old English attests that they had some interest and perhaps relevance to the scribes and their patrons.

WILLS AND CHARTERS

Charters and wills, although a useful source of general information about Anglo-Saxon material wealth and landscapes, are among the least useful of later documents for the purposes of understanding childhood in the Anglo-Saxon period. They represent the legal documentation of a literate, Christian society, and are in their content indicative of an increasingly urban economy, looking towards impersonal, nationwide legal structures to uphold standards and property rights, rather than the more rural, kin-orientated society of the earlier period. The transactions in the surviving wills and charters are predominantly designed to safeguard the interests of the Church; on the whole, the transactions involve wealthy people, and are not representative of the holdings of the ordinary Anglo-Saxons. That said, wills and charters do provide occasional glimpses of Anglo-Saxon family structure and attitudes towards offspring which have comparative value for the earlier Anglo-Saxon period.[23]

GENEALOGIES

At first glance, the Anglo-Saxon genealogies of the kings would appear to present an ideal source of information for studies of the number of offspring and overall size of recorded Anglo-Saxon families. A man's connections determined to a large extent his place and status in earlier Anglo-Saxon society, and kings were anxious to legitimise their claims to the throne by recording their royal pedigree. The chief purpose of a genealogy was to prove noble lineage and rights of inheritance. These lineages have impressive depth – tracing kings' ancestors back through their pagan gods and further back, in some cases, to Noah and then Adam – but they lack width: brothers, sisters, aunts and uncles are never mentioned unless the line has passed through them. Wives, too, remain unrecorded, and even where a king's wife is mentioned, it is impossible to tell if she was his only partner. It is only by an incidental reference in Bede, for example, that we learn that Redwald had at least two wives; there is no mention of them in the East Anglian genealogies.[24] The recorded lists of kings and their heirs, and the reconstruction of royal families from Bede and other Anglo-Saxon sources, offers little in the way of useful information on family size, structure, or the experience of childhood.

LANGUAGE AND VOCABULARY

The size of the Anglo-Saxon vocabulary relating to childhood is impressive. Arguably, a society which barely recognised childhood as a separate state from adulthood, and which never noticed attributes or conditions of childhood, might be expected to have a limited range of terms for a limited concept. What you do not have the words to say, you do not have the concept to articulate. Janet Nelson hinted at such a principle when she claimed that there is no word for 'childlike' in medieval Latin.[25] If, as she suggested, childhood is a construct, then without the language to describe that construct, there is no childhood.

As discussed in the introductory chapter, the Anglo-Saxons not only had words for children (*cild*, *bearn*), but also for the state of childhood (*cildhad*), and, perhaps most importantly, could identify and describe behaviour relevant to childhood: childish (*cildisc*), childishness (*cildsung*). There was also a limited, but nonetheless relevant, set of words to describe artefacts belonging peculiarly to the world of children, such as children's clothes (*cildclaðas*), a child's bed or cradle (*cildcradol*, *cildatrog*), and a child's nurse (*cildfostre*), as well as the more sinister '*bearnmyrðra*'

*The infant Jesus wrapped in swaddling (*cildclaðas*) and lying in a cradle (*cildcradol*).
(Bodleian Library, Rawl B.484, f. 85)*

– the murderer of a child. To this may be added the expressions to describe youth: state of youth, adolescence (*geoguðhad*) , youthful (*geoguðlic*), joy of youth (*geoguðmyrð*) and youthful passions (*geoguðlust*). These expressions all come from the surviving written documents, which are not in themselves concerned with writing about children, and we may assume on this evidence that a much wider vocabulary of childhood may have existed in the vernacular.

On the whole, children have a marginal place in the documentary sources. The only child to receive detailed and concentrated discussion is Christ, for whose childhood the starting point was the Gospels, translated into Old English and elaborated in Old English poetry. Other children make only fleeting appearances in the literature, largely because the literature, like the furnished burial ritual, was designed by adults for adult audiences. Children are not entirely absent either, though, and the literature is studded with expressions of concern by parents about children, and descriptions of their activities and their welfare.

CHAPTER 4

Age Thresholds and Rites of Passage

The majority of grave goods buried with children are adult artefacts belonging within the context of an adult burial ritual, but occasionally, recognition of the childishness of children manifested itself in this adult domain. The tiny brooches with burials 17 (aged six) and 28 (aged eight) from Sewerby are the only iron brooches on the site, and are all smaller in size than the corresponding bronze brooches in adult graves – they may also have been cheaper. These brooches would seem to have been tailored to fit the diminutive wearers, and can reasonably be regarded as part of the children's personal equipment. The skeleton in grave 28 was also accompanied by a large number of miniature beads of a type not found in any other grave, which the excavator speculates may have been particularly suitable for a child.[1] Similarly the skeleton of an eleven- to twelve-year old in grave 35A, Abingdon, thought by the excavator to be female, was buried with a spearhead, which appears to have been ground down from one much larger. At Empingham II, Rutland, grave 72 was of a girl aged five or six who was buried with a small pot and was accompanied by a tiny annular brooch (22 mm in diameter), the smallest brooch on the site.

The evidence provided by grave goods in the pagan period presents clear discrimination against the under-tens. Pins, brooches and belts are usually taken as indicators that the body was clothed for burial. Child burials rarely include such goods; are we to infer that children were buried naked? Infants would perhaps be buried in archaeologically untraceable swaddling, but what about older children? The idea of naked juveniles should not be discounted immediately. In the anonymous *Life of St Cuthbert*, the embryonic saint, aged eight, was described as playing with a gang of boys of his own age, some of whom were unclothed.[2] Boniface, born in about 675 of noble parents, was described as going out without his shirt and also frequently without his tunic when he was a child.[3]

Archaeological evidence supports the age of ten to twelve as a probable threshold between childhood and adulthood in the early Anglo-Saxon period. At Portway, Hampshire, the occupant of grave 60, identified as an eleven- to twelve-year-old, is buried with the 'adult' grave features of a partially flint-lined grave with a wooden baulk.[4] Only females over the age of twelve to fourteen are buried with girdle-hangers or chatelaines on most sites. An indication of the transitional

An illustration to Psalm 17: 'may their children have more than enough'. Naked children eat with their hands around large tables. (British Library, Harley 603, f. 8v)

age between childhood and adulthood for girls may be interpreted in burial 93 at Abingdon, Berkshire.[5] The grave contained the remains of a fifteen- to sixteen-year-old buried with beads, disc brooches, a knife and a possible girdle-hanger; in other words, with all due respect. She was clearly pregnant at the time of her death, and her manner of burial gives no hint that the burying community found anything 'wrong' about a girl of this age bearing a child. Her 'marriage' must have been contracted when she was around fourteen years of age or younger, and for matrimonial purposes she must have been considered an adult. The conclusion is inescapable that the age of ten to twelve marked the difference between childhood and adulthood in the burial ritual.

In Anglo-Saxon manuscript illustrations, attempts were made to depict children and to distinguish them from adults. Within the *Harley Psalter* a mid-eleventh-century illustrated copy of the Psalms, children are relatively easily recognisable. They are consistently depicted as being smaller than adults, and there is even some attempt to scale artefacts to the diminutive size of the children. In the illustration to Psalm 17, two groups of nude children feast at two tables. A few of the children are clothed in short tunics. The tables are too large for them – they stand around them rather than sitting (scenes with adults eating show the

A woman gathers children around her. All the children wear tunics, and all but the tallest (standing on the right) have a cropped hairstyle with high foreheads. (British Library, Harley 603, f. 7v)

adults sitting at normal-sized tables). Arguably, the children are also given childlike characteristics within the picture – they eat with their fingers rather than using knives or other tools, and two of the children are shown either fighting or playing over the food.

Throughout the *Harley Psalter*, children are also clearly distinguished by their dress. Children are always shown either naked or wearing short tunics cinched at the waist. Some adults wear these clothes, but adults are also shown wearing cloaks, which are never given to the smallest children. It is noticeable that the children have the same hairstyles as many of the adult males: short bobbed hair, with a high forehead – perhaps shaved?

Some attempt was made in the *Harley Psalter* to differentiate between babies and older children, partly in dress (babies are swaddled), but also in posture and, to a lesser extent, size. The illustrator of the *Harley Psalter* was copying a Carolingian model, the *Utrecht Psalter*, but his was not entirely a slavish copy: in an illustration to 'the children of Israel', the Anglo-Saxon illustrator typically adds children to the scene where none were shown in the original, showing mothers holding the hands of their offspring as they are led away captive.

In his study of medieval High German literature pertaining to childhood, James Schultz noted that, although childhood was a recognised stage of life, vocabulary indicated that other factors were considered more important in social development than mere youth. None of the terms for young males, he contended, rigorously distinguished between child and adult, and women were categorised by whether they were virgins (*maget*) or married. There was an age class (*kint*), but

The Children of Israel. Note the two children at the back of the group: one wears a cloak rather than just the simple short tunic of the other children, and may be an older child. (British Library, Harley 603, f. 51r)

there was no gendered class of boy or girl.[6] Even in modern English, although 'boy' and 'girl' have a normal application to children, these same terms may also be used in very different circumstances; our own terminology is not rigorously specific either, and would surely fail the Schultz test. Within the Old English lexicon, however, age categories do seem to follow the medieval High German pattern. There are several terms to describe boys and boyhood in the Old English lexicography. By far the most common is *bearn* or *cild*: both terms can be used of girls too, but more often a male child is assumed. Occasionally boys and girls are distinguished by the use of a gendered compound – *waepcild* (weapon child) for boys and *wifcild* (weaving child) for girls.

Beyond this, there is significant evidence to suggest that boys went through several distinct phases before achieving full adulthood. In the tenth-century Old English translations of Bede's *Ecclesiastical History of the English People*, boys and male children are referred to either as *cniht/cneoht* or as *cild*. A monk, looking back at his childhood, describes it as his *cneohtwerendum*, and at Sigeberht's new school in East Anglia, two age groups were to be taught – children and young men – described as *cneohtas and geonge menn*. In book III of the *Ecclesiastical History*, there is an implication that male immaturity was divided into three phases: boyhood and youth, as we have already seen, but also

Captives being led away by soldiers. No children were shown in the original version of this illustration, but in the Anglo-Saxon copy, children have been added to represent the People of Israel. (British Library, Harley 603, f. 29r)

cildhade – there is a reference to Ecgberht looking back on the sins of his '*cildhade oððe cneohthad*'. However, the period of *cildhade* must have been short, or the term flexible, because later we read of a '*cneohtcild*' called Æsica, aged three years at the time of his death.[7] An Anglo-Saxon male, then, had three categories of youthfulness: he might be a son (*sunu*), but he was also a *cild*, a *cniht/cneoht* and a *geogoð* (youth).

The concept of sequential transitional phases for males was given clearest expression by the homilist Ælfric, who specified that growing up was about development through different stages. His intention was to contrast spiritual rebirth through baptism – where you would immediately achieve full spiritual status – with physical birth – where you had to pass through stages of maturation. These stages started with *cild*, then *cniht* before reaching adulthood.[8] Similarly, in Brythferth's *Manual*, the four seasons of the year were likened to the stages of male growth – childhood (*cildhad*) followed by youth (*cniht gioguð*), succeeded by full maturity (*geðungen yld*) and very old age (*swiþe eald yld*).

Just as there are no precise modern chronological definitions for 'child', 'lad', 'boy' and 'youth', so the terms *cild*, *cnapa* and *cniht* appear to have been loosely associated with age bands and appropriate context, rather than with rigid age categories. Cuthbert was described as an eight-year-old *cild*, while elsewhere we read of a seven-year-old *cnapa* and a ten-year-old *cnapa*. The social status and activities of boys through these stages of *cnapa* and *cniht* are discussed in the chapter on adolescents.

It is more problematic to identify any term to distinguish female children. Terminology for girls appears to have been more loosely age-related than for boys, and for girls, the distinctive rite of passage they passed through was marriage. Within the Old English Bede, women on the whole fall into three categories: they are either *dohter* (daughter), *faemne* (virgin, unmarried woman), or *wif* (wife, woman). The most common definition of a woman's status in Bede is as a daughter, but these women are also termed *faemna*, which has implications of youthfulness. However, *faemna* are not always young, even though the term is used specifically to indicate virginity – the church of St Mary is described as the church of the '*eadigan faemnan Sancte Marian* (the blessed woman St Mary)', while Etheldreda, twice married without ever losing her virginity, is referred to as a *faemne* rather than as a *wif*. Equally, the epithet *wif* need not mean specifically a married woman: Hegiu, the first Northumbrian woman to become a nun, was described as a *wif*. No specifically age-related terms for females were used. In other documentary sources, *mægð* (maidens) was the equivalent to *fæmna*. All girls were 'maidens', but some older women who were unmarried or holy virgins, and even wives, were also described in the same way. Again, a *mægð* was not specifically equated with virginity, so that when the Virgin Mary or a female saint were being described, a qualifier would be added – Mary was 'a clean maid' or 'a spotless maiden'.[9]

An examination of the surviving Anglo-Saxon lawcodes leaves no room for doubt that there existed a traditionally accepted age of transition from childhood to adulthood. On occasion this age was considered so self-evident that it was not even specified, as in law 38 of Ine of Wessex (AD 688–725): 'If a man and his woman have a child between them, and the man dies, the mother will have custody and care of her child. She will be given 6 shillings to look after it, a cow in summer, an ox in winter; the kinsmen will manage the property, until the child reaches maturity.'

In the late seventh century Kentish laws of Hlothhere and Eadric, an exact legal age of responsibility is given in law 6, and it should be noted that a legal 'adult' is considerably younger than might be expected: 'If a man dies leaving a wife and a child, it is right that the child should remain with the mother, and one of its father's relatives who is willing to act, shall be given it as its guardian to take care of its property, until it is 10 years old.' Ine's laws held ten to be the age of criminal culpability; a ten-year-old was considered as an accessory to theft. By the tenth century, this age of passage to adult responsibility was raised to twelve in the reign of Æthelstan. That this was the traditional age of transition among the mixed Danish and English populations was demonstrated by the tentative and ultimately futile efforts of Æthelstan to raise the age after which the death penalty could be exacted to fifteen – with Canute's kingship, the age was firmly lowered to twelve.

There appears to have been a legal threshold age for girls, since one of the codes of King Alfred of Wessex deemed that if anyone raped an under-age girl, she should be given the same compensation as an adult. There is no indication as to whether the girl is to be considered under-age by an absolute chronological determination, or whether her maturity was assessed on her personal development. As we have discussed, the archaeological record suggests that girls may have been accorded some adult status from the age of about twelve, but a late Old English text indicates that, for some legal purposes, a girl could be under her parents' guardianship until sixteen or seventeen years of age.[10] It is probable that a girl remained in her parents' care until she married. Law 81 of Æthelbert of Kent (*c*. 595–616) legislated that if a married woman without children wanted to leave her husband, her goods and bride gift reverted to the care of her father's family.

The most important transitional age for boys and girls appears to have been between about ten and twelve, the age at which a child became, in legal terms, an adult, and when marriage and the establishment of a family became a theoretical, if not physical, possibility. A certain amount of status could be achieved, it seems, simply by becoming part of procreative society, and if status was derived in part from the ability to produce a family, then children even of extremely wealthy and influential parents can never have achieved the same status as poor but fertile adults. This point was explored by J.F. Shephard in his analysis of isolated Anglo-Saxon barrow burials, where it was noted that there were no certain instances on record of infants or juveniles as the sole occupant of an isolated barrow. J.F. Shephard argued that isolated barrow burials represented territorial landmarks and the establishment of an ancestral claim to land. This being so, infants and juveniles would automatically be excluded from such élite burial rituals because the 'attainment of adulthood (or potential to be an ancestor, perhaps) was a *sine qua non* for membership of this superordinate class'.[11]

Within the late antique world, childhood was usually divided into three phases: *infantia* which lasted up to the age of seven; *pueritia* which covered the years seven to fourteen; and *adolescentia* which spanned fourteen to twenty-eight. In this system, recorded by Bede, true adulthood did not begin until the late twenties, and adolescence lasted rather longer than the modern interpretation of the word. In the later Middle Ages, *adolescentia* was described by Avicenna and Johanitius as lasting from birth to thirty-five years of age.[12] Within the Anglo-Saxon ecclesiastical world, these definitions may have had some validity, but there is no hint of this system in the vernacular lawcodes.

DEFINITION OF INFANT

Whatever the Mediterranean views on the duration of the first phase of the human lifespan, the Old English vocabulary indicates that the period of infancy was short and clearly defined by physical development. There was no specific Old English word for 'infant', but when the Latin *infans* was translated into Old English, a literal description of what 'infancy' meant to the Anglo-Saxons was offered, giving us a clear picture of the duration of this period. *Infans* was translated by Ælfric in his *Grammar* into '*unsprecende cild*' – the child without speech.[13] Infancy was a period of utter dependence and lack of communication, and by these terms, an Anglo-Saxon child might emerge from the state of infancy about eighteen months to two years after birth. In the Old English Psalters, the phrase '*infantium et lactantium*' is translated as 'children and milk suckers.'[14]

Documentary sources indicate that between the ages of two and three, children effectively passed through their first threshold, or moved from one phase of childhood to another, to the extent that significant decisions about the future of the child could be taken at this time. In two separate hagiographic tales containing an element of competitiveness, two royal princesses, Edith and Eadberga, were offered the choice between the jewels and garments of royalty or the dark veil, Psalter and cross of the religious life. They were aged two and three respectively at the time of this test, and both infants moved instinctively towards the ecclesiastical items, thus 'choosing' to dedicate themselves to the Church and effectively demonstrating self-determinism, ending their infancy as a period of total dependency. The precocious Æthelwold achieved this distinction at an even earlier age: as his mother sat nursing the baby Æthelwold on her lap, regretting that she could not go to church, the infant, reading her thoughts, miraculously transported them both there. Thereafter, Æthelwold was dedicated to an ecclesiastical career.[15] This testing of infants might seem, at first glance, to be a fantasy unique to the hagiographic tradition, yet in the laws of Ine of Wessex, an orphaned child was to be cared for until it was three years old, and then it was to be assessed 'according to its appearance'. Perhaps the testing of the princesses and the assessment of the orphaned child were both based on a belief that even from a very early age, all behaviour determined a child's ultimate destiny. St Guthlac's very name was supposed to have revealed his future, because according to his hagiographer, 'it being as though by divine plan, because by virtue of its formation, it fitted and matched his qualities'.[16]

The theory implicit in this statement is not so far from the secular superstition recorded in the tenth-century Old English translation of *Peri Didaxeon* that pregnant women, offered a rose or lily, would reveal the sex of their child by their choice of flower.[17] Naturally, there comes a point in the normal course of a child's development when greater social awareness and learning ability are shown; the child has a competent grasp of speech, and is able to start taking a more independent part in the community life. It may be the observation of this natural point of transition, associated with learning to walk and speak, that is responsible for the sporadic references in Old English texts associating three- to five-year-olds with new events and adult choices. At the age of four or five, the young Alfred was encouraged by his mother to enjoy literature and taught to learn by rote by his teacher; he was also taken to Rome by his father to take part in a ceremony interpreted by his biographer as an act anointing him as a future king.[18] Perhaps in memory of this, Alfred presented his own grandson with a sword at the same age in a ceremony reported by William of Malmesbury.[19] The accounts of the testing of Edith and Eadberga may fall into the same mould. The precocity of the saints was being emphasised, but there may have been an acknowledgement and exploitation in these tales of an accepted rite of passage, a transitional age between the total dependency of infancy and part-participation in the anticipated life of the adult.

AGE THRESHOLDS IN THE *LIVES* OF THE SAINTS

The constrained and stylised form of the Old English *Lives* of the saints obliged the hagiographers to accommodate the activities of men and women living within an Anglo-Saxon culture to the confines and restrictions of an essentially alien and late antique genre. The table overleaf reveals the trends in social expectations for

*Recorded Events in the Childhoods of a Selection of Anglo-Saxon
Saints*

Saint	Age	Event	Lifespan
Oswald	13 years 30 years	Exiled from Northumbria to Scotland Converted to Christianity Came to the throne	*c.* 604–42
Hilda	13 years 33 years	Converted to Christianity Became abbess	*c.* 614–80
Wilfred	14 years *c.* 21 years 30 years	Left home, took up arms Went to Rome Elected bishop	*c.* 634–709
Cuthbert	8 years *c.* 26 years	Passed from infancy to boyhood Entered Melrose as a monk	*c.* 635–87
Guthlac	8 days 15 years 24 years 26 years	Baptised Left home, took up arms Entered Church Finished education	*c.* 674–714
Æthelwold	Infancy Adolescence	Performed translocation miracle In Royal Household	*c.* 909–84
Edith	2 years	Chose Church over secular world	*c.* 961–84

some of the saintly children in Anglo-Saxon England, and illustrates some
common patterns in the lives of these élite, idealised members of society. It is
noticeable that childhood as such is not a prerequisite in the narrative of a saint's
life; we know nothing, for example, of the childhood of Ælfric's saints Edmund,
Swithun and Oswald, king and martyr.

For many of the saints, the most significant transitional point in their lives
came at around the time of puberty, from thirteen to fifteen years of age, but
their entry into their final adult role might be delayed into their mid-twenties or
later.

A review of the evidence indicates that the Anglo-Saxon child's place in society
changed as the child matured, as we would expect, but while there were
transitional stages within the life of the child, there were no clear age-related
thresholds and no specific rites of passage. Infants were baptised, but so were

adults, and while marriage marked entry into the adult world for some girls, not all girls married. For those children who spent their adult careers within the Church, entry into it did not necessarily mark an age-related rite of passage either, because children could be dedicated to the Church at birth, and some, like Eadberga, would be reared in a convent from earliest infancy. Either Anglo-Saxon society barely registered developmental stages of children, or it was sufficiently sophisticated to recognise, as modern society does, that emotional and physical development depended on the individual, and rigid hierarchies of age limitations would have been unreasonable or unworkable.

CHAPTER 5
Conception, Birth and Babies

Conception, pregnancy and childbirth have always been fraught with difficulty and anxiety in any period, and for both the Anglo-Saxon child and mother, the risk to life during pregnancy and birth must have been high. Mortality rates for infants in modern non-developed societies before the introduction of contraceptives have been calculated as being up to 100 deaths per 1,000 live births, and similar figures must have predominated in the Anglo-Saxon period.[1]

INFERTILITY AND CONCEPTION

In the teachings of the Christian Church, sex was immoral outside marriage, and the only purpose of sex within marriage was procreation. According to Alfred's law 85, if a man was so badly wounded in the genitals that he could not have children he was to be given eighty shillings as compensation. Law 81 in the late sixth-century laws of Æthelbert of Kent implies that, in a union without children, the wife could end the marriage and return to her family home. The late tenth-century remedies for women who could not conceive children relied heavily on chants and ritual practice, a sure indication that the doctors had no ready cure for the problem. To help a woman conceive she was advised to find a bone in a hart's heart or belly and tie it tightly to her arm.[2] Alternatively, she could drink a concoction made by slicing and drying a hare's belly, pounding it to dust and sprinkling it in a drink. If both the partners drank the preparation, a son would be conceived, but if the woman drank alone, the child would be androgynous.[3] A drink of hare's genitals in wine would also be effective for conceiving a male child, or, if the couple wished, hare's rennet – from a female hare for the wife and from a male hare for the husband – was to be drunk before intercourse. Afterwards, the couple were to abstain until the wife became pregnant. She was to eat mushrooms instead of meat and rub herself with oils instead of bathing, and 'wonderfully she will be pregnant'.[4] An easier option for the infertile woman might be to try the Latin charm entitled 'For a woman who cannot bear a child': '*Solue iube deus ter eatenis. Ad articulorum dolorum constantium malignantium diabolus ligauit angelus curauit dominus saluauit in nomine medicina. Amen.*'[5]

Not all remedies assumed that a male child was the desired outcome, and if the remedies seem bizarre and inadequate from a modern point of view, it must be recognised that there was, in practice, almost no way a society without the benefit of modern medicine could have influenced or affected the chances of conception beyond ensuring an adequate diet for the mother. Under these circumstances, the psychological value of the charms and complicated remedies cannot be underestimated. It may be that the Anglo-Saxon doctor deliberately accentuated the psychological value of these treatments. A woman who could not conceive was advised to eat and drink a soup of fieldmore in milk and water, and to have seeds of henbane or coriander tied to her thigh to produce a boy or girl. The remedy warns, with great confidence in its powers, that 'when the child is born, remove the medicine to prevent the uterus from prolapsing'.[6]

A significant cause of infertility in Anglo-Saxon women may have been malnutrition, as indicated by the many remedies to provoke periods. The most common reasons for the interruption of the menstrual cycle, apart from pregnancy, are either extreme fitness or malnutrition. Little is known of the Anglo-Saxon diet, but iron deficiency would not be unlikely, especially in the winter and early spring, when sources of iron – green vegetables, fresh meat and fish – would have been in short supply.[7] The presence of endemic malaria in the Anglo-Saxon population would also have contributed to iron deficiency, leading to both infertility and problems in childbirth for women.[8] Similarly, intestinal parasites – roundworm, whipworm and tapeworm – were a commonplace, and vitamin and iron deficiencies would have been chronic, especially for women. Under these circumstances, the remedy for infertility that recommended replacing meat with mushrooms in the diet would have been positively harmful if followed.

MISCARRIAGE

Recipes in the medical texts to prevent miscarriage are not particularly prominent, possibly because there was so little that herbal remedies could do for this problem, although, frustratingly, a whole section on gynaecology indicated in the index has been lost from *Bald's Leechbook*. There exists nonetheless a significant body of material on the subject. Borrowing from the Latin, an Old English text recommended that a woman who was having a miscarriage or whose foetus had died should drink dust of hare's heart with frankincense dust in clear wine for seven days – an impossibly expensive remedy, making it unlikely that any woman would test its efficacy. If a woman suffered repeated miscarriages, she was advised to continue the treatment for thirty days, drinking the dusts either in wine or with an unspecified collection of herbs. After a successful delivery, if the woman felt ill, the same preparation was to be applied.[9] By contrast, a remedy also borrowed from a Continental source offered to prevent miscarriages by giving the pregnant woman advice on her lifestyle: she was to avoid drink, horse-riding and salt and sweet food.[10] This advice may have resulted from the observation of gestational diabetes, where a woman fails to produce enough insulin to keep her blood glucose levels normal during the pregnancy, and which would have been detectable to a medieval doctor because of the increased sweetness of the urine. However, if the pregnant woman was already suffering from a poor diet, the advice to limit her intake of sugar and salt could have been more harmful than beneficial.

Remedies within the Old English Leechbooks were often effective. Treatments for harelip, a fractured skull and gangrene within *Bald's Leechbook* were all clearly described and clinically correct. The Anglo-Saxon doctor's normal practice was to observe the symptoms of the disease, to make a diagnosis and to treat that problem with herbal drinks or poultices. As a general rule of thumb, if an Anglo-Saxon doctor could see it, he could treat it with a modicum of success. Experience also taught Anglo-Saxon doctors when a disease was beyond their control: in diagnosing a swollen neck, the doctor is advised to carry out a simple test still used today by general practitioners – can the patient look down? If not, then both the Anglo-Saxon doctor and the modern GP would concur that the disease could be serious (probably meningitis) and would need immediate treatment or, in the environment of the Anglo-Saxon doctor, 'he will be dead in about 3 days'. Against this background of observation, diagnosis and treatment with poultices and drinks, much of the advice for pregnant women stands in stark contrast, emphasising a sense of helplessness as the doctors took refuge in ritualistic practices and the aid of the spiritual world. To ensure her health, a pregnant woman was instructed to write a Latin prayer on fresh wax and tie it under her right foot.[11] To ward off the dangers of an overdue birth and congenital disorders, the Old English collection of recipes known as *Lacnunga* advised a woman to 'go to the grave of a dead man, and step 3 times over the grave, and say 3 times: may this be my protection against loathsome late birth, may this be my protection against miserable still birth, may this be my protection against loathsome deformities at birth. Then let the woman go to her sleeping husband and say: up I go over you stepping with a live child not with a dying one, with a full-term birth, not with a doomed one. And when the mother feels that her child is alive, let her go to a church and go before the altar and say: I said this chant to Christ.'[12]

The same collection of recipes offered an alternative set of rituals: 'Let the woman who cannot give birth take the milk of a cow of one colour in her hand and sip a mouthful of it and then go to running water and spit the milk in it and then scoop up with the same hand a mouth full of water and swallow it, then say these words: "I carried the great, powerful man everywhere; I will give birth to the same." Then she is to go home, go to the brook without looking around or back when she leaves it, and then let her go into another house from the one she left and taste food there.'[13] Both of these remedies appear to continue old insular traditions about charms and magic and are not borrowed from a classical model.

A number of early inhumation burials corroborate the view that amulets were considered particularly powerful charms for women during or immediately after childbirth. Boxes that may have contained perishable herbs and charms have been found in a number of graves containing females and babies. At Lechlade, Gloucestershire (grave 107), a woman buried with a newborn baby had a box among her few grave goods. At Barton Court Farm, Oxfordshire, a sixth-century burial (grave 271) consisted of the remains of an adult woman buried with a newborn infant. The woman's grave goods included a cast bronze ring with a haematite pebble, and amber and crystal beads, which the excavator cautiously interpreted as a purse/amulet group.[14] At Camerton, Somerset, in a cemetery dated to the seventh century, a woman who died in the course of her pregnancy

0   5cms

A copper box from a child's grave, Updown, Kent. Such boxes may have contained herbs or materials thought to have healing properties.

(grave 100), and who was buried with a seven-month-old foetus, had a cowrie shell and a boar's tusk at her feet.[15] Audrey Meaney ascribed amuletic powers directly concerned with childbirth to these symbols.[16] Interestingly in this context, at Castle Dyke, Humberside, another seventh-century cemetery, only two women were buried with animal-teeth pendants. One was next to an infant buried with a mammiform pot while the other was also neighbouring an infant burial.

Double burials containing the casualties of childbirth are much less common in the mortuary record than one might expect. Many of the larger excavated cemeteries such as Alton, Hampshire, have no such multiple burials, and in Anglo-Saxon inhumation cemeteries as a whole, infant burials are rare. At Berinsfield, Oxfordshire, of 114 individuals represented by whole or partial skeletons from the cemetery, only one was newly born (grave 38). This infant was buried in what appeared to be an earlier pit feature containing a sheep; it is not possible to say whether the buriers were aware of the sheep burial, or even aware of the pit, although the choice of burial location may not have been coincidental.[17]

Some advice for pregnant women had a clear and non-medical agenda. In one homily, women were warned that, when they were pregnant, they were to 'avoid all extravagance, not to carry heavy weights, nor to exercise either quickly or slowly', but the point of the warning is to tell women that if a child was miscarried, the mother would be guilty of condemning the soul of the unborn child to hell: 'because it shall arise on Domesday if it was alive in the womb, and it will be punished in hell if it died a heathen'.[18] The male guardians of Church values, it seems, were not averse to adding extra guilt and stress onto a woman at what must already have been an extremely anxious time.

The fatalities associated with childbirth were plainly understood within the later documentary sources. An Old English copy of a text on the formation of a foetus records that by the third month of the pregnancy, the child will have a soul, that by the eighth month of gestation it can be considered to be alive, and that if the ninth month comes and goes without birth, then in the tenth month 'the mother will die'.[19] Advice to women to help in the delivery of their babies and to ensure a speedy birth was as varied and ultimately futile as the remedies to promote conception: 'When a woman has a difficult delivery, take parsnip, seethe it in water, give it to her to drink and bathe herself with: she will be healed.'[20]

Foetal death during pregnancy was of concern to the Anglo-Saxon doctor, who had a range of treatments to prescribe. Foetal death and stillbirth must have been relatively common: even in 1950s Britain, the stillbirth rate was 19 out of 1,000 live births, and the incidence increases with malnutrition, maternal disorders and infectious disease.[21] If the foetus was not expelled naturally as a miscarriage or stillbirth, the outlook for the mother was not good. Modern treatments include induced labour using prostaglandins, or surgical intervention. The Anglo-Saxon doctors eschewed surgery except of the most superficial type – given the high risk of infection at the time, any incision in the body would have been highly likely to lead to death. Instead, the woman was given dittany juice, either in wine or warm water, if she had a fever: 'It will expel the foetus immediately without harm'.[22] Dittany was recognised as a herbal plant into early modern times; the sixteenth-century herbalist John Gerrard recommended it for drawing out splinters of bone and wood and for arrow wounds, but he commented that, not being native to Britain, it was extremely difficult to grow, and would not survive a cold winter.[23] The Old English remedy was a copy derived from Dioscorides, and would have been an impractical prescription for the sick woman. Pennyroyal, another Mediterranean plant recommended to expel a dead foetus, might have been more accessible and would have had some chance of achieving its aims: a member of the *labiatae* family, pennyroyal is noted in modern herbals as being a uterine stimulant which should not be used during pregnancy.[24] Equally difficult to obtain, and useful only as a palliative, was the drink of wolf's milk mixed with wine and honey: 'immediately it will be better' is the optimistic prediction.[25]

Removal of the afterbirth occasioned medical intervention too. Old lard used as an emollient, or brooklime and hollyhock boiled in ale and given as a drink, were the options of choice, or fleabane used as a suppository.[26] Illustrations in documentary sources indicate that women would be accompanied by midwives during their confinement. After the delivery, the baby would be washed and swaddled by the midwife or 'birthing-servant' (*byrðinenu*) while the mother recuperated in bed. Males are noticeably absent from these scenes.

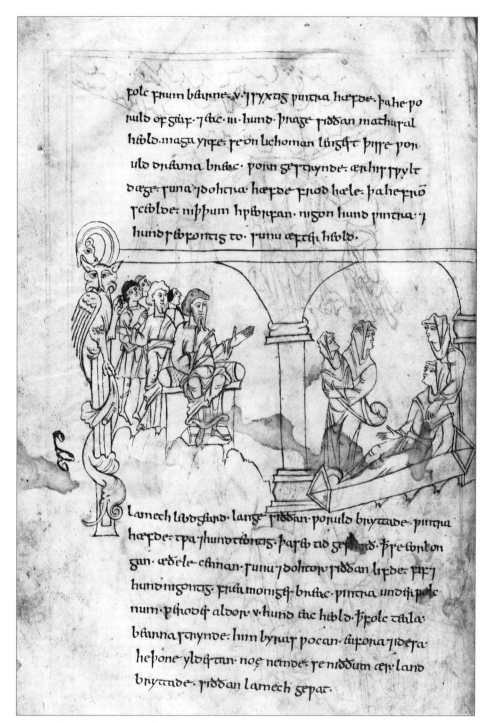

Lamech's first child. His wife is in bed with midwives in attendance, one supporting the mother, and one holding up the swaddled baby. (Oxford, Bodleian Library, Junius 11, f. 56)

FEMALE MORTALITY

Although there are relatively few women in the Anglo-Saxon mortuary record who unquestionably died from the complications of childbirth, mortality statistics for Anglo-Saxon women are usually interpreted as corroborating the impact of childbearing on female health. At the fifth- to seventh-century cemetery site at Berinsfield, Oxfordshire, adult female deaths below the age of thirty were considerably greater than those of males in the same age group. Calvin Wells interpreted the mortality rates at North Elmham, Norfolk as indicating that males were better fed than females, and at the site of Beckford A in Hereford and Worcester, male remains were more robust than those of female, and more females than males died as young adults in cemetery B.[27] At the late Anglo-Saxon rural church cemetery of Raunds, Northamptonshire, 44 per cent of all adult females died between the ages of seventeen and twenty-five, that is, during their optimal period of childbearing.[28]

In the archaeological record, it is only possible to be sure that a woman died of childbirth if the infant skeleton is still in place in the pelvic girdle (although even in these circumstances it is not impossible that the pregnant woman may have died of causes unconnected with her condition), and while such cases are not numerous, those that have been excavated offer a grim reminder of the risks for women. At Great Chesterford, Essex, a site with relatively high numbers of infant burials compared to the average Anglo-Saxon cemetery (5 foetuses, 12 stillborn and 26 neonates – birth to two months), two of the women (burials 32 and 127) apparently died from the complications of childbirth.[29] Burial 32 was of a woman aged between fifteen and twenty-five years, resting on her right side with her knees drawn up. She had an iron ring-headed pin at her shoulder and a knife at her left elbow, and her unborn child was at thirty-two weeks. Grave 127 was an older woman aged between twenty-five and thirty-five, who was buried in a supine position with a knife, two tinned bronze disc brooches at her shoulders, a string of beads and an iron pin at her right waist; she, too, died during pregnancy.

CONTRACEPTIVES, ABORTION AND INFANTICIDE

Recent work on infanticide and abortion in pre-industrial Britain indicates that this form of birth control was 'a normal and persistent form of human behaviour'.[30] Reasons for wishing to dispose of unwanted births may be many – the child may have been illegitimate or socially unacceptable, the family might have been unable to support any further children, or there may have been a wish for a particular sex of child.

It is difficult to assess how far any stigma attached to a pregnancy may have been relevant in the pagan Anglo-Saxon period. Tacitus in his *Germania* related that the Germanic people in the fourth century – ancestors of the Anglo-Saxons – showed a high moral stance towards illicit unions and their unwanted products, but Tacitus was writing before the Anglo-Saxon period, and he had a particular agenda: he wished to shame his Roman audience into better standards of conduct by demonstrating how pure and uncorrupted was the life of the barbarian savage by comparison, so Tacitus's warm appreciation of Germanic morality should not be taken at face value.[31] By contrast, later Christian writers looking back on the pagan Anglo-Saxon period had a vested interest in demonstrating how immoral the pagan forebears were. Emphasis was laid on their casual liaisons, but much of this must have had some foundation in reality. Kings, in particular, were castigated for having several wives, as witnessed by Boniface's stiff letter to King Æthelbald of Mercia, a Christian king and a supporter of St Guthlac who nonetheless had 'improper' relationships.[32] The offspring of these polygamous relationships were, by the light of the Christian Church, illegitimate, but it is interesting to note that one Christian king, Aldfrith, who was, according to Bede, 'a most learned man', generous and famed for his piety, was the bastard son of Oswy.[33] For royalty, at least, even in the early Christian period, a bastard child was not necessarily an unwanted child, and would suffer no stigma in its later career.

Strict marriage codes are necessary to concepts of illegitimacy, and for the earlier Anglo-Saxon period it is difficult to make a case that such rigid social structures existed. The earliest lawcodes of Æthelbert of Kent (c. AD 595–616) imply that marriages could be contracted and broken with relative ease. Lawcodes 79 and 80 advise that, in case of the breakdown of a relationship, a mother may leave with her children and take half the joint wealth with her, or if the husband wishes to keep the children, she may have compensation of goods 'worth a child'. If, however, there are no children, then it is the woman's father's family, rather than the woman herself, who benefit: they receive back the money they gave to her partner at the marriage. On the basis of this evidence, it would seem that a child was a positive advantage to a woman involved in a relationship. Complaints about polygamous unions persist into the late Anglo-Saxon period, and their frequency perhaps reflects a commonplace practice. The Viking period laws of Edward and Guthrum legislated against two brothers or near relatives having one wife, while those of Æthelred attempted to deal with priests having two or more wives.

The linguistic evidence, too, indicates that there was always a certain ambiguity in the terminology used to differentiate a properly contracted marriage from a couple simply living together. The earliest and most commonly used expression for a union between woman and man is *haemen*, a word also associated with *ham* (home) and *hiwung*, *hiwan* (family, farmstead), and one which can be translated as 'to have intercourse with', 'to cohabit with' and 'to marry'. The earliest lawcodes use *haeman* and *haemed* (which can be translated, according to context, as 'cohabitation', 'marriage', 'adultery' and 'fornication') without distinction between the legal types of relationships, to the extent that Margaret Clunies Ross has suggested that 'traditionally both wives and concubines were regarded as part of a man's household'.[34]

Towards the close of the Anglo-Saxon period, however, the Church had successfully established the concepts of lawful marriage and adultery, and the documentary sources indicate that this distinction was tending to create an environment where the rights of a child born out of adultery were in question, to the extent that some clerics could voice as a common opinion the question of why God should create a living child out of an adulterous relationship.[35] The eighth-century laws of Ine of Wessex gave a man the option of acknowledging an illegitimate child, and provided a word for such a baby: *dearnunga bearn* (secret child). A bastard could also be described as a *hornungsunu*. The prospects of such a child were not necessarily poor: the place name Horningsea in Cambridgeshire may derive from land held by an illegitimate Anglo-Saxon. However, the laws concerning the children of nuns were particularly harsh. In law 8 of King Alfred, a nun who was abducted from a monastery and had a child was not entitled to any of the father's property if he died, and nor was their child. If the child was killed, the father's kindred would receive compensation, but the king would take the mother's share.

Abstinence, as a contraceptive technique, was not specifically advocated, but was certainly used by two Anglo-Saxon noble ladies, although for different reasons. Æthelthryth, daughter of Anna, King of the East Angles, refused to consummate her marriage in 652 to Ealdoman Tondberht, and after his death she apparently maintained her virginity when she was married in 660 to Ecgfrith, fifteen-year-old King of the Northumbrians. When Ecgfrith began pressing his demands, Æthelthryth was helped by Bishop Wilfred to leave her husband and enter the convent at Coldingham. Æthelthryth's abstinence seems to have been due to the desire to maintain her virginity. Another notable queen who was regarded as having had a chaste marriage was Edith, sister of Harold II, last of the Anglo-Saxon kings, and wife of Edward the Confessor. The union was childless, and this may be why it was later seen as abstinent.

It has been suggested by Sonia Hawkes that some formal marriage arrangement was a necessity even for a young woman of the pre-Christian period, and that evidence for an illicit union in the shape of a pregnancy would lead to the punishment of both the mother and the unborn child. Such, at least, was her interpretation of the burial of a pregnant woman who died in the pagan period and was buried in grave 78 at Worthy Park in Hampshire. The woman was aged between thirteen and fifteen years when she died. She had no grave goods, and was buried face down in the grave. Sonia Hawkes commented: 'It is nearly certain that this girl had been raped and that the unusual posture of her skeleton in some way reflects her punishment for the tarnish she had brought upon her family's honour. Hampshire has no peat bogs [a reference to earlier Continental burial ritual] but the shame of a muddy grave bottom would have served as well. Naked, bound, lacerated and perhaps still alive, with the howl of human jackals in her ears, her passport to a merciful oblivion is likely to have been the slime and mire of this chalky trench.'[36] Although this account of the prone burial of a young pregnant woman may be dramatic, the interpretation of the injuries evident on the skeleton, and the idea of the girl having been raped have been called into question. Nonetheless, prone burials are rare in an Anglo-Saxon pagan context, and this burial cannot be considered 'normal' or 'respectable', but whether her pregnancy contributed to the ignominious burial of the teenager or not must remain open to speculation.

On the whole there is little in the Anglo-Saxon cemetery evidence to support an argument for infanticide, in part because there is a notorious dearth of infants in the archaeological record as a whole.[37] What is evident is that disposal of unwanted infants in the pagan period, if such existed, is not comparable to the treatment of such infants in the preceding Romano-British period, where finds of neonates associated with villas (e.g. Barton Court Farm, Oxfordshire, or Hambledon, Buckinghamshire) are not uncommon.[38] A recent study on Romano-British infanticide carried out by the Ancient Monuments laboratory at English Heritage examined the skeletons of 164 children who died at or around birth. Of these, 86 came from cemeteries and 78 from villas and settlements. The high proportion of infants found around Romano-British settlements is to be attributed to the belief that newborn infants were not 'proper' humans and therefore were exempt from the laws insisting that burial should take place outside the settlement.[39] It is perhaps because infants were considered as subhuman that infanticide could be justified. By contrast, while there are few enough Anglo-Saxon infants in cemeteries, they are only rarely found at settlement sites; if infants were hastily dispatched and casually buried around the settlement areas it was in such a way as to leave little archaeological evidence.

One Anglo-Saxon cemetery that is unusual in containing a high proportion of child burials is Great Chesterford in Essex. There, six of the fifteen foetuses at the site were found in one grave. The infants were all aged between thirty-six and forty weeks at the time of death. As the report comments, 'it is difficult to imagine how six or more foetuses of the same age can be buried in the same spot, unless the grave was marked and reopened each time for the burial of a full-term stillborn'.[40] A number of foetuses in one grave does not predicate infanticide, but it is a peculiar occurrence, and if nothing else it demonstrates that, for the pagan Anglo-Saxons, even infants who had not come to full term were worthy of burial in the main cemetery – as, at this cemetery, were horses and dogs.

Margaret Clunies Ross argued in her paper on concubinage that, with the introduction of Christianity, the Church had a vested interest in limiting the number of wives a man could take, and in reshaping attitudes to children.[41] It is in this period, arguably, that the concept of legitimate relationships, and with it the concept of social stigma attached to children born out of sanctioned wedlock, began to have an impact. This change in attitude is illustrated by comparing Æthelbert's relaxed laws on the disintegration of a couple's union, written before 616 – 'if [a woman] wishes to leave with her children, she shall have half the goods: if the man wishes to keep the child, her share equivalent to a child' (Æthelbert, laws 79 and 80) – to those of Alfred (reigned 871–99), where marriage has become a sacred and indissoluble union, and revenge is only due to those who are legitimately related: 'a man may fight without liability if he finds another man with his lawful wife . . . or with his legitimate daughter, or sister, or with his mother, if she was lawfully married to his father'.

The same, however, might not have been true of lower social groups for whom, probably, economy would have played a larger role in promoting the limitation of family size. There is surprisingly little in the writings of the later Christian Anglo-Saxons about infanticide – surprising, because homilists such as Ælfric and Wulfstan seem to have criticised the moral failings of their countrymen at every opportunity. Ælfric was clear that, among the list of sinful activities in the population, infanticide was one: 'Some of them [women] kill their children before they are born, or after birth, that they may not be discovered, nor their wicked adultery be betrayed. Then the child perishes, a loathsome heathen, and the wicked mother, unless she ever do penance for it.'[42] Such behaviour was the inevitable result of the success of the Church in instilling fear in the hearts of women who had conceived illegitimate children. Anglo-Saxon medical texts contain a number of remedies that may be interpreted as methods of terminating unwanted pregnancies. The most plausible of these comes in the *Herbarium Apuleii*: 'This plant fleabane, sodden in water, and used as a suppository by a woman purges the womb.'[43] If this is indeed a veiled recommendation of an abortifacient, it is of the most ambiguous kind, and could equally number among the many other remedies to expel a dead child from the womb. However, a late Anglo-Saxon penitential warns of a ten-year penance as punishment for a woman who 'kills the child within her with drinks or other things . . . or kills it after it is born'.[44]

Other remedies that may be construed as abortifacients are concerned with inducing or preventing menstruation. There are seven such remedies contained in surviving Old English medical books, and all recommend herbal remedies. Bonewort is clearly considered to be the most efficacious, as it crops up in five of the prescriptions in the *Herbarium Apuleii*, and in a sixth to relieve 'sore and heat of the womb'. Sea holly was recommended as a diuretic, to provoke periods and to relieve stomach ache. To stop periods, an alternative remedy recommended a drink made out of brooklime and centaury boiled in ale, followed by a hot bath and the application of a poultice made of beer dregs, green mugwort, wild celery and barley meal applied to the genital area.[45] As Christine Fell pointed out, remedies to promote periods are as likely to be a response to amenorrhoea caused by malnutrition as an attempt at abortion.[46] Remedies recommending warm baths, hot poultices and warm drinks made from herbs rich in iron content would all be comforting and practical to a woman with iron deficiency, and since the addenda to the remedy to stop menstruation was a further recipe for a woman suffering from menorrhagia (excessive bleeding), rectifying an iron deficiency would have been appropriate treatment, even if it would not have cured the condition. Furthermore, since one of the early signs of miscarriage is bleeding, the remedy to stop bleeding might equally be construed as an attempt to avert a miscarriage. One of these remedies could perhaps be interpreted as a method of terminating a pregnancy: 'To stimulate menstruation, take ten pennies weight of the seeds of this herb [bonewort], pounded in wine and drunk, or bruised with honey and laid on the genitals; initiates bleeding, and draws the child out of the womb.' Again, this might equally be interpreted as a method of aborting a dead foetus rather than a living child from the womb; there are many other remedies to this effect. Dittany, drunk in wine or hot water was recommended for a woman who was carrying a dead foetus, as were fresh shoots of pennyroyal in wine. The recommendation to use fleabane to purge the womb is followed in the next line by a remedy in which the same weed is to be soaked in wool and placed on the genitals, as an infallible cure for infertility. The emphasis in Old English medicine is more on preserving the baby and mother than on ridding the mother of an unwanted live burden.[47]

EARLY INFANCY

After a successful birth, care of the Anglo-Saxon baby followed the paths we might expect – the baby needed to be fed, clothed and amused. Nonetheless, given many of the comments some historians are prepared to make about the treatment of children in the past, it is worth stressing that the list of activities performed by the new mother Mary in an Anglo-Saxon description of the nativity of Jesus contained everything we might recommend and nothing of which we could disapprove: 'she bathed him and . . . put cream on him, and carried him, and . . . swaddled him, and rocked him'.[48]

Swaddling

Once the child was born, it was wrapped in clothes dedicated to the purpose: the Old English homilist Ælfric described them as '*macum cildclaðum*' (soft children's clothing). Ælfric was describing the birth of Christ, and the same subject in the poem *Christ* described the baby wrapped in cloths.[49]

Were children tightly wrapped, according to the later medieval practice, or were these loose infant wrappings? The illustrations are ambiguous. In one manuscript the baby seems to be closely wrapped, but the mother tucked into bed has the sheets twisted around her feet in a similar way. Anglo-Saxon illustrations do not show the tight, plaited bandaging familiar in later medieval representations of swaddling, and at the current state of knowledge it might be safer to argue for babies having been wrapped rather than tightly swaddled.

The infant Jesus being bathed. (Oxford, Bodleian Library, Rawl B.484, f. 85r)

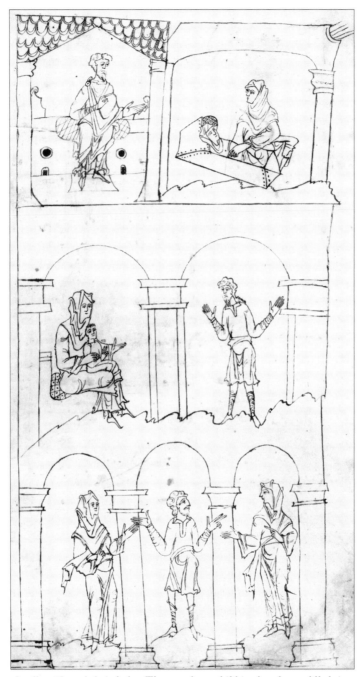

*Irad's wife and their baby. The new-born child is placed, swaddled, in
a cradle (top panel) while Irad sits apart and looks on. The middle
panel shows the young child being dandled on his mother's lap; again,
Irad looks on as his wife cares for the child. (Oxford, Bodleian
Library, Junius 11, f. 53)*

Breastfeeding

Notwithstanding Pope Gregory's complaint to Bede that mothers were giving their babies to wet-nurses (Gregory could hardly have had good knowledge about Anglo-Saxon women, and was more likely to have been commenting on Roman practices), most mothers probably breastfed their own children.[50] The medical remedies for the later period include advice for women who are having problems: 'for lactating women whose breasts are sore and swollen: take [knotgrass], pound it and mix it with butter; apply to the breasts and it will wonderfully drive away the soreness and swelling.' For women who could not produce milk a foreign plant, whose Old English name was unknown to the scribe, was recommended.[51]

By the Christian period, however, the élite at least did use wet-nurses. The *childfestran*, literally the nourisher of the child, is specifically mentioned in Ine's law 63 as one of the necessary members of a thane's personal retinue: 'If a thane travels, he may have with him his reeve and his smith and his children's nurse'.[52] It is a peculiar lawcode, and sheds extraordinary light on the ordering of the élite Anglo-Saxon family. The smith, reeve and nurse were all clearly vital servants in the thane's retinue, either because their services could not be dispensed with or because these servants represented the thane's superior status. If the latter, this would imply that lower-status families were most definitely not entitled to have

A female demon nurses triplets. (British Library, Harley 603, f. 4r)

nurses for their children even if they wanted them; if the former, it suggests that the high-status mother might have taken relatively little responsibility for the care of her own children.

Weaning

Calvin Wells, after studying the skeletal evidence from the cemetery at Worthy Park, Hampshire, declared that infants were expected to go straight from breastfeeding to solid food; this belief was based on his analysis of dental evidence, and was used to explain the sudden increase in the mortality among children at three to five years.[53] Wells's sample is not large enough to make this a certainty, but it is an interesting possibility. If there is genuinely a sudden degradation of teeth at two or three years, then this could as easily be caused by the grinding-down of adult food to pulp – known quern-stones and grinders seem to have given off a lot of grit in the process of grinding corn – as by the consumption of solid food. Ælfric assumed that children would go straight from breastmilk to bread.[54] The baker in Ælfric's *Colloquy* stressed that his produce was important to 'little children'.[55] This bread was likely to have been a soft, finely ground white bread, and was considered strengthening food, both for children and invalids.[56]

In support of Wells, there is the grave goods evidence of knives. Knives were not regarded as weapons but as general-purpose tools, and especially as eating equipment, and knives are among the most ubiquitous finds in adult male and female burials. According to the cemetery evidence, children might be buried with knives at the age of two or three years, although the percentage of burials of children with knives rises steeply at age eight or nine and there is another surge at sixteen to twenty. The incidence of children buried with knives varies from site to site, however. At Abingdon, Berkshire, a two-year-old was buried with a knife, although the next oldest child with a knife was aged six. At Alton, Hampshire, the youngest child buried with a knife was aged four. At Buckland, Dover, a number of children aged less than six were buried with knives, although none were definitely toddlers. At many sites, children were still not being buried with knives at six or seven, such as Sewerby, Yorkshire, where the youngest burial with a knife was aged ten to twelve, and Winnall, Hampshire, where the youngest burial with a knife was aged eleven. There is a likelihood, of course, that the knives buried with children were not their own personal knives, but part of the adult symbolism of the burial ritual; the apparent rises in the incidence of knives according to age might support this view. However, grave goods can perhaps be reasonably divided into two categories: those that children could have used in life and those that they clearly could not. The evidence of children buried with knives might serve to emphasise either the lack of interest parents took in the safety of their offspring, or the domination of the adult ritual over children's burials once more.

It has been argued that the length of the knife blade increased according to the age of the person buried, and if this were so, the knives were arguably not simply a requirement of the burial ritual, because under those circumstances, any knife would have done for a dead child. Far from being adult equipment foisted indiscriminately on children, like pots and brooches, these smaller knives would

Length of Knives in Children's Graves

Age Band	0–5 (n=152)	6–10 (n=92)	11–14 (n=38)	15–29 (n=229)	30–44 (n=137)	45+ (n=144)
Length (cm)	9.6 (n=10)	9.4 (n=16)	12.8 (n=6)	11.2 (n=75)	11.6 (n=53)	13.6 (n=54)

appear to be the personal possessions of the children, and were smaller in recognition of the child's relative lack of dexterity and size.

However, again, care must be used in how 'child' is used in the creation of the statistics from which such arguments are derived.[57] Using a population derived from thirteen furnished inhumation cemeteries, there were 207 burials with knives where the *maximum* age of the deceased was twenty-five or under at the time of death, but there were only fourteen cases where the child was aged five or under at the time of death, and of these cases only two were aged about two years old. Within cemeteries, knife blade lengths did not show a consistent increase with age. At Buckland, for example, of those buried with a knife and aged twenty-five or under, the longest measurable knife blade at 20 cm was buried with a six- to twelve-year-old, and the smallest measurable blade at 9 cm was buried with a twelve- to eighteen-year-old. At Lechlade, Gloucestershire, there were only three children buried with knives. None of these had knife blades longer than 14 cm, but two of the blade lengths were in the average range for the site. The blade lengths at this site do appear to form a pattern, though: the four- to five-year-old is buried with a blade length of 9.3 cm; the seven- to ten-year-old's measured 12.9 cm, and the eleven- to twelve-year-old's measured 13.7 cm, but with such a small sample, it is not appropriate to draw any more than cautious inferences. Although the figures are not conclusive, they do indicate that, in some communities, some children were carrying knives at less than five years of age, but this was not a common occurrence, and if children were being weaned suddenly onto solid, adult food at the age of two or three as rapidly as Wells suggested, they were not using adult utensils to eat this food. A scene from the *Harley Psalter*, illustrating the words from Psalm 17: 'may their children have more than enough', depicts children using their hands to eat food, and this seems a more likely practice.

One of the more obscure medical remedies may support the idea of rapid weaning. The remedy discusses a child who is *ahwaened*, which Oswald Cockayne translated as 'vexed', to give: 'in case any child be vexed, then take thou the same wort [smearwort], and smoke it with this; then wilt thou render it the gladder'.[58] This is a puzzling remedy, since it seems to be for no specific ailment, unlike the other remedies for which smearwort is prescribed; the other ailments are 'strength of poison', 'stiffest fevers', 'sore of nostrils', 'chill', 'bite of adder' and 'ulcer on nose'. The remedy for '*ahwaened cyld*' follows immediately after that for 'bite of adder', and it may be a continuation, i.e., if the child is vexed by the bite of an adder, then take roots of this same plant. . . . However, if this is the case, then the children's remedy is very different from that for adults, which involves frequent doses of the plant to be taken internally. Smearwort (*Aristolochia clematitis*) contains aristolochic acid, which has tumour-inhibiting properties.[59] In overdoses it may produce violent gastrointestinal irritation. The Old English *ahwaened* translated the original Latin *contristatus*, which Cockayne knew to be 'sad, gloomy', but is this what the Old English translator intended? The Old English verb *awenian* means 'to wean', and if this was intended then we have a less ambiguous remedy for a child reluctant to be weaned. The much later account *Life of St Anselm* includes a reference by the saint to children being encouraged to wean by the method of smearing something sharp and bitter on the mother's breasts, though this reference may have more to do with Italian and Norman childrearing practices than Anglo-Saxon ones.[60] The bitter smoke of smearwort, applied to a child asking to be fed, might have the same effect, although this would be a somewhat drastic remedy.

The tentative conclusion from the little circumstantial evidence we have about the age of weaning would suggest that it happened relatively late by modern standards, at about two or three years of age. By the standards of present non-industrial agricultural populations, however, this is not a particularly late age for weaning: often a mother's milk is the surest source of food in poorer societies, and water from the local well, unless boiled, could be lethal to a baby not yet immune to the local pathogens, so children who were breastfed until the last possible moment might have been strong enough to survive the contamination in food and water.

An illustration to Psalm 113: 'he gives the barren woman a home, making her the mother of children'. (British Library, Harley 603, f. 58r)

Whether they were aware of it or not, a late age of weaning would have had considerable implications on the fertility of Anglo-Saxon women. It has been established that breastfeeding postpones the return of ovulation after birth, so that in populations where lengthy and intensive breastfeeding is practised, there is a substantial contraceptive effect.[61] The number of children a woman might produce in her lifetime has a distinct effect on attitudes towards offspring: the fewer the children, the more they are likely to be cherished by their parents, or to receive their undivided attention. In addition, the sustained breastfeeding suggested by Wells would have obliged the mother to be in close contact with the infant for at least its first few years, and this contact could hardly have failed to produce a bond of affection between mother and child during this period. The evidence and the possibilities it suggests are tantalising, but inconclusive.

The evidence from the various Anglo-Saxon sources indicates that Anglo-Saxon women were as anxious about conception, pregnancy and childbirth as any modern mother. Because of the obvious dangers, and perhaps because of the influence of Christian teachings, some women chose abstinence rather than risk childbearing, but there is little substantial evidence to support widespread use of induced abortion or infanticide as alternative contraceptive devices.

Once born, the baby would be cared for by wrapping it in its special children's clothes, would be fed, possibly even until it was a year or two old, on breastmilk, supplemented later by soft bread, and would be rocked in its own cradle. However, just as childbirth was a potentially fatal enterprise for the mother, so the earliest years of its life were the most dangerous for the baby, in spite of the best care of the mother. In the next chapter, attitudes towards the infant, a liminal and vulnerable member of society, will be assessed.

CHAPTER 6

Infancy, Baptism and the Afterlife

An Anglo-Saxon mother could never have felt confident that her new baby would survive in the difficult and dangerous environment out of the womb, and her practical experience must have been that the child she was caring for was as likely to die as to live. Given the precarious hold of the infant on life, at what point did parents accept their new child as a permanent member of the family, and how did parents react to, and cope with, the potentially brief life and sudden death of their child?

Mortality rates recorded for non-developed countries before the introduction of contraceptives give some indication as to what infant mortality in pre-industrial societies, like that of Anglo-Saxon England, might have been like. These comparative statistics show that there must have been anything up to 100 deaths per 1,000 live births, or up to 108 deaths per 1,000 children aged between birth and four years, that is, a 90 per cent chance of producing a live child, and a similar chance of keeping a live birth alive until its fourth birthday.[1] Shulamith Shahar suggested that, in pre-industrial Europe, 200–300 out of every 1,000 infants died in their first year and only half of that number reached the age of five.[2] Even recent figures for England (issued by the Royal College of Midwives, 25 January 1990) give, as the poorest rates in the country, 10 deaths per 1,000 live births in the West Midlands, where deaths are from stillbirths or in the first two weeks after birth, yet, as a measure of how many infants are missing from the archaeological record, these modern figures appear to be roughly comparable to the rates found in furnished Anglo-Saxon cemeteries.

It has long been recognised that infants are under-represented in earlier Anglo-Saxon inhumation cemeteries and cremation cemeteries.[3] Infant mortality can hardly have been as low in the Anglo-Saxon period as the mortuary statistics indicate, so other considerations must be responsible for this situation. One possibility is that infant bones are more easily dissolved than adult bones, and may simply not have survived in the archaeological record, but comparable sites from Romano-British cemeteries and the churchyards of later Anglo-Saxon cemeteries suggest that post-depositional decay is not the answer. At the Roman site at Owlesbury, Hampshire, 34.8 per cent of the burials were of under fives.[4] In the Anglo-Saxon monastic cemetery at Jarrow, Northumbria, 42.9 per cent of the mortuary population were seventeen or under at the time of death, and 30 per cent of burials in this juvenile category were four or under at the time of death.[5] In the late Anglo-Saxon cemetery at Norwich, of those to whom it was possible to assign an age, 45 per cent of the late Anglo-Saxon cemetery population were infants.[6] At the late Anglo-Saxon church cemetery at Raunds, a 20 per cent level of infant mortality was represented in the excavated area, while at Winchester, in the church cemetery in use from the seventh century to the late ninth century, of the 250 graves excavated, 27.2 per cent were of children under two years of age.[7] There is clearly an increase in infants in the mortuary population from the pagan Anglo-Saxon period to the Christian Anglo-Saxon period. This is unlikely to have been caused by increased mortality rates; it is much more likely to be the result of change in burial practice.

It is possible that infants were included within the pagan cemeteries, but they may have been buried more shallowly than adults, reducing their likelihood of survival. Burial 198 at Lechlade, Gloucestershire, was of an infant or foetus with a gestational age of six to seven months buried so close to the top of the gravel that it was largely removed during the mechanical stripping of the site, and furthermore, the burial was cut by another adult grave. At Lechlade again, burial 95/2, a foetus with a gestational age of seven months was only discovered during the analysis of the female burial 95/1. The position of the baby's bones did not indicate that it necessarily belonged to the female, and the excavator argued that the two bodies were deposited in the grave at the same time.[8] Shallow burial might be indicative of a relative lack of care over the disposal of infants. It is true that it is difficult to dig deeply where the hole is of narrow width and length, but there are practical implications for shallow burials, not least the possibility of scavenging dogs or wild animals disinterring the remains.

Infants and children may not normally have been buried in adult cemeteries in the pre-Christian period. Other methods may have been used to dispose of infants, such as cremation without subsequent burial. There has been some evidence from the cremation cemetery at Spong Hill, Norfolk to suggest a proportionately high number of juveniles in cremation pots, and at Caistor-by-Norwich the sample of rescued cremations was weighted towards infants.[9] Cremation burials do not always present larger numbers of infants than their inhumation counterparts, though. At Millgate, the experienced bone analyst Mary Harman noted that infants were badly under-represented in the cremation record.[10]

There are exceptions to the general rule that pagan Anglo-Saxon sites contain low numbers of infant burials. The late pagan site of Lechlade, Gloucestershire, contained forty-four burials of children aged six years or less, making up 20 per cent of the cemetery population, of which twenty-five burials were of infants under three years of age. Of these forty-four infants, thirteen were in double burials with adult females, males or older juveniles. Taking a sample of Anglo-Saxon furnished inhumation cemeteries generally, of those infants that have been recovered, about 17 per cent are included in double burials (22 out of 130 infant burials), compared to the rest of the older age groups in the mortuary population, of which 9 per cent are buried in double or multiple graves (95 out of 1,141 burials). The double infant burials may represent the only infant burials within a site. At Empingham II, Rutland, in a mortuary population of over 150 bodies, there were no neonates and only two burials of infants under two years of age, both of whom were interred with 'wealthy' adult females. At Nassington, Northamptonshire, out of over forty burials, only two infants were found, in the form of a skull buried by the hand of female burial 31, and another skull in the crook of the arm of female burial A.[11] Where infants do occur in the adult cemetery, then, they often appear as an addition to the graves of adults. Arguably, the double burials may represent two members of the same family who died simultaneously, but if two deaths coincided, it may have been a matter of convenience to bury the bodies together. Equally, if disease attacked a community, weak infants might be expected to die with their carers.

Perhaps infants were normally buried away from the adult cemetery sites. As mentioned earlier in relation to infanticide, Roman infants were exempt from normal mortuary taboos, and were frequently buried in or around sites of domestic occupation. At the Romano-British villa at Barton Court Farm, Oxfordshire, later reused by the Anglo-Saxons for burial, there was a cluster of twenty-six infant burials dating to the late fourth and early fifth centuries, and the Romano-British villa at Hambledon, Buckinghamshire, also yielded high numbers of infant burials.[12] The practice of burying infants in and around settlements does not appear to have been adopted by the Anglo-Saxons. Excavated Anglo-Saxon settlement sites rarely contain burials of any sort, although King Edwin's palace complex at Yeavering, Northumbria, does include human burials which may be associated with an early church. One exception to this rule is Sutton Courteney, Berkshire, where an infant and female adult were buried together in a pit in house XXIV. This, according to the excavator, was clearly an abnormal burial: an over-large pit had been dug, into which the bodies appeared to have been hastily thrown.[13] A further case of an infant buried in the floor of a sunken-featured building was uncovered at Barrow Hills, Oxfordshire in 1983.[14] Later in the medieval period, the settlements of Tattenhoe and Westbury included two burials of infants, one an *in utero* foetus of five to seven months associated with a late eleventh-century building and showing signs of gnawing marks from rodent activity, and the other dating to the late thirteenth century, below building 4, carefully buried with a few animal bones. The excavator hesitantly guessed that both these burials represented foundation deposits.[15] There are insufficient numbers of such burials within settlements to argue for a widespread practice of settlement burial for the earlier Anglo-Saxon period, but the strategy in many settlement site excavations is to reveal the outline of post-hole buildings and analyse deposits within sunken-featured buildings, rather than to look for the tiny bones of infants buried near such habitations.

WHEN DO INFANTS BECOME HUMANS?

If parents were prepared to bury their children shallowly, and allow the graves to be disturbed by later burials, or to bury their children away from the community cemetery, it might imply that the pagan Anglo-Saxons regarded infants as being less than full humans. We have little evidence about earlier Anglo-Saxon attitudes towards very young children, and there is no firm information to show when the pre-Christian baby was supposed to develop a human personality, though by the Christian period, it is apparent that even stillborn children 'counted', to the extent that when Asser recorded the size of Alfred's family, he noted that the count included 'those who were carried off in infancy by an untimely death and who numbered . . .'. Unfortunately, the scribe copying the manuscript failed to record the number, but nonetheless, King Alfred and his biographer were counting and wanted to include all the children, not just those who survived, in the narrative of Alfred's life.[16]

Within the furnished burial ritual, children who were included in the adult cemeteries may have been specifically selected from the set of children who died and were disposed of elsewhere. The majority of dead infants may not even have been formally buried, and there is a possibility that some were simply thrown away: Dominic Powlesland reported infant bones in the rubbish pits at the settlement of West Heslerton.[17]

If this is true, then the infants within the cemeteries have not been given 'normal' burial ritual for their age group, and on further analysis, it can be seen that this specially selected group of young children did not receive a 'normal' pattern of burial within the adult ritual either. The infants buried within the adult cemetery were distinguished by a lack of grave goods in comparison to other age groups.[18] At Lechlade – a late sixth-/seventh-century site, with an unusually high number of infants – twenty-three were buried without grave goods; a further six were buried with only beads, while the remaining fifteen were given slightly more luxurious burial. At Alton, Hampshire, where again there is a relatively high proportion of infants (eight out of fifty inhumations), six of the infants were buried without grave goods, while of the remaining two, one was buried with a bone bead, and one, a four-year-old, was buried with a bead and a knife. This pattern is in keeping with that for other sites. Rarely buried with weapons, and usually buried without grave goods or only a single bead, buckle or pot, children under the age of five represent the 'poorest' members of the mortuary community. If grave goods are a representation of status in life, then infants had little value to society, and certainly no status in death. If grave goods within Anglo-Saxon cemeteries represent any form of belief in an afterlife, then infants were clearly expected to arrive in the new life as helpless and useless as they left the old. Having said that, there are some extraordinary exceptions to this rule, whose wealth of grave goods sets them apart from infants, children and adults alike. At Finglesham, Kent, for example, there were no burials of infants under eighteen months old, but there were nineteen burials of infants aged between eighteen months and five years. Of these infants, twelve were buried with no grave goods and six were buried with only one or two items, but three children were buried with expensive necklaces. The most spectacular was grave 7, with a probable girl aged between two and five years who was buried with a wheel-thrown bottle, a Roman flagon, a knife, chatelaine and pouch, and an elaborate necklace including a gold solidus of Sigeberht II/III.

The selected group of younger children in the burial ritual were sometimes distinguished from the 'normal' burials not by their poverty or wealth of grave goods, but by unusual burial ritual. Double burials are not uncommon in fifth- to seventh-century inhumation sites, and the occurrence of infants within such graves has already been discussed. Multiple burials of more than two bodies are less common and less easily explicable in terms of simultaneous natural death. At Empingham II, of the three triple burials, two included child burials, and the one odd quadruple burial included an infant overlain by three adult male burials. The ritual at Empingham II, a fully excavated site, was inhumation. Only one cremation burial was found – that of a child aged five or six years.[19] At Holborough, Kent, the seventh-century cemetery contained exclusively west–east burials, except for one infant, buried north–south. At Appledown, West Sussex, structure 32 consists of four post-holes arranged at each corner of a square, with a fifth post-hole in the centre of the structure containing the cremated remains of an infant or child. While this is not the only post-hole structure at the site, it is noticeable that this feature has drawn particular comment as the 'most striking example' of a post-hole burial.[20]

Cemeteries whose use straddles the transitional period between the arrival of Christianity and the abandonment of these sites for church graveyards show a particularly high level of what may be described as 'uneasiness' about infant burials. The case of Lechlade has been mentioned, where, within the context of Anglo-Saxon cemeteries, a surprisingly high number of infants are buried in the cemetery. At Marina Drive, Dunstable, Bedfordshire, the cemetery did not come into use until shortly before the coming of Christianity in the late sixth century. It produced a number of grave goods which may be confidently defined as amuletic. These included two beaver teeth, three cowrie shells, one faceted crystal, one ox rib and one quartz crystal. Apart from a bag of human teeth, these were the only 'amulets' within the cemetery, and they were all found with children between the ages of one and six years.[21] Within the Anglo-Saxon burial ritual, amulets are by no means exclusively buried with infants and children, but it is not uncommon for infants to be buried with such items, and Marina Drive offers the most remarkable case of this tendency. Whatever it was about an individual's death that motivated the buriers to include amulets among the grave goods, infants often qualified for the distinction.

So called 'Final Phase' sites, such as Marina Drive, are cemeteries dating to the seventh and eighth centuries. The number of burials with grave goods in these cemeteries is low – only about 25 per cent – and the repertoire of grave goods changed to become more restrained. Weapon burial declined in male graves, and brooches and long strings of beads for women were replaced by pins and smaller necklaces. Arguably, the restraint illustrated in the Final Phase cemeteries was not merely coincident with the arrival of Christianity, but was a reflection of it, to the extent that Final Phase burials represent a Christianised burial population, or one where Christianity had challenged the older Anglo-Saxon belief systems. It is interesting to note that, while a new ritual was being developed for adults in these cemeteries, there are indications that the burials of children retained a more conservative tradition. Final Phase cemeteries such as Marina Drive, Bedfordshire; Didcot, Oxfordshire; Lechlade, Gloucestershire and Winnall II, Hampshire all include either abnormal or anachronistic approaches to children's burials. At Marina Drive, as we have seen, the juveniles were the ones buried with amulets, and children also have the richer necklace sets. At the partially excavated cemetery at Didcot, of the seventeen burials, the richest belonged to the youngest to perish – grave 12 – whose three- to five-year-old occupant was buried with a buckle, a silver ring, six beads, a knife, an iron pin, a copper alloy workbox and miscellaneous iron fragments.[22] The Final Phase of the cemetery at Castledyke, Barton-on-Humber included the grave of a ten- or eleven-year-old whose grave goods were all together in a bag, and included such amulets as a polished pebble and, like the pouch of amulets at Marina Drive, human teeth – in this case, eleven teeth from a nine- or ten-year-old.

Interestingly, the phenomenon of children being accorded a more old-fashioned and conservative burial ritual at a time when adult burial ritual was in a period of transition appears to have been mirrored when pagan furnished ritual changed from inhumation to cremation in the Anglian areas. At the large cremation cemetery of Caistor-by-Norwich, the report noted that children's cremation urns showed a higher level of decoration and associated objects than those of adults, implying that more care was taken over these burials. The writers of the report explained these findings by suggesting that 'the ritual appropriate to child funerals remained conservative at a time when the belief in its value to adults . . . was breaking down'. They also noted that the cremated children might represent the offspring of the wealthier members of the community who might have a more traditional approach to burial than the poorer or more casual families.[23] At the cremation cemetery of Lackford, Suffolk, it was noted that 'children were frequently cremated, often very young ones'.[24] It may be that the cremation burials at Empingham II and Appledown also reflect this traditional approach to children's death and burial.

At Winnall II, the excavators noted that this peri-conversion site contained a number of burials marked by stones placed over their bodies, which, it is speculated within the site report, may represent attempts to lay ghosts. These possibly 'revenant' burials include the juveniles in graves 9, 18, 24b and 33 – occupants were aged four years, eighteen months, eight years and eleven years respectively. Not all children were buried with stones over their bodies, and some adults were, but a very high proportion of the children (four out of nine) received this treatment.[25] At Lechlade, the body in grave 140, aged about nine or ten, was buried with stone blocks over the head, by the pelvis and over the knee; the burial dates to the late seventh or early eighth century, right at the end of the site's use for burial. The undatable burial 177, of a two- or three-year-old, was buried with a stone between the right arm and chest and over the feet. Other methods of burial associated, perhaps, with preventing the dead from walking are also found at Lechlade. Grave 74 is of a nine- to ten-year-old, buried prone, with its head at knee-level to one side of the body. The other two prone burials are of a female aged over forty and a fourteen- to fifteen-year-old. At Empingham II, grave 113 contained a double burial, of an adult male, prone, with his hands in front of his face, overlying a child, also face down.[26] Prone burial is uncommon in Anglo-Saxon cemeteries, and is usually interpreted as indicating punishment or sacrifice.[27] Again, what we are seeing is not a ritual aimed exclusively at infants and children, but a ritual provoked by some condition of life or death that children and infants were more likely to fulfil than adults.

In the case of the Final Phase cemeteries, it is arguable that two influences were at work. The new Christian beliefs seem to have been encouraging adults to move away from burial with grave goods to a new ritual, which was shortly also to include a new spatial significance, as burials developed within churchyards. What was the place of children within this new belief system and within this new burial ritual? Children's burials had never, before, had parity with adult burials. Were children to be buried in exactly the same way as adults under the new rules? Would children, particularly if they were unbaptised (or even if they had been baptised but were too young to comprehend the new teachings and were effectively ignorant of Christianity) be given the same afterlife as adults? The 'safest' response to these problems may have been to emphasise children's difference to adults, either by giving them a more traditional and conservative burial ritual, or by altering the new ritual to mark out the graves of those for whom an afterlife within the new Christian theology could not be guaranteed with confidence.

Not all prone burials of adults and children need have sinister interpretations. At Chesterford, Essex, a child aged about eight years was buried prone. There is another, adult, prone burial at the cemetery, of a woman buried apparently without her costume because her grave goods were collected together in one corner of the grave. Her burial, both prone and with the unorthodox deposition of her costume merits interpretation as anomalous and deliberately dishonouring, but the prone boy has more orthodox deposition of a relatively rich range of grave goods – he has a dog carcass at his feet and a spear and mended shield.[28] This burial must either be interpreted as the deliberately prone burial of a child who needed the symbols of unusual wealth to honour his burial but nonetheless required the ignominy of interment face down – an attempt to appease the spirit and prevent revenantism at one and the same time? – or might be interpreted more prosaically as accidental, in that the buriers might not have realised that the body was prone. To argue accident rather than a deliberate deposition, you would, however, also have to argue some obscuring grave furniture such as a coffin, for which there is no evidence, or stunningly inattentive mourners at the burial, and given the care with which the grave goods were deposited around the body, this seems unlikely. Here, then, there seems to be a case of deliberately mixed messages. The boy was buried with an adult weapon set, indicating maturity and status, but the shield was mended – symbolism was more important than the material value of the item. A dog – one of very few animal burials within Anglo-Saxon mortuary contexts, and usually indicative of high status – was included, and possibly sacrificed, in the burial, yet the boy was buried prone, a mark of dishonour and, feasibly, fear on the part of the burying community. The messages are impenetrable, and whether the child's manner of death, youth, or other circumstances contributed to this burial ritual is not determinable.

Later documentary evidence sheds little light on any interpretation of these pagan burial rituals, but in the Scandinavian *Njall's Saga*, Hrafnkell piled up a cairn over the boy whom he was forced to kill in fulfilment of his vow; in the sagas, generally only murdered men were covered with stones or turf, or witches or wizards who had been stoned to death for their crimes.[29] It is not sensible to use late Scandinavian sources to elucidate pagan Anglo-Saxon material, but this example does provide an interesting context for attitudes towards the dead that might lead to such behaviour. Graves marked by stones over the bodies might indicate an exceptional or threatening death, or perhaps exceptional or threatening times, such as a period of religious conversion.

The infants included within the pagan cemetery tend to be marked out in some way, either by their very presence in the adult cemetery, or by some unusual feature of the burial. Towards the end of the use of the pagan cemeteries, at a time when Christianity must have been influencing ideas about burial and the afterlife, there is a suggestion that infant burials begin to receive greater emphasis. Why should the archaeological record indicate greater worry about the infant afterlife in the conversion period?

The Church taught that adults, and babies too, unless they were baptised, would not reach heaven.[30] This meant that all infants, not just those who died in peculiar or threatening circumstances, had the potential to hold a grievance against the living if they died before baptism. The idea that the dead could have malign intentions towards the living, and that even dead infants could be susceptible to this behaviour, might not seem obvious and needs some illustration. Already suggested are examples from the pagan archaeological record where infants are given unusual treatment in death, but no actual intention to 'lay' a ghost can be deduced from this even though there is a strong temptation to interpret the presence of amulets and stones in graves in this way. A persuasive case might be made for the dramatic burial 38 at Worthy Park, Hampshire, which illustrates that the emphasis in cases of violent death was on the infant, rather than the adult, burial. In this example, the grave contained a woman with a newly born child lying head down between her thighs, its feet still apparently enclosed within the woman's pelvic girdle, as if the infant and mother had died at the moment of childbirth. The infant's body was deliberately covered by a layer of chalk. The fact that there was no chalk over the mother suggests that it was the infant, not the adult, whose death presented a particular problem and whose burial deserved special treatment.[31] This burial poses problems of interpretation, in that the foetus must have been visible to the buriers. Its articulated feet bones appear to lie undisturbed in the pelvic girdle, rather than to have fallen through after decomposition, as would have been the case if the infant had been lying on top of the body of the woman, indicating that the foetus may have been expelled after the woman had died. This is not beyond the bounds of possibility: when the body of a pregnant woman decomposes, the foetus may be expelled after about 48–72 hours.[32] This gives an interesting insight into pagan Anglo-Saxon burial practice: the woman would seem to have been dead for at least two days before her burial. However, a simple explanation might be that the umbilical cord had become wrapped around the child prior to labour, obstructing its delivery and making it impossible for the midwives to decently remove the baby from the mother.[33] The upsetting expulsion of her stillborn child after the mother's death might be sufficient cause to explain the peculiar circumstances of this burial.

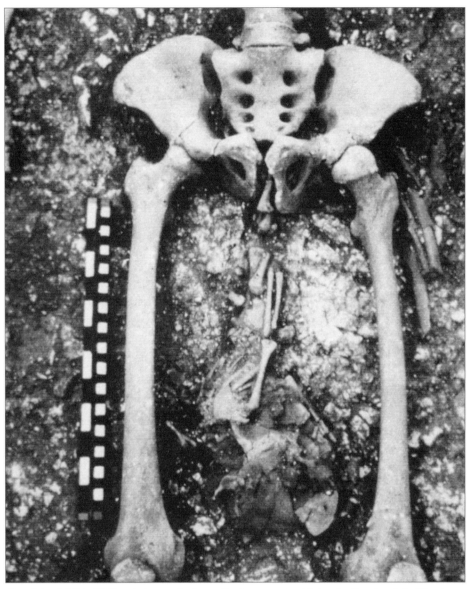

Death in childbirth? The skeleton of a foetus lies between the thighs of a female adult, Worthy Park grave 38.

There are few documentary sources relating to infant burials. In a charm from the *Lacnunga*, a late Anglo–Saxon text, there are hints that a dead infant could in some way influence or prevent birth. A woman who had miscarriages was to take a bit of her own child's grave, wrap it in black wool, sell it to a trader and then say: 'I sell it, I have sold it, this black wool and these grains of sorrow.'[34] Ælfric terrorised listeners of his homilies with tales of ghosts and of the fates awaiting those who died in sin. Characteristic of the tales that he felt his audience would be prepared to accept was the story of a child monk who missed his parents so much that he ran away from the monastery. He died the instant he arrived at his parents' house. Whenever they tried to bury him, the next day his body was found thrown out of the grave, until Benedict intervened with a consecrated wafer to lay on his breast. The earth would reject an unholy body; this story was an old one.[35]

Revenantism

Paul Barber's work on traditional European beliefs in revenantism (the belief that the dead may return to life), drew attention to the particular susceptibility of infants to have a malign existence after death in the popular imagination. He offered two plausible suggestions as to why this should be. In the first place, he demonstrated the link between disease and the phenomenon of revenants. The common belief in large parts of Europe was that when there was an outbreak of hauntings – of corpses coming to life, taking life from the living, and turning the newly dead into revenants – the culprit was invariably the first person who died. His victims were his nearest friends and relatives, those with whom he was most regularly in contact. The root of this superstition, Barber deduced, was the attempt by the ignorant to explain the introduction of fatal infectious disease into the community. Naturally, infants were the most vulnerable to disease, and thus were most likely to die under these sinister circumstances.[36]

Within the Anglo-Saxon documentary sources, sick children are recorded as calling the living to follow them to the grave, although a positive Christian slant is given to the picture. According to Bede, a child oblate called Æsica was too young to live as a monk and was being brought up by nuns. Æsica fell fatally ill:

> When he came to his last moment, [he] cried out three times upon one of the virgins consecrated to Christ, speaking to her, as if she were present, by her own name, 'Eadgyth, Eadgyth, Eadgyth', and therewith ending the temporal life entered into life eternal. But that virgin which he called at his death, straightway in the place where she was, being there taken with the same sickness, the very same day that she was called was taken out of this life, and followed him that called her to the kingdom of heaven.[37]

Our modern understanding of infections enables us to give a scientific explanation to this kind of incident, and it is clear that an infectious child may well pass on its infections to its carers. An explanation for the story might be that Eadgyth had formed some bond with the child, probably by acting as its carer/surrogate mother. She was absent at the time of the child's death; small wonder then that Æsica should call on her in his last moments. In Bede's time, a different, and in this case mystical, explanation was sought.

Scavenging dogs around a cemetery also play a part in the European story of revenantism. Barber cites numerous examples from European folklore in which the action of dogs and wolves grubbing out fresh corpses was reinterpreted as an attack by the animals on revenants attempting to rise from the dead. Dogs thus became the traditional enemies of vampires. One is reminded inexorably of Ælfric's child who would not stay in his grave until an amulet was placed on his chest. Wolves and dogs certainly inhabited the Anglo-Saxon countryside, and the early cemeteries, on the periphery of settlements, must have been targets. It appears that infants were buried more shallowly than adults (and therefore fail to survive in the archaeological record), and thus one could suppose that they were the most convenient prey for dogs and other scavengers. The discovery of an empty infant grave so shortly after the death of the child could easily give rise to extreme fears and superstitions, and might be the explanation for the stones placed over the graves of some children and adults – not so much to prevent a putative ghost getting out, but to prevent scavengers (and grave-robbers in the case of some of the richer adult burials) from getting in.

Baptism

Could the introduction of Christianity have put an end to these superstitions, or, as the late pagan cemeteries indicate, could it indeed have heightened the superstition? It has already been suggested that Christianity placed all those who were not baptised in a vulnerable position, and it is not unlikely that the rite of baptism may have been regarded by the new converts as a further charm against the spirits of dead infants. A long Christian tradition asserted clearly by St Augustine at the beginning of the fifth century argued that a child dying unbaptised was condemned to the fires of hell, with a consequential penalty for the parents who were responsible for the failure to baptise.[38] The teachings of the Anglo-Saxon Church reiterated that children, even though they had no understanding, had to be baptised, although there seems to have been some resistance to this idea. Even at the end of the Anglo-Saxon period, Ælfric felt obliged to reiterate the idea that infants had to be baptised, even though they could not understand the ritual. The subject arose in his sermon on the Lord's Epiphany, on the Second Sunday in Lent, and on the Sacrifice on Easter Day, all traditionally baptismal days. Ælfric was one of a long line of ecclesiastics attempting to preach this message. Augustine's eighth question to Gregory, according to Bede's account, was about baptism, including how soon after birth an infant could be baptised, particularly if it was in danger of dying. Gregory replied that it could be baptised the very hour it was born, even though it lacked understanding.[39] This may have been merely a forum for the discussion of theological matters that were more an issue to Rome than to the pagan English. Offsetting this objection is the presence in the vernacular lawcodes of severe penalties incurred by those who failed to baptise their infants. Law 2 of King Ine of Wessex (reigned 688–72) is uncompromising: 'A child shall be baptised within 30 days. If this is not done, 30 shillings shall be paid in compensation. If it dies without being baptised, he shall pay for it with everything he owns.'

To fail to baptise the child was not a serious offence – thirty shillings was not a large penalty compared to fines for other crimes – but to allow a child to die

Infant baptism? Naked adults, their feet in water, look on as a child is lifted up to the heavens. (British Library, Harley 603, f. 72r)

unbaptised was. The law indicates that many parents were reluctant to baptise their apparently healthy infants; perhaps there was an unintentional correlation in their perception between death and baptism. The *Northumbrian Priest's Law* reinforced the haste to baptise – 'each child shall be baptised within 9 days: if not, 6 oras [Danish coins]'.[40] Guthlac, the model child of model Christian parents was, we are informed, baptised after eight days, and Bede noted that the very first Northumbrian to receive baptism was Eanflaed, the newly born daughter of Edwin.[41] Other children of Edwin's died apparently at the moment of baptism – they were still wearing the chrism.

It may be that the references to baptism in the surviving documentary evidence represent no more than the continuation of an ecclesiastical debate that had no relevance to the actual state of affairs. After all, by the time Ælfric was writing, England had been Christian for some centuries, and baptism of infants ought to have been a matter of course. However, a late account from Cornwall, written about 1200, suggests that even notably pious Christian parents could fail in this duty. The manuscript concerns the life of Peter of Cornwall and Launceston, and describes the events occurring to his pious family. One family member, Ailsi (a corruption of the Anglo-Saxon name Æthelsige), had visions through the medium of his dead fourth son, Paganus – so called, we are told, because 'he was a long time a pagan, living 12 years before he was baptised'. We are given no reason why Paganus was not baptised by his parents, although his name may indicate that he was unusual in this respect. Within the same family, we are told of a child who died at the same time as her grandfather: 'she died in a state of innocence, immediately after baptism, and still dressed in white'; moreover, she died at precisely the same time as her grandfather, and was buried in his coffin.[42] Why should Paganus have remained unbaptised all through childhood while other children in his family were baptised almost at birth? Perhaps the circumstances of the granddaughter's death provide the key. Baptism was for sickly children, used as a last-minute resort to save the child's life or to ensure its smooth entry into heaven. A lively child had no need of baptism.

This view is exemplified in the attitude of one of the new converts to Christianity who came to Wilfred on one of his missionary journeys into the countryside. The woman 'held in her bosom the body of her first-born child, wrapped in rags and hidden from sight; she uncovered the face of the corpse for the bishop to confirm it among the rest, hoping thus to be able to bring it back to life'.[43] The bishop, discovering the ruse, baptised the child only after some persuasion. The woman's expectations were confirmed – the child was revived, and she hastened away with it. Subsequent events showed that the woman remained a heathen even after this demonstration of Christian power.

Wilfred's miracle is not an original one. Augustine in the early fifth century recorded a similar miracle attributed to St Etienne. An African woman accosted the martyr with her dead child in her arms and tearfully begged him to revive the infant. That done, the baby was taken to the priests for baptism, whereupon he died immediately.[44] The differences between the two versions of the miracle story are instructive. In St Etienne's case, the woman's anxiety is not so much that her child has died as that it has died unbaptised; in the seventh-century Anglo-Saxon version, the pagan woman's earnest desire is that the child should live, even if that required the act of baptism.

Burials

Baptism is not an archaeologically identifiable rite, but burials in excavated Christian Anglo-Saxon graveyards may throw light on the question of Anglo-Saxon attitudes towards infants and their Christian afterlife. One peculiarity of infant burials in this period is that they tend to be clustered under the eaves-drips of the church, possibly because the water dripping from the holy roof might be thought to 'double-bless' the infants. Such clusters are noticeable at Raunds, Whithorn, Jarrow and Winchester. Indeed, for Hartlepool, the presence of a cluster of infant burials has been used to locate the probable site of the lost church.[45] It must be stressed that the habit of burying infants under the eaves-drips is by no means unique to the Anglo-Saxons: Pliny noted that it was customary to bury the bodies of very young infants *in subgrundariis*, and this was interpreted by Fulgentius as referring to infants who had not been alive more than forty days.[46] In excavated Merovingian cemeteries such as Frénouville,

Giberville-le-Martray and Verson, children are as badly under-represented as they are in the furnished cemeteries of Anglo-Saxon England, even though, on the Continent, the population using these large rural cemeteries was nominally Christian. In the Carolingian period, these cemeteries were relocated to the churches in the heart of villages and in towns, as they were in eighth-century England, and in Carolingian France, as in England, the numbers of infants in these cemeteries rises dramatically. Clusters of infant burials have been excavated from these later Continental church cemeteries. At St Martin de Trainecourt, at Mondeville in Calvados, 106 children in the cemetery were located in a space to the north-east, along the cloister. At Courneuve, the excavations of the church of St Lucien revealed 85 per cent of the burials found along the south side of the building were of young children.[47]

The change in burial ritual accorded to children needs some explanation. It may be that the earlier cemeteries, situated away from the domestic spaces, were not perceived to be sacred spaces in the same sense as the consecrated ground of a church cemetery, and there may not have been the same pressure to bury everyone in the community within the furnished burial grounds. The sudden enthusiasm for burying infants in the church cemetery may also reflect the level of control Christianity exerted over the customs of the newly converted. Arguably, this change in behaviour towards dead children could represent the augmentation of pagan superstitions about children who died suddenly and inexplicably, by the additional fear over what would befall the soul of an unbaptised child. Under such circumstances, a place under the holy roof within holy ground must have offered an ideal burial site. That this special area for infants was seen to have peculiar properties is reinforced by the 'children's cemetery' at the Anglo-Saxon monastic site of Whithorn in Galloway. Here, the ground to the east of a small building identified as a chapel had a graveyard 'densely populated with infants and young children'.[48] The site at Whithorn represented a monastic community, so the presence of such young children is puzzling. The excavator Peter Hill suggested that they must have been local children, and that 'it may have been appropriate for the very young to be buried at the gateway to the inferred area of consecrated ground'. In fact, there is some evidence that children, even infants, were included in Anglo-Saxon monastic communities, so it is not necessary to assume that these children were laity, but nonetheless the grouping of child burials is interesting. This children's cemetery was only in use for a short period – perhaps thirty to forty years, from about 735 to 760. In the earliest phase of this cemetery, there were fourteen burials, tightly packed, but arranged in rows. Nine of the burials were identified as infants. In the second phase, the graves covered a wider area of ground, but also a wider age range – up to ten years old. The last two graves (possibly coinciding with a period of difficulty for the Anglian Christians at Whithorn) were of a 'child' and a 'young juvenile'. The reason for the change in the function of this space is open to speculation, but a possible answer might be that, as Christianity was placed under strain, and the fate of those who died unexpectedly appeared less certain, the population using the cemetery may have felt that it was just as well to give older children the benefit of this holy space too. Fears that this might not be enough to keep the spirits of the dead quiet are hinted at in the spread of cremated human bones that seal the last phase of the 'children's cemetery'. Cremation, of course, was a pagan practice, and the last resort of those trying to rid themselves of revenants.[49] Among the thirty-seven skeletons in this 'children's graveyard', two are buried with amber beads – remarkable amulets within the context of a 'Christian' burial site.

Not all children associated with early death and marvellous deeds were malevolent. The extraordinary and hugely popular tale of St Rumwold demonstrates how the wise infant, the *puer senex*, could fascinate an Anglo-Saxon population. St Rumwold was born, prophesied and died within three days, yet his cult was of major importance, and several towns claimed the saint as their own.[50]

INFANT SACRIFICE/DEDICATION

We have already seen that the infant was expected to go through the ritual of baptism in Christian Anglo-Saxon England. On the whole, the homilists attempted to persuade parents that it was necessary to perform baptism as quickly as possible to prevent a child dying a heathen. The apparent reluctance of even Christian parents to baptise their children may be due to a superstition that to baptise the child was to attract an early death, but it may be that dedication of an infant to any god was considered a significant rite of passage. There are strong hints that baptism may have been seen in the light of a sacrifice, and that baptism, pagan rites of infant dedication and donation, and death may have been subtly interwoven in a difficult and ambiguous pattern.

In 626, when the pagan King Edwin of Northumbria was deliberating whether or not to convert to Christianity, and furthermore was contemplating a major offensive attack into West Saxon territory, he used his newborn first child as a bargaining counter with the Christian god. If he won a victory, he would be converted to Christianity, and as an earnest of the bargain, he would give his daughter to the Church to be baptised. Janet Nelson interpreted this act as Edwin using his daughter as a 'thank offering' for victory, and it is worth noting that the Frankish Clovis also converted to Christianity and used his newly born child as a dedication to the Christian god in the same way.[51] However, Bishop Paulinus, who had come north from Kent with Edwin's Christian bride in 625, had already been actively teaching the Christian faith, and at the time it was perfectly acceptable, within the *Rule of St Benedict*, for children under the age of ten to be given as oblates to monasteries.[52] Ælfric, writing in the tenth century, specifically likened the act of baptism to a sacrifice: children were brought to Christ through baptism, in the same way that Abraham offered a sacrifice of his son Isaac, or Anna offered Samuel.[53] Ælfric also noted, however, that some priests carried out additional – heathen? – ceremonies at the baptism of infants: 'They set their fingers into the child's ears with their spittle, and in the child's nose'.[54]

Ælfric warned several times of a practice that seems to indicate the dedication of an infant and its mother to heathen gods. The most commonly cited version of this warning is in Ælfric's *Lives of the Saints* , where he reminded his audience of those 'witless women who draw their infants through the earth at crossroads and so commit them to the devil'.[55] The meaning is obscure but unpleasant, and the text then goes on to warn against women who deliberately kill their children. The act of drawing the child through the earth has therefore been interpreted as a means of infanticide, but other references by Ælfric to this rite suggest that it may be more of an initiation or dedication ceremony. Ælfric returned more than once to this idea of parents drawing their children through the ground, but equated it to other pagan customs. In one homily he warned against the seeking out of wells, stones and trees (presumably for heathen worship), and at the same time forbade men from drawing their children through the earth, because it would commit both the child and the mother to the devil.[56] In another homily, Ælfric described women who brought their children to crossroads to draw them through the earth, again consigning both the mother and the child to the devil.[57] In a further reference, women who taught their children witchcraft or drew them through the earth by the road were condemned.[58] Finally, in a law of Canute, priests were called on to forbid all forms of heathen practice, including the worship of wells, trees and stones, necromancy and augury, wizards, the devil's work of drawing children through the earth, and various other forms of sorcery.[59] It is difficult to interpret what this act of drawing children through the earth might have entailed, and what it signified. The influence of the Vikings on Anglo-Saxon society at this time may have had some impact in a revival of pagan customs. The connection between the child, death and rebirth may be significant in this ritual. Just as a Christian child is sacrificed in the waters of baptism, effectively to die to allow for a rebirth in Christ, so these children were being given a symbolic death in the ground, presumably as an act of dedication to another deity, leading to a new life in the service of, or under the protection of, that god. A connection between death and rites of passage is one that has been explored in some detail by sociologists; it is expressed with the greatest clarity by M. Eliade in a discussion of the dichotomies between child/adult and profane/sacred: 'The journey from the profane world to the sacred implies in one way or another the experience of Death: one dies in one life to achieve another . . . one dies to infancy and the irresponsibility of childhood, that is to say, the secular world, to be able to arrive at a superior life, one where it has become possible to participate in the sacred.'[60]

While the true meaning of the behaviour described by Ælfric must remain obscure, it seems clear, taking all the cases where 'drawing through the earth' is described, that it was not intended by the participants to lead to the death of the child, that it could involve both parents, and that the ritual led to the dedication of both the mother and child to the deity being worshipped. It is tempting to speculate that a pregnant mother may have called on some deity for aid in birth, and the ritual was a form of 'thank offering' of the child and mother for a successful outcome, just as Edwin gave his daughter to the Christian god to ensure a victorious campaign in Wessex.

There are clear signs within the pagan period that the burial of infants was often seen to involve peculiar rituals, such as burial contrary to the prevailing orientation, burial with stones over the body, or burial with amuletic artefacts. That such treatment was not exclusive to infants suggests that the decision to bury the deceased in an unusual way may have had more to do with the manner of death than with any specific age-related rituals, but that a high proportion of infants are buried with such peculiarities implies that infants were particularly susceptible to the kind of deaths that would lead to this behaviour. Infant death is characterised by often being unexpected and inexplicable, as the Anglo-Saxon prognostications illustrate. The advent of Christianity may not have resulted in a decline in the superstitious treatment of infant burials; rather, late pagan cemetery sites are characterised by a spate of peculiar or more frequent infant burials, such as occur at Marina Drive and Lechlade, and these peculiarities may even be extended to include older children, as at Winnall II or the apparently Christian site of Whithorn. Later documentary evidence suggests that, far from alleviating fears about the spiritual fate of infants who died under mysterious circumstances, Christianity, with its emphasis on the necessity for baptism, increased anxieties about infants. There are hints that baptism might have been popularly misunderstood as applying particularly to infants on the brink of death, acting either as a cure or an assurance that the spirit of the dead infant would sleep quietly. The child Paganus – who, although of Christian family, was not baptised until his twelfth year (it is tempting to speculate that this took place just before he sickened and died, though of course the evidence does not support this) returned to haunt the living in the form of benign visitations, indicates the force of the belief that the spirit of the unbaptised dead child would be unlikely to rest. Superstitions towards infants, common in many pre-industrial societies, and arising out of the high infant mortality rates, would appear to have been present throughout the pagan period, and to have continued in some form into the Christian period too in Anglo-Saxon England.

CHAPTER 7

Health and Childcare

> It was considered idle to attempt to rear a sick or weak child, for he would
> probably die of hardships before he came to man's estate; and it was worse
> than useless to rear a timid one, who could only be a 'nithing' and a disgrace
> to a nation of brave men.[1]

So argued John Thrupp in his portrayal of a primitive Anglo-Saxon world where a
crude form of eugenics by abandonment and neglect ensured that only the
strongest children survived. In practice, the archaeological and documentary
sources indicate that sick and weak children were given great care by their parents.

There can be no question of the high level of infant and child mortality in
Anglo-Saxon England from the fifth to the eleventh centuries. Dysentery,
infectious disease and starvation were probably the most serious threats to the
health of children as well as adults. Death often came swiftly: Bede describes the
children of Edwin dying at the point of baptism; King Alfred lost an unspecified
number of infant children; and fevers could be sudden and deadly. Wilfred's
'adopted' son, Bishopson, died of a fever, and all the oblates but one were killed
by a plague that swept through Bede's monastery. Two young Englishmen,
Æthelhun and Egbert, went to study in a monastery in Ireland where plague
killed all their companions and they themselves were dangerously ill with the
disease. The same plague also devastated the population of the East Saxons to the
extent that they apostatised from the true faith in the hope that their old gods
might help them.[2] In the South Saxon monastery on Selsey Island, a little boy
'who had lately been converted to the faith' died of a virulent plague. The
conversion of the South Saxons to Christianity in the late seventh century
followed a period of three years of drought and famine during which time,
according to Bede, starving men and women would join hands and throw
themselves off cliffs into the sea.[3] The *Annals* in the Moore Manuscript recorded
that for the year 759, 'a great pestilence occurred and continued for nearly
two years. The people were wasted by various kinds of malignant diseases but
especially dysentery.'[4]

In addition to disease and famine, violence was a facet of Anglo-Saxon society,
and children as well as adults suffered brutal deaths. Child murder was viewed,
however, as a particularly unpleasant crime. The story of the Massacre of the
Innocents was a popular theme in late Anglo-Saxon art: variations on this topic
are given in gruesome detail in the *Harley Psalter*, and this motif reinforced the

*A soldier kicks a child, a cradle is ransacked and children flee in an illustration of Psalm 109:
'may his children wander about and beg: may they be driven out of the ruins they inhabit'.
(British Library, Harley 603, f. 56r)*

concept of child slaughter as a pagan, non-Christian characteristic, to be condemned as such. King Cædwallan, a Christian, joined forces with the pagan Penda to fight Edwin of the Northumbrians in 633. After Edwin's death, Penda and Cædwallan carried the battle into Northumbria, slaughtering the population as they went. Bede regarded Penda's inhumanity as inevitable, but he heaped invective on Cædwallan, who: 'although a Christian by name and profession, was nevertheless a barbarian in heart and disposition and spared neither women nor innocent children. With bestial cruelty he put to death all by torture.'[5] This was in direct and deliberate contrast to the behaviour of King Edwin, felled in battle by Cædwallan, in whose reign a woman and her new-born baby could travel from one end of the kingdom to the other without coming to any harm.[6]

Children, then as now, were always casualties in times of war. If not directly caught up in the conflict, they would suffer from the consequent famines, or endure the trauma of upheaval as refugees. After Edwin's death, many of the leading Northumbrian children were sent into exile for safe keeping, including Edwin's daughter, Eanflæd, his son Uscfrea, and grandson Yffi. Edwin's widow obviously believed Oswald, the new claimant to the throne, to be capable of killing his infant rivals. The two boys were sent to Dagobert of Gaul, where shortly afterwards they died of unnamed causes and were buried 'with the honour due to their birth and innocence'.[7]

The most likely causes of infant mortality in the Anglo-Saxon period, as in any pre-industrial period, were complications associated with birth, congenital disorders and infectious diseases, but some of the documentary evidence, in particular the *Penitential*, might indicate that a proportion of infant mortality was brought about through the carelessness or negligence of the very adults who were supposed to be nurturing the helpless child. In the late seventh century, Theodore of Tarsus, a missionary to England who became Archbishop of Canterbury, included in his list of penances for crimes the injunction that: 'if a woman place an infant by the hearth, and a man put water in the cauldron, and it boil over so that the child is scalded to death, the woman must do penance for her negligence but the man is acquitted of blame'.[8] One homily of Ælfric warned against the foolish women who share their beds with their children but roll over on them and suffocate them, and the woman who breastfeeds her child and then falls asleep and smothers the child with her own breasts.[9] Both these cases might be plausible, and we must accept that such mortality must have occurred in Anglo-Saxon times as in others. Before we start accusing Anglo-Saxon parents of exceptional carelessness and callousness, it is worth emphasising that Theodore, of Mediterranean and Roman upbringing, may have been simply working within a long-established Roman ecclesiastical tradition when he created his *Penitential*, and we need not assume that it had a close and meaningful relevance to Anglo-Saxon life. Furthermore, the homilist giving examples of mothers accidentally killing their babies was doing so as a scaremongering campaign to persuade parents to baptise their infants as soon as possible. Like an insurance salesman with unwilling customers, he was drawing pictures of the awful and unpredictable events that might lead a child to die in infancy, and playing on the fears of new mothers in showing how they might inadvertently cause their child's death. Incidentally, it is worth noting that the homilist assumed mothers would breastfeed their own babies rather than give them to wet-nurses.

CHILDHOOD MORTALITY

Barbara Hanawalt produced useful comparative figures for child mortality rates in the Middle Ages, drawn largely from coroners' records. Interestingly, most infant deaths recorded were from cradle deaths by fire. Infants remained in the cradle until their fifth year.[10] The number of accidents dropped dramatically after the age of four: Hanawalt postulated that at this age, children had sufficient mobility to follow their parents to the field and were thus better supervised, but if the example of Cuthbert may be credited, Anglo-Saxon children appear to have been allowed unsupervised play up to at least eight years of age, and if such unsupervised playtime was a characteristic of Anglo-Saxon childhood, this perhaps might have contributed to the apparent rise in mortality rates for children over three or four years of age.[11] Within the Anglo-Saxon furnished inhumation cemeteries, there was a gradual increase in child mortality as age increased, with a high at seven to nine years, significantly at the age when Cuthbert was reproved for his foolish play, and the age at which Bede considered infancy to end and boyhood to begin.

Individual burials from Anglo-Saxon cemeteries do indicate that there was a reasonable level of care and medical knowledge among the Anglo-Saxon communities. Occasional examples of children and adults with cleft palates – like the six-year-old from Burwell, Cambridgeshire or the nine-year-old from Raunds, Northamptonshire – demonstrate that care was lavished on children: a child born with a cleft palate cannot suckle, and therefore it would take a considerable effort

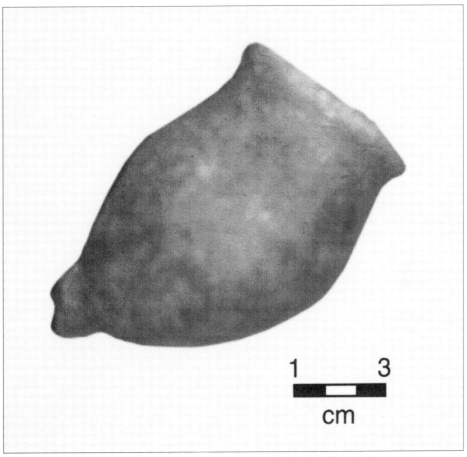

A feeding bottle buried with an infant in a cemetery at Castledyke, Humberside.

to keep such a child alive in the crucial early months.[12] Remarkable material confirmation of individual effort to keep a baby alive has been made at Castledyke South, Barton-on-Humber, where grave 133 has revealed an infant buried with a mammiform pot, presumably a feeding bottle. The pot was 11.1 cm high, with a rim diameter of 63.7 cm.[13] The bone preservation at the Castledyke cemetery was extremely poor, so no reason for the feeding bottle can be ascertained from the skeletal evidence, but among the possibilities are that the child's own mother was incapable of producing milk, or the child may have had a cleft palate. Unfortunately the contents of the bottle have not yet been subject to analysis, so we cannot say anything about what fluid the child was being given to drink, although it may have been expressed mother's milk. The use of such a feeding bottle, with the attendant possibility of infection or contamination in the milk, would have dramatically decreased an infant's chances of survival, and clearly the infant buried with this pot succumbed to an early death. Feeding bottles have not been discovered anywhere else in Anglo-Saxon England, but a parallel may come from a fourth- to fifth-century cemetery site at Hjemsted in Denmark in the form of a small pot with a spout.[14] The pot is only 7.7 cm high, with a maximum diameter of 6.7 cm. The pot is included in the inventory for grave 318, but the plan of the burial indicates that the pot was actually outside the grave cut. The skeletal survival here was also extremely poor – most bodies had completely disappeared, and due to the intercutting, it is impossible to say what size of grave pot 387 belonged to.

Although the feeding bottle is a rarity, evidence of Anglo-Saxon parents struggling to sustain sickly infants is not. At West Hendred, Oxfordshire, excavation revealed a tiny grave and fragmentary bones. The grave cut was only 35 cm in length, and the initial assumption was that the burial was that of an infant. Bone preservation was again very poor, but analysis of the surviving teeth indicated that the tiny child was in fact two to three years old at the time of death. There are a number of illnesses that could lead to the failure in growth of a baby, leading ultimately to death: a hole in the heart, for example, and some such explanation must be assumed in this case. What is beyond doubt, however, is the care that must have been lavished on the infant to keep it alive past its birth.

Even more significant are Anglo-Saxons who survived childhood with congenital deformities. At the furnished inhumation cemetery of Worthy Park, grave 38 was of an adult with a congenital absence of his left arm. At birth, this infant must have been obviously deformed, but his community did not reject him. At the later Christian cemetery of Raunds, Northamptonshire, the burial of a probable victim of poliomyelitis was a male aged twenty to thirty years, who suffered from the failure of growth of his right femur, right tibia, right fibula and right foot, and tuberculous arthritis of the right knee and left shoulder. His survival of a disease contracted in childhood is indicative of real care of a deformed child in the later Anglo-Saxon period, evidence which directly contradicts any theory that juveniles were regarded as 'disposable goods', or that no care was given to them until they reached maturity.

Many deformed babies would have had little chance of survival simply due to medical ignorance. Even in modern times, survival rates are poor. A recent survey showed that malformed children have only a 51.3 per cent chance of survival in modern England.[15] The deformed Anglo-Saxon adult burials show that what care could be given, was given.

MALNUTRITION

The many recipes and charms in the Leechbooks to provoke conception and against infertility discussed in Chapter 5 may indicate anaemia or malnourishment in the population as a whole, and children would certainly have suffered from malnutrition alongside their parents. The most visible form of malnutrition for an archaeologist is rickets, which is extremely rare in an Anglo-Saxon context, and when it does occur, it tends to be seen on only a few skeletons in later Anglo-Saxon church cemeteries. The Anglo-Saxon population may have suffered from debilitating stomach parasites, and possibly anaemia, but there was no vitamin D deficiency or lack of calcium, which cause rickets. Vitamin D comes from milk, butter, eggs, liver and oily fish; and the action of the sun on the skin also leads to its formation. This vitamin promotes the absorption of calcium, which is necessary for the proper formation of bones and teeth. Calcium is present in quantity in milk, cheese, fish and bread, all of which may have been available to Anglo-Saxon children in greater or lesser quantities throughout the year.

The skeletal evidence corroborates the view that the Anglo-Saxons had adequate supplies of calcium. Teeth are generally in good condition in this period, showing little sign of caries, though since the Anglo-Saxons had no remedy for caries when it occurred, the protection of teeth must have been a high priority. Audrey Meaney believed that beaver teeth were especially prized as an amulet to protect teeth, and identified beaver teeth in the graves of infants at Marina Drive, Dunstable, Bedfordshire, and Burwell, Cambridgeshire (a Christian cemetery), as having served this function.[16]

Dental enamel hypoplasia may indicate the ages at which children suffered the stress that caused the defect. At Empingham, the defect formed between two-and-a-half and four-and-a-half years of age.[17] Simon Mays has drawn attention to the problems of correctly sexing skeletons by the shape and size of the teeth. Results indicate that it is relatively more difficult to sex males than females, and he argues that this may be because environmental stress has an impact on tooth growth, which implies that males might be more sensitive to environmental stress than females in childhood.[18]

Another skeletal indicator of malnutrition is *cribra orbitalia*, which manifests itself as small holes or pepper-pot lesions in the eye socket. It is occasionally identified in juveniles and less often in adults. Calvin Wells drew attention to it in his analysis of the skeletal material from the early Anglo-Saxon cemeteries at Worthy Park, Hampshire and Finglesham, Kent where the most advanced case of the disease was in the skeleton of a two-year-old (grave 4) and in that of a five- or six-year-old (grave 31). Wells argued that the presence of this disease in juveniles rather than adults must be because it 'was usually a self-limiting condition or because it was part of a lethal syndrome which killed them before they attained adulthood'. More recent studies have cast serious doubt on this interpretation. *Cribra orbitalia* is observed in children, but its causes are obscure. The pepper-pot lesions may be caused by a physiological response to iron deficiency anaemia, which may have been induced either by nutritional deficiency or by the chronic intestinal parasite infestation most Anglo-Saxons must have suffered. Periodic bouts of malaria would also have contributed to iron deficiency anaemia.[19] The presence of *cribra orbitalia* in a cemetery population is usually taken as an indicator of a diseased or impoverished community. At Whithorn, the 'children's cemetery' dating to the eighth century showed a high incidence of *cribra orbitalia*. There were several multiple burials in this group, leading the excavator to suggest that some were victims of an epidemic. However, both adults and children had *cribra orbitalia* at this site, the most severe examples being found in the adults.[20] At Raunds, Northamptonshire, the occurrence of *cribra orbitalia* was frequent in children from the age of two years to adolescence, and was more common in females than males.[21]

MEDICINE FOR CHILDREN

The Leechbooks are less informative about childhood diseases than about pregnancy and childbirth. On the whole it seems that adult remedies were to be applied to juveniles, though a clear awareness is demonstrated that medicines should be adjusted to suit the age and strength of the sufferer: 'And always observe when you are applying powerful medicines, what the strength is, and what the body of the patient is like; whether it is strong and hardy and may bear strong medicines easily, or whether it is delicate and tender and thin, and may not bear the medicines. Apply the medicines according to your observation of the patient, because there is a great difference in the bodies of a man, a woman, and a child.'[22] Occasionally, recipes do recommend modifications for juveniles: for example, for 'matter in the neck', for children's worms, 'water sickness' and 'scabby head'.[23] There are, in addition, two recipes specifically about children teething, one remedy for children's tapeworms, and one about general constipation in children.[24]

Of the medicines that refer to children, then, four out of the ten are about stomach worms and general stomach disorders, but medicines for stomach complaints are common in the Leechbooks as a whole. Archaeological findings suggest that the early Anglo-Saxons, living off a meat diet of pig, sheep and cow, probably did not have the technology to heat their food through sufficiently, or if they did, they did not apparently recognise the importance of high temperatures in food preparation. Their cooking pots are of notoriously porous and fragile clay, which could not have withstood high temperatures. Anglo-Saxons must have inevitably suffered from debilitating parasitic infections, and excavations of medieval cesspits at Amsterdam and York, which yielded eggs of *Trichuris triciura* (whipworm) and *Ascaris lumbricoides* (roundworm), indicate the type of infections that may have been common in the earlier period.[25]

The most sensitive approach to children's eating problems is in a remedy for stomach-ache and constipation: 'About children's stomachs, and overfilling, and if they do not digest their food properly, and if they sweat and stink. When this is diagnosed, then they will be offered a variety of foods rather than one kind, so that the novelty of the food may be good for them.'[26]

A simple variation in diet might have been effective in that it may have included fresh fruits and other delicacies, which would undoubtedly have eased the problem. A lack of roughage may have caused many of the stomach problems experienced by the Anglo-Saxons, such as juvenile constipation. Of course, there is no skeletal evidence for this condition, but there is an example of a celebrated sufferer in the form of King Alfred himself, who quested as far afield as Jerusalem for a remedy for his painful piles, which were believed to have contributed towards his death. As a member of the royal family, it has to be assumed that Alfred ate finer foods than the average Anglo-Saxon, but it is noted by his biographer that he was a sickly child.[27]

DEFORMITY

Deformity at birth appears to have been as feared by mothers in the Anglo-Saxon period it is today, but there was little that could be done about such a catastrophe.

Of the medicines dealing with this problem, chants and divinations predominate. 'Hateful deformed birth' and 'hateful black birth' are both included in a chant to ward off the evils of childbirth, while another remedy translated advice on how to predict a deformed baby: 'If the pregnant woman is four or five months gone, and she frequently eats nuts or acorns or any fresh fruits, then it sometimes happens that the child is silly. Again, there is another matter, if she eats bull's meat, or ram's, or buck's, or boar's or cock's or gander's flesh or that of any begetting animal, then it sometimes happens that the child is humpbacked and ruptured.'[28] A further remedy suggests the apparently hopeless treatment of washing the new, deformed child in a dip of cucumber. Archaeological evidence for the survival of deformed children does exist, and examples were given at the beginning of this section.

While the examples from the archaeological record, and the remedies in the medical texts, do indicate that children were worthy of care, even the 'ugly misborn' ones, the most compelling evidence of parents caring for their seriously ill children comes from the *Lives* of Anglo-Saxon saints. These tales give some insight into diseases which were considered incurable (though we hardly need the evidence of the *Lives* to guess those), but the *Lives* are generally uninformative about the details of the illnesses suffered by children – it is not their purpose to discuss the child's health, merely to illustrate that the saint was capable of curing the apparently incurable. Children suffered from paralysis, blindness, lameness, pestilence and madness. Only occasionally is it possible to offer any meaningful diagnosis: Bede drew on the *Life of St Germanus* for the tale of a chieftain called Elafius who carried his sick son with him to meet the missionary Germanus. The boy was suffering from a wasting disease not unlike the archaeological case of poliomyelitis at Raunds – the limb was withered and contracted so that he could not walk.[29] Very rarely, we are given hints as to what other methods of treatment were attempted before divine intervention was sought. The young Cuthbert, on becoming lame in the knee, was carried outside to rest in the sunshine where he was unexpectedly healed by a passing messenger from God.[30] The most interesting example comes from Bede's account of the activities of John of Beverley, who was asked to cure the sick daughter of an abbess who was taken ill with violent pain and swelling in the arm after having been bled. The illness is, to risk anachronism, iatrogenic, as John explained to the abbess: 'He asked when the girl had been bled? And being told that it was on the 4th day of the month, said "You did not act sensibly or skilfully in bleeding her on the 4th day of the moon; for I remember that . . . bleeding at that time was very dangerous, when the light of the moon and the tide of the ocean is increasing; and what can I do to the girl if she is likely to die?"'[31]

John was a skilled healer for his day, and one of his most remarkable miracles demonstrated relatively sophisticated medical care. John had been searching for a suitable pauper to lavish alms on, and a young man was brought to his attention. The youth came from a local village, and had been dumb, apparently, since birth. In addition, the young man had a scabby, scurfy skin and alopecia. The bishop ordered a house or hut to be built for the youth, where he lived and received an allowance. One Sunday, the bishop made the youth put out his tongue, then he made the sign of the cross over it and began to teach him to speak: 'Say "A"', and he said it. 'Say "B",' he said, and he said that too. After a session of medieval speech therapy, the youth was able to speak fluently, 'the bonds of his tongue being unloosed'. It may have been the sign of the cross that cured the youth, but there is a minor medical condition known as ankyloglossia or tongue-tie, in which the band of tissue attaching the underside of the tongue to the floor of the mouth is too short, limiting the movement of the tongue and causing speech defects. Today, an operation would be performed to divide the band of tissue, but the same effect might be achieved by giving the tongue a sharp wrench which would literally break the bonds of the tongue.[32] Having cured the youth of dumbness, John sent him to his own doctor to treat his skin condition, whereupon the youth 'gained a clear complexion, ready speech, and beautiful curly hair, whereas he had once been ugly, destitute and dumb'.[33] The ease with which the skin condition was cleared may indicate that a nutritional deficiency, remedied by the food the youth had access to, may have been part of the problem, and while a malnourished youth might be interpreted as indicating a lack of care on the part of the parents, the fact that the youth not only survived his village life with his disabilities, and actually chose to go back to his family rather than remaining with the bishop on a permanent basis, are indication of the care the family did attempt to give him.

Bishop John was able to cure the dumb youth as much through knowledge as divine power, and the medical texts indicate that some medical interventions were based on good observation and sensible treatments. A harelip could be cured by minor surgery, involving cutting the lip and sewing the wound together with silk. Tooth and gum ache in children could be remedied either by rubbing the gums with boiled hare's brain or dog's milk; the ingredients would not have had much effect, but massaging the gums might have brought some relief. A child with a scabby head, like the youth healed by John of Beverley, could be cured by rubbing the scalp with a head of garlic. Garlic has antibacterial properties, and while the treatment might have been smelly, it might also have been effective.[34] Treatment for intestinal worms included the use of pennyroyal and spearmint, both of which have carminative properties.

The life of the earlier Anglo-Saxon was undeniably precarious. At any time, disease or accident could lead to a rapid death, in the face of which the doctors were helpless. The whole business of birth, as the Leechbooks illustrate, was mysterious and beyond human interference, and the child, once born, was extremely vulnerable. It is not surprising that in a primitive society, medicine had as much to do with ritual and superstition as with medical knowledge; no doubt the Anglo-Saxons made no distinction between these three sides of healing. But the treatment of children seems to have drawn on all the medical resources the leeches of the day were capable of bestowing, and must have been inextricably bound up in the social apprehension of the child. Contrary to the theories proposed by Ariès, and followed by Stone and others, the remedies outlined in this chapter suggest a committed expenditure of time and energy in encouraging children through the dangerous years. The number of remedies dealing with conception and childbirth, coupled with the complete absence of any contraceptive remedies, seems to imply that children were very much wanted, and women would go to some lengths to secure a child. If a deformed and 'useless' baby could survive to adulthood, as illustrated in the archaeological record, it seems unlikely that equal care was not invested in 'normal' children. The evidence of the Leechbooks, hagiography and archaeology provide a powerful argument for rethinking the status of children in Anglo-Saxon society.

CHAPTER 8
The Family

It is still not known exactly whether the Anglo-Saxons, on emigrating from the Continent, came to a land deserted by the native British, or whether the newcomers were obliged to find living space where they could. Probably a mixture of the two possibilities occurred. An understanding of the population density and the pressure on living conditions at the time is crucial if any estimation of the size and type of the earlier Anglo-Saxon family is to be made, although certain knowledge of the Anglo-Saxon demographic pattern can never be achieved. However, the intensity of population pressure will have a direct effect on the size and shape of the family group: 'A community in the early stages of growth is likely to contain many young families, still with few children and a simple structure. The big and complex households, once thought typical of

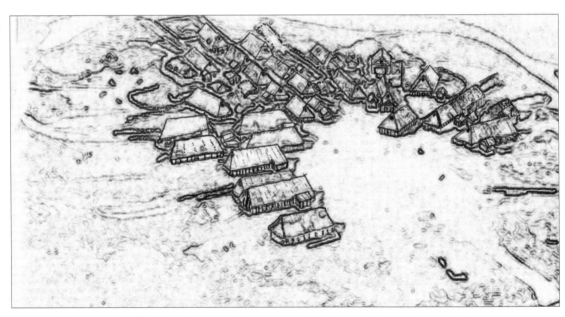

A reconstructed Continental terpen village, representing the complex, highly organised community life familiar to the Anglo-Saxons before their migration, but not adopted when they came to England.

traditional society, are typical only of certain periods of high population densities.'[1] A group under pressure from lack of land space would naturally tend towards an extended family living structure, whereas land space and relative wealth would promote nuclear family structure as each new couple set out to build their own farmstead.

The Continental evidence from the settlements abandoned by the people who then apparently migrated to England indicates that the immediate ancestors of the Anglo-Saxons dwelt in large communities under severe pressure of land space and with strict stratification. Feddersen Wierde, near Bremerhaven, and Wjister have both been carefully uncovered.[2] At their abandonment, somewhere around AD 450, these villages consisted of thirty or so dwellings with outbuildings laid out in a manner indicative of a highly organised society. These complex and fairly large villages were developed from single farmsteads in the first century AD. The increasing pressure on land from the rising sea level was probably one factor that forced the inhabitants of these mound-villages or *terpen* to build up their settlements. These conditions of pressure on the availability of land would lead naturally to concentrations of population in the available areas, and would imply that household sizes may have been large, because sons and daughters, even after marriage, would have had no opportunity to move away from the family home.

A comparison of these sites with the early Anglo-Saxon settlements in England suggests that, on emigration, a new form of settlement type was quickly established and with it, by implication, a new family structure. While Feddersen Wierde and Wjister contained thirty or so dwellings, English settlement sites give very different figures. At West Stow in Suffolk, the settlement began in the fifth century but was abandoned by the seventh century. There were a range of outhouses and sheds associated with it, but only seven larger timber buildings. The excavator suggested that these represented family units surrounded by peripheral work sheds.[3] At Mucking in Essex, a site in use from the fifth to the seventh centuries, a population of about eight to ten families inhabited a shifting settlement with little structural evidence to suggest an organised community. The picture is that early Anglo-Saxon settlement consisted of small farmsteads or hamlets, without evident hierarchies of settlement, and showing little signs of pressure on land space – settlements sprawled without order, lacked fences or other boundary markers between properties, and new houses were erected in new spaces rather than being built on the sites of old ones.

Where there are cemeteries associated with the settlement, an even clearer picture of the population density in the early Anglo-Saxon settlement sites may be obtained. At Bishopstone, Sussex, in use until the late sixth century, the buried population was 124 people, while the settlement, occupied for two centuries, contained only ten major buildings.[4] The mortuary population is unlikely to represent everyone who lived at Bishopstone, but even so, ten major buildings over the fifth and sixth centuries can hardly be called a village; even 'hamlet' would be a grandiose term for the settlement. West Stow, Suffolk, and Mucking, Essex, offer the same story, of farmstead settlements persisting over a period of time, but not developing into villages of any substance in the earlier period.[5] The evidence so far strongly implies that families were free to break up and the younger generations to move on, because the early settlements never appear to grow over time, and Anglo–Saxon inhumation cemeteries tend to be fairly small – many Anglo–Saxon inhumation cemeteries of the earlier period contain fewer than fifty bodies and must be assumed to represent the burials over time of families belonging to one farmstead, and even in the larger cemeteries containing around 200 bodies, we may be looking at the burials over time of not more than five to ten households. Chris Scull, in his study of state formation in East Anglia, proposed a model whereby the society indicated by the archaeological evidence – an agrarian Anglo–Saxon society with no market economy or specialised industry – may have developed. According to his model, the settlements found by excavation were the homes of patrilineal descent groups, farming their own territory, with each generation establishing a new home within the community until pressure on land space (placed arbitrarily by Scull at the fourth generation) forced a member of the family in the junior line of descent to move away from the home territory to establish his own farming settlement.[6] The study of the archaeological and documentary evidence indicates that rarely would the extended family model apply in the rural areas of Anglo–Saxon England, because married children would set up a new home away from the parental dwelling.

In some cases, it appears that new land may have been in short supply. At Puddlehill in Bedfordshire, excavations revealed a tiny community, with two associated graveyards containing half a dozen burials, all adult (although 'wide areas were excavated and the quarrying carefully watched'). The site was eventually abandoned and never cultivated again by later settlers. The report suggested that this group may have been under considerable land pressure, perhaps from the British people who were still a force to be reckoned with, or by other groups of settlers.[7] This case is a reminder that much of the settlement archaeology for the Anglo–Saxon period comes from liminal sites, where the archaeology survives because no further habitation has taken place. Only 'failed' sites leave an undisturbed archaeological record. Most of the known Anglo–Saxon settlements were located in upland areas. However, discovery of such valley bottom sites as St Botolphs, Sussex, suggest that there may have been many sites on the richer, lower-lying lands which have been subsequently buried by silt or built over by later settlements.[8]

CEMETERY EVIDENCE FOR FAMILY GROUPS

The settlement evidence, coupled with the size of the average Anglo–Saxon cemetery, indicates that many pagan cemeteries represent the burial plots of only one or two families over several generations. This is supported by the epigenetic evidence at the Anglo–Saxon inhumation cemetery of Berinsfield, Oxfordshire, where inherited skeletal characteristics such as a cleft neural arch, a sixth lumbar vertebra, a septal aperture, wormian bones and metopic sutures have been identified in a number of skeletons on the site. These epigenetic characteristics appear to be determined by genetic influence; the presence of one or several of these characteristics in several burials may indicate familial relationships. It is interesting to note that one of the earliest burials on the site, the female in grave 8, exhibits half of the six epigenetic characteristics. The excavator notes that the epigenetic traits at this site seem to indicate that there are three main burial groups or families. The group in the south-east of the cemetery is the only one to exhibit the occurrence of sixth lumbar vertebrae and a combination of septal apertures and wormian bones. No epigenetic traits were present in the south-west group, where the graves were predominantly orientated west–east, leaving a final group to the north where several members share the characteristic of lamboid wormian bones. This creates a putative three families, each of which includes a mix of males and females and a range of dates of burial, indicating that parts of the site were used by coherent groups over a period of time. Of course, the numbers are small. The southern limits of the site have not been established, but the northern group, if correctly identified, may be taken as a complete household burial. It consists of about fifty burials, including eight certain males and twice as many certain females. Two burials belong to the first phase of the site's use, twelve to the second phase, only two to the third phase, and four to the fourth phase, the mid sixth century, with a high proportion of the burials, particularly those of the children, undatable due to lack of diagnostic grave goods. If we accept that this plot was in use from about 450 to 575, a period of about 125 years, and that the generational interval was about 25 years, then we can argue for the northern plot containing the burials of five generations of the same household, which ideal construct leads us to the probability of ten members in each generation. Within this northern group, twenty died before the age of fifteen or sixteen, indicating that no child can have experienced a large communal family, and the membership of the household must have fluctuated dramatically. Each generation at Berinsfield, by this example, could expect to lose two of its new members before they left adolescence.[9]

At Castledyke, Barton-on-Humber, the cemetery was in use over 200 years, with an excavated mortuary population of 147 and a probable total population of about 200. There were probably about 45–60 individuals alive at any one time in this community, which the excavator supposes to represent about 6 families, and there was some evidence for family plots within the cemetery.[10]

At Empingham II, Rutland, the predominantly inhumation furnished cemetery site, in use from the late fifth to the early seventh century, has been completely excavated. Forty-five adults were found to have shovel-shaped incisors, and there were thirteen cases of hypodontia or microdontia. All three conditions are considered to have a genetic component in their causation. The cases were plotted on the site plan to try to find burials of family groups, but there was no evidence for any such clustering.[11]

There are larger cemeteries available for analysis, such as the massive cremation cemetery at Spong Hill in Norfolk, consisting of over 2,000 burials, but the nature of the evidence makes identification of possible family groups within cremation cemeteries very difficult. In some cemeteries, family groups have been tentatively identified, and in cases where bodies appear to have been deliberately inserted into the chambers of earlier burials, some close relationship might be presumed. At Portway, Hampshire, grave 63 contained cremation vessels. The excavator's interpretation of the finds was that vessel 67b had been placed at the foot of the grave, then 67b had been replaced by 67a. When the rim

*Burials of Two or More Bodies in One Grave From a Sample of
Anglo-Saxon Cemeteries*

Age Band	0–5 (n=152)	6–10 (n=92)	11–14 (n=38)	15–29 (n=229)	30–44 (n=137)	45+ (n=144)
0–5	2	2	2	7	3	3
6–10	2	0	0	3	1	0
11–14	2	0	0	0	1	1
15–29	7	3	0	3	3	2
30–44	3	1	1	3	0	1
45+	3	0	1	2	1	0
Totals	19 (12.5%)	6 (6.5%)	4 (10.5%)	18 (7.8%)	9 (6.6%)	7 (4.9%)

and shoulder of 67a later disintegrated, the vessel was crushed. The broken
pottery was collected and replaced in the space left by the pot. This
interpretation would imply a fairly long period of remembrance on the part of
the 'family group'. On this site also, a possible family group of the rich burials 6,
33, 48 and 54 has been postulated.

At Polhill in West Kent, Brian Philp remarked on the high number of multiple
graves at the site. One contained three skeletons and sixteen contained two, and
four of the bodies in these multiple graves had been inserted at a later date.
These, Philp suggested, were family graves. A similar case might be made for the
multiple burials at Lechlade, Gloucestershire.

The comparative rarity of these multiple graves in earlier Anglo-Saxon
cemeteries, however, must argue against the concept of a 'family burial chamber'
being a normal concept, and other explanations for the phenomenon should be
sought. These multiple burials, for example, bear no comparison to the family
vaults of Victorian England either in size, scale or consistency of occurrence. The
table of multiple burials derived from a selection of Anglo-Saxon cemeteries
indicates that, while the burial of two or three bodies in the same grave may
indicate close blood relationship between the deceased, there are no consistent
patterns, and such burials normally only involved two bodies.

One example of a possible family plot comes from the barrow excavated at
Stanton Harcourt, Berkshire in 1940.[12] Six of the graves were of adults, while
thirteen were of children of varying ages. In four graves, no remains were
preserved, but these were also probably children. This sample is much more in
keeping with the mortality figures expected of this period, and this group may
reasonably be assumed to represent a small family from an isolated farmstead.
There were no other graves in the immediate vicinity. There were two cases of
overlapping interments, and three possible cases of miscarriages. There were
grave goods associated with some of the burials: one old woman had a silver pin,

three of the children had knives and other objects (a pricker, a bead, a bootlace tab, two buckles and a spearhead between them), but this was a poor collection, indicating either a late seventh-century date, or merely poverty.

Careful study of settlement patterns in the West Midlands in the later Saxon period reinforces the idea that settlements were small and that new families usually moved on rather than staying within the parental homestead. Della Hooke used boundary clauses, place-name evidence and archaeology to build up a picture of the settlement patterns of the region, and concluded that, alongside the main village nucleus, many subsidiary settlements were to be found. These minor settlements never became dominant, and many failed to survive.[13] One explanation for these minor settlements might be that they represented the enterprise of couples setting up home on their own.

It is evident, on the basis of the settlement archaeology, that settlement structure changed through the Anglo-Saxon period. In the earlier phases of settlement, the Anglo-Saxons lived in small, sprawling hamlets typified by Mucking. There appears to be increasing stratification of settlement into the middle Anglo-Saxon period, as typified by the enclosures and fences at Catholme, Staffordshire, and in the middle Saxon period more concentrated populations occur, notably at the *wic* sites such as Ipswich and Hamwic. By the later Saxon period, there were small towns or *burhs* scattered throughout the area of Anglo-Saxon settlement. House plots were small, and population pressure must have been significantly denser – perhaps sufficiently to affect the type of family. It is within the cemeteries belonging to these towns that the clearest signs of malnutrition in Anglo-Saxon communities occur, such as in the cathedral cemetery at Winchester, although signs are still limited. Excavations of the house plots in late Anglo-Saxon York demonstrate how constrained the population must have been, and analysis of the floors at this site indicates a relatively squalid existence to go with it; in the later, urban environment the family experience may have been very similar to that recorded by Pollock for later medieval urban populations. Conditions in late Anglo-Saxon Oxford were sufficiently crowded for houses even outside the town walls to be built with cellars, implying that there was simply not enough room to expand houses sideways. Even so, the majority of Anglo-Saxons continued to live in relatively small agricultural communities. The later documentary sources also make it clear that, notwithstanding the pressures of urban living for some proportion of the population, the typical family unit was seen as nuclear to the very end of the Anglo-Saxon period.

Documentary evidence certainly supports the idea that grown-up children were not all expected to stay at home, and were almost definitely expected to move on when they married. The Anglo-Saxon word for 'bachelor' was *hægsteal*, literally, one staying at home. *Hægsteal-had* was the unmarried state, or virginity. King Alfred's children Edward and Ælfthryth were still living at home at the time Asser wrote his *Life* of the King. Both were past puberty: Edward was not more than twenty-three years old at the time the *Life* was written; and Ælfthryth did not leave home until her marriage to Baldwin II, Count of Flanders. The

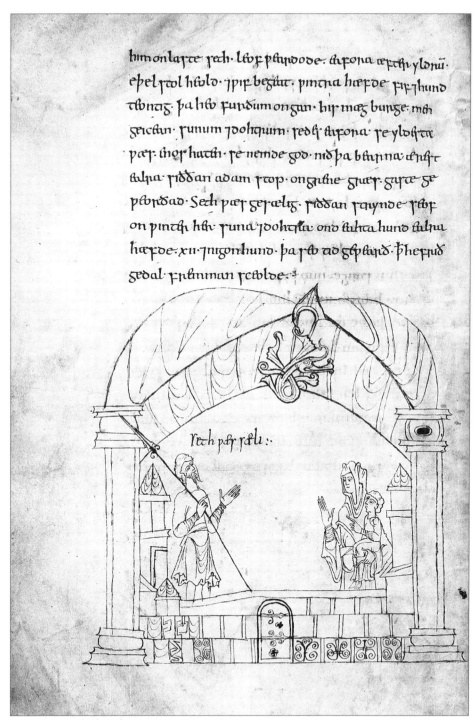

An ideal Anglo-Saxon nuclear family. The caption reads 'Seth was blessed'. (Oxford, Bodleian Library, Junius 11, f. 56)

lawcodes portray the family as consisting normally of a man, his wife and children rather than any more extended group, such as in-laws or grandchildren, although the household for the élite might include servants. In Ine's law 7, if a man steals without the knowledge of his wife and child, then they will not suffer, but if he steals with the cognisance of his *hired* – household, family – then the penalty is slavery for them all. In this instance, it appears that *hired* is being used as a synonym for 'wife and children'. A lawcode of Canute uses a similar format: a householder (*bonda*) who has no charges relating to his property may pass the place on entire to those who dwell in it – his wife and children – when he dies. The family perceived by the lawmakers as common to the average man seems to have been nuclear. It is only in the upper echelons of society that the lawcodes hint at larger households such as that of the thane whose mobile household unit was to include his smith, his reeve and his children's nurse (Ine, law 63). The late Anglo-Saxon wills also emphasise the importance of the nuclear family (although here Christian mores about the 'normal' family must come into play). Most wills, when they refer to family, mean a wife and children, although kinsmen, brother's sons and siblings, foster-parents and god-kin are mentioned as recipients, and servants, priests and slaves are also referred to in wills.[14]

KINSHIP NOMENCLATURE

What is known of Old English kinship terminology emphasises the importance of close kin, as might be expected, but does not indicate that more distant kin were considered an integral part of the family group. Within the Old English family group, parents, grandparents, children, paternal or maternal uncles and aunts, nephews and nieces (with a particular emphasis on the relationship between a man and his sister's son) are all given distinct names, demonstrating a non-unilineal kinship structure, in which affiliation with the mother's family held as much importance as the father's. More distant relatives fade into obscurity; cousins were not distinguished, and Lorraine Lancaster noted that the 'kinless man', so frequently referred to in poetry as well as the lawcodes, was a man without close kin – a brother or a father – rather than a man without any relatives at all.[15]

MARRIAGE, FERTILITY AND LIFE EXPECTANCY

Throughout the Anglo-Saxon period the normal 'family' consisted of parents and children, although servants and slaves might also be part of the wider household belonging to this nuclear group. The question of whether this nuclear family was presumed to be small, consisting of only a few children, or much larger remains open. Some reasonable inferences about family size can be drawn from a study of Anglo-Saxon life expectancy and by comparison with other pre-industrial groups. By assessing life expectancy, probable age of menarche and marriage, and length of the breastfeeding period after birth, a guess at the number of offspring per woman might be made. The statistics drawn from analysis of the Anglo-Saxon skeletal evidence give a clear indication that life expectancy for women who

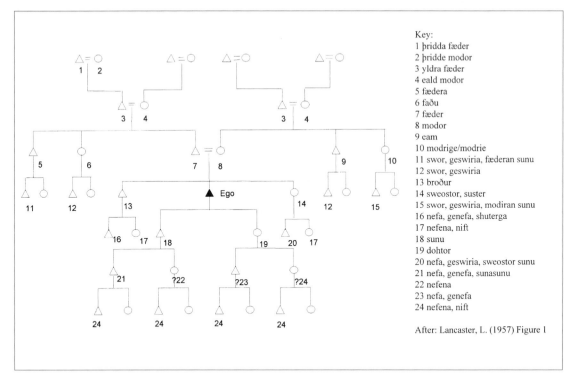

Key:
1 þridda fæder
2 þridde modor
3 yldra fæder
4 eald modor
5 fædera
6 faðu
7 fæder
8 modor
9 eam
10 modrige/modrie
11 swor, geswiria, fæderan sunu
12 swor, geswiria
13 broðor
14 sweostor, suster
15 swor, geswiria, modiran sunu
16 nefa, genefa, shuterga
17 nefena, nift
18 sunu
19 dohtor
20 nefa, geswiria, sweostor sunu
21 nefa, genefa, sunasunu
22 nefena
23 nefa, genefa
24 nefena, nift

After: Lancaster, L. (1957) Figure 1

Relationships and kinship terms between members of an Anglo-Saxon family.

survived childhood was not high by modern standards. A life expectancy of about thirty years has been suggested for females in this period, although recent advances in techniques of determining the age at death may push this figure up. Nonetheless, while over half the population of Anglo-Saxon women survived to twenty-five years of age, few lived into old age (in this context, over forty-five years). Levels of nutrition are equally problematic. Low nutrition would lead to delayed menarche and reduced fertility. The skeletal record shows little sign of malnutrition in women, but the number of remedies to promote periods in the Leechbooks is evidence of some malnutrition and reduced fertility.

The limited skeletal evidence of women who probably died due to the complications of childbearing offer the only archaeological clue to the average age of childbearing in Anglo-Saxon England. It could be argued that the most dangerous birth – and the one most likely to cause a fatality – would be the first, but in practice the risk to the mother remains high during any pregnancy and delivery. The age at death of pregnant women in the archaeological record ranges from fifteen to over thirty-five, with the majority of cases occurring after the woman had passed twenty years of age. It would be tempting to interpret this as an indication that Anglo-Saxon women delayed marriage and childbirth until after their teens, which would lead to a reduced risk of miscarriage, stillbirth or death in childbirth, but with such a small sample it would not be statistically viable to make such an assertion.

Burials of women and infants may give some hints as to typical ages for childbearing. Many of the infant burials occur in double graves, where the infant is buried with an adult. Within the sample cemetery population four of the recognised under-one-year-olds are buried in double graves; this is a higher proportion of double burials than occurs in any other age group. Of these four, one is buried with a fifteen-year-old, two are buried with women in their twenties, and one is buried with an adult over forty-five years of age. It is difficult to resist the notion of mother/child burials as the explanation for many of these multiple burials, but note the relatively late age of those adults buried with infants. The first pregnancy was often dangerous, and the second was also critical, when the woman had not yet recovered from her first confinement and was actively engaged in caring for the first child. Given a probability that infant deaths represent the first or second child, it could be suggested that the Anglo-Saxons may have 'married' at a relatively late age. It is medically attested that the probability of death in childbirth is highest in the teens, falls off in the twenties, when the body is stronger and more fully developed, and then increases in the thirties and forties. The statistics from the multiple burials perhaps indicate that Anglo-Saxon women were waiting until the optimum age for safe childbirth before producing their offspring; this would positively influence infant mortality rates.

Studies of later medieval peasant populations in Europe corroborate the likelihood that Anglo-Saxon women would have married at a relatively late age. According to the Halesowen records, before the plague peasant girls tended to marry after eighteen years of age, although daughters of richer parents who could afford a dowry would marry younger.[16]

None of the women in the pagan cemeteries who died during pregnancy were exceptionally young. The woman buried at Abingdon in Berkshire (grave 193) was about fifteen when she died, and her pregnant state must have been obvious.[17] Her grave goods suggest that a woman of relatively high social status (grave 193 is comparatively wealthy for the site) could begin a family as a young teenager.

It has been suggested that 'striations' on the pelvic girdle may indicate the number of children a woman may have given birth to during her childbearing life, and if this were a reliable method it could be used to say something about the age of childbearing, but as a method it has not yet been proven, and one remains sceptical as to its uses.[18]

The age at which girls were married is also open to debate. The grave goods evidence indicates that girls were buried with adult female grave goods such as chatelaines and brooch sets from as early as ten or twelve years of age, and it must be assumed that this was a feasible age for marriage. By contrast, the hagiographer of Guthlac commends the saint's parents for their seemly marriage: 'he [Guthlac's father] took to himself a wife, in accordance with the seemly laws of marriage, a damsel of like age from among the ranks of noble maidens; her name was Tette'.[19] Felix, Guthlac's biographer, appears to have frowned on the idea of adolescent girls marrying older men, or vice versa. Whether his comment reflects a common Anglo-Saxon practice, or whether he was holding Guthlac's virtuous parents up as an example of what Anglo-Saxons should have been doing but were not is a moot point.

The lawcodes do, however, imply that there was an age before which it was socially unacceptable for a girl to be involved in a sexual relationship: a law of Alfred legislates against anyone raping an under-age woman (*ungewintredne wifman*), but frustratingly, no hint is given as to what that age was.

Firm evidence for the male age of marriage is not available, but there is some justification for arguing that boys did not reach marriageable age until they had passed through a 'warrior' stage and had accumulated sufficient funds to found a family, although royalty, as ever, provide the exception to prove the rule: Ecgfrith, King of Northumbria was only fifteen when he was married to the widow Æthelthryth in 660. Absence of evidence is not evidence for absence, but it is worth making a cautious note that Anglo-Saxon writers were well aware of the Roman model of early marriage for girls, but conspicuously did not adopt this exemplar in their accounts of their own saints. Ælfric, for example, copied out stories of this Continental practice when he wrote about Petronilla, who died to avoid the fate of being married to a nobleman at an early age, or of the celebrated St Agnes of Rome who also died, at thirteen years of age, to avoid an arranged marriage with a man much her senior. Anglo-Saxon saints do not seem to have followed this exemplar. The homilist Ælfric also recommended that young men should avoid intercourse until they married an equally virginal woman.[20] Less fatal methods were ascribed to Anglo-Saxon virgins who wished to avoid the marital bed: St Æthelthryth, already mentioned, simply refused to have sex with her first and second husbands, and when the young Ecgfrith insisted that their marriage be consummated, she left her husband to become a nun. In a secular aristocratic setting, William of Malmesbury recorded that the Mercian Lord Æthelred's wife Queen Æthelflaed, Alfred's daughter, suffered so badly during her first delivery that she refused to have any more children: 'Because of the difficulty experienced in her first, or rather, her only labour, she ever afterwards refused the embraces of her husband, protesting that it was unreasonable for the daughter of a king to give way to a pleasure which after a time produced such painful consequences.[21]

The *Anglo-Saxon Chronicle* recorded that, on his return from Rome in 855, King Æthelwulf, passing through France, contracted what was probably a political marriage with Judith, the twelve-year-old daughter of Carloman. Æthelwulf was already an old man with grown sons and a married daughter; he died two years later. This royal marriage of convenience seems to have caused no stir in England. The big scandal was when the widowed Judith subsequently married her step-son. Even for men, we have relatively little information on marriageable age, though they may have married later, since they may have required sufficient status and funds before acquiring a wife. King Alfred, one of the few males for whom we have details, did not marry until he was twenty, but his biographer recorded that he had, for 'many years' before his marriage, been suffering from a divine illness which caused him to restrain himself from 'carnal desires'.[22] This story was part of the myth of saintliness that Asser was possibly trying to ascribe to his subject, and the issue of Alfred's mysterious disease follows shortly after a statement that 'even from childhood', King Alfred was an enthusiastic visitor of holy shrines. While we may question Alfred's continence and the divine nature of his disease (which miraculously disappeared before his wedding), it is interesting to note that Asser believed the period between King Alfred's marriage and the 'first flowering of his youth' (when he first felt carnal desires) was a long one.

The documentary sources for information on age at marriage and duration of marriages (based on royal alliances) may support the idea that royal women married fairly late, and the young Judith was an uncommon phenomenon. Of Edward the Elder's four daughters, only one, Eadgifu, married before she was twenty: her sisters Eadhild, Eadgyth and Ælfgyfu married in their mid-twenties. Edward was forty when he married Edith, who was considerably younger, but at over twenty she was not unreasonably young to marry an older man, and Edward and Edith were married for the next twenty-one years, from 1045–66. The reluctant mother Queen Æthelflæd married Æthelred of the Mercians in 888 at the age of eighteen, and the union lasted until 911, when Æthelred died, but they only ever had one child, their daughter Ælfwynn. Another long marriage was that between Oswiu, King of Northumbria, aged thirty-one at his wedding, to Eanflaed, aged seventeen. They were married for twenty-seven years and had four recorded children, although Oswiu may have had one son by a previous relationship.[23]

In an overview of demographic patterns in past times, Fekri Hassan engaged in detailed and complex calculations to assess the average number of offspring of a woman in prehistory, and concluded that 'the potential total fertility can be estimated at 4.71 children'.[24] This was thought to be somewhat of an overestimation, but even if the average Anglo-Saxon woman worked extremely hard to improve on her 'potential total fertility', mortality rates must have led to the actual surviving number of offspring of any one mother rarely exceeding four or five, and it is difficult to find documented cases of larger Anglo-Saxon families: they are certainly not typical.

The length of time between the onset of sexual activity and the age of death of women is crucial to any estimation of the size of a nuclear family, but information is scanty and conflicting. One of the youngest burials of a female with an infant within the earlier Anglo-Saxon inhumation cemeteries comes from Abingdon, where the girl was aged about fifteen at the time of death. Adult female-related grave goods – chatelaines, keys, sets of brooches – are buried with girls in the pagan inhumation cemeteries from the age of ten, suggesting that by ten or twelve, girls were given adult status in the burial ritual. Given the lawcode references to orphans receiving full property rights at this age, it remains open to question whether these ritual 'adults' were married girls, girls who could technically marry but in practice might be expected to wait, or girls who, due to family mortality, had inherited wealth and responsibility. Grave attributes that might distinguish married from unmarried women have not yet been identified, but to complicate the picture it must be remembered that, in the earlier period at least, 'marriage' was not the binding contract it later became, and that one man might have many 'types' of partner, ranging from his 'wife' to his 'concubine'. The later Christian documents emphasise the importance of the nuclear family as we would understand it, but in practice the boundaries of the marriage appear to have been fluid.

Few children can have grown up in the care of both parents. If the average life expectancy was low, then the youngest children in a family could expect to experience the death of one or both parents in their very early childhood. A compelling example would be that of King Alfred, whose family, as royalty, might have been expected to have a longer life expectancy due to better nutrition. However, a combination of causes, including conflicts with the Vikings, proved fatal to several members of Alfred's immediate family. By the age of twenty-one, Alfred had outlived his father, mother, step-mother and all his older brothers. Alfred himself had five children (boys and girls) who survived into adulthood, in addition to an unnamed number who were 'carried off in infancy by an untimely death'.[25]

The impact of the mortality rates on the probable size and structure of the Anglo-Saxon family cannot be underestimated. Jack Goody calculated that in English communities between 1574 and 1821, 42 per cent of the registered population were children, of which 20 per cent were orphaned. Only 2.3 per cent of these children had a living grandparent, and the mean size of a sibling group was 2.76. In addition, Goody found that the size of a family tended to increase with wealth, from three to four household members in the family of a pauper to an average of six members in the household of a gentleman.[26] The lawcodes emphasise the central place of children in the family unit. Æthelbert's laws 79, 80 and 81 leave no doubt that children were necessary for a successful marriage, and it is notable that a later law of Æthelstan thought it worth using the affection of a man for his children as a useful lever for forcing the offender to stay within the law. Although the early lawcodes indicate that one of the perceived purposes of marriage was procreation, not all couples did have children. In a document recording the history of the estate of Wouldham, Kent, the childless Alfeah granted his property to the childless widow of his brother Eadric.[27] Eadric's widow remarried, but by this time, the line of Alfeah and Eadric had ended without issue. Such cases cannot have been uncommon. Conversely, Edward the Elder, King of the Anglo-Saxons between 899 and 924, was married three times and had about fourteen children.

PARENTS, FAMILY AND KINSMEN

Useful evidence for the range of adults who were considered to have a direct responsibility for caring for children comes from the documentary sources, and these emphasise that the most important bonds were between parents and children, although ties of affection could be built up between other relatives and carers. In the *Lives* of the saints, for example, sick children are frequently brought to the saint for healing. Of course, the image of the saint healing a sick child was an inevitable topos of the *Lives*, and was intended to emphasise the similarity between the actions of the saint and those of the ultimate perfect man, Christ. We need not assume that the miracle ever occurred or even that the children ever existed, any more than events and characters in modern novels are considered to be 'real', but in order for the audience to believe in the saint, his actions must have seemed plausible, and the children and their carers must have reflected 'real' Anglo-Saxon life. A variety of carers take both boys and girls to the saints for miracle cures. According to Bede, St Germanus cured a nobleman's daughter of sickness; the father and kin brought the child to the saint. Also in Bede, a noble child aged ten was brought for healing by its father and mother, and a demoniac boy was taken to a nearby monastery by his father. Sorrowing noble parents brought their mad son to Guthlac for a cure, and in one cure effected by John of Beverley, workmates of the father brought his son for healing. Within the *Lives* of the saints, boys and girls were equally worthy of being brought to the saint for healing, and while the parents had the primary role in caring for the child, other members of the kin and community also took on some of the burden of responsibility. Grandparents are virtually absent from miracle stories, presumably reflecting the short life expectancy of the adult rather than reflecting any lack of love or participation in child nurturing by the grandparents.

Mothers

There can be no doubt of the importance attached to the bond between mother and child in most societies, nor that this bond must have been as important in the Anglo-Saxon period of human history as in any other.[28] The bond between mother and child is axiomatic in the Anglo-Saxon record. It has been a popular misconception that illustrations of children in the medieval period before the fifteenth century were unrealistic and poorly proportioned, and that mothers were never depicted in warm and affectionate contact with their children but were always shown in stiff, unnatural poses, rarely, if ever, touching their children.[29] Ariès thought that it was not until the twelfth century that children were portrayed as infants, rather than as miniature adults, with tender and sentimental depictions of mothers and children embracing, caressing and hand-holding. In fact, children do appear in Anglo-Saxon manuscripts; if child and parent are perceived in stiff relationship to each other, it has more to do with the art style of the day than with any commentary on a mother's affection for her child.

In the *Harley Psalter*, children populate the scenes from the Psalms. The manuscript, drawn in the mid-eleventh century, was produced at Christ Church, Canterbury and was based on the *Utrecht Psalter*, produced near Reims in the early ninth century. The Anglo-Saxon copy of the Carolingian original is close, but not slavish, and one of these deviations in particular emphasises the central role: the visibility of children in Anglo-Saxon society. Illustrations to the Psalms in the *Harley Psalter* are peopled with Anglo-Saxon crowds engaging in everyday activities – farming, fighting and observing. Among the characters are women and children in various attitudes – women cradling babies, women holding the hands of older children or resting their hands lightly on their heads.

Documentary sources corroborate the assumption of the bond between women and children. In the Old English poem *The Fates of Man* it is the duty of both the parents to care for the child until it reaches maturity, but other – more telling

Five children gather around their distressed mother. (British Library, Harley 603, f. 50r)

because less intentional – examples are available. What of the description of the banishment of Cain in Genesis 'from his mother, his kinsmen and his family'?[30] This innocent phrase raises many questions, but relevant in this context is the implication that the mother is the person who will be most missed by Cain. In the context of outcasts and their mothers, the most notorious mother in Anglo-Saxon literary history deserves a mention. In the poem *Beowulf*, Grendel, the hideous monster described as the spawn of Cain, is an outcast in the desolate wastes, but his exile is shared by his mother. Grendel's mother is remarkable, not for her hideous and malevolent strength, but for the devotion to her son whose miserable death she tries to avenge. This is not the only notorious partnership in crime of a mother and son in the Anglo-Saxon world. An historical example was recorded in a document confirming the exchange of lands between Wulfstan Uccea and the Bishop of Winchester. A woman and her son forfeited an estate because they had practised witchcraft on Wulfstan's father.[31]

Poignant evidence of the bonds between mother and child comes from the archaeological evidence, where the skeletons of females are found with their arms curled round the bodies of infants who, it is not unreasonable to suppose, were their own children or foster-children. While such cases are not common, they still occur with regularity. For example, cases occur at Empingham II, where of the two infant burials (less than two years old) at the site, one (49b) was resting within the crook of the arm of the richly accompanied adult female buried with it; at Barrington, an infant/foetus resting under the head of a severely disabled woman who may have been the mother; at Portway (grave 13), Nassington (grave 31) and Beacon Hill (grave 33) – for these cases to represent a general feeling amongst Anglo-Saxon families that when mothers and children died at the same time it was appropriate that they should be buried together in this sympathetic manner.[32] Of course, not all mothers had harmonious relationships with their children. The example of Enneawn, who publicly disinherited her adult son after he had equally publicly accused her of keeping estates that belonged to him, is a case in point.[33]

Fathers

In the family scene in *The Fates of Man*, where parents were described rearing their children, the emotional investment in the child was divided equally between the parents – it was not only the mother who was supposed to care, the father was expected to love his child too.[34] Ælfred added to his translation of Boethius the comment that nothing could be more sorrowful to a father than to see the death of his child. In the *Harley Psalter*, men as well as women are depicted in close contact with children, and perhaps the most evocative portrayal of close bonds of love between father and son may be seen in the extraordinarily intense embrace of God the Father, seated, holding Christ the Son on his lap. Their two heads are pressed close together, eye to eye, nose to nose and lip to lip.

Mothers were the primary carers in Anglo-Saxon England during the earliest stages of a child's life, but fathers do seem to have been actively and emotionally involved in rearing their children: there was no social expectation that fathers would distance themselves from their children. In the *Lives* of the Saints, mothers and fathers were both active in seeking cures for their sick children, either together or individually. Wulfric, who died early in the eleventh century, seems to have been trying to protect a sick or disabled daughter in his will, because he described her as his 'poor daughter' (*min earman dehter*) when he bequeathed estates to her, and he urged his brother to protect her and her land.[35]

The existence of a close relationship between fathers and their children may seem banal to the modern reader, but in view of later trends towards the active distancing of the father from the upbringing of children, the Anglo-Saxon assumption that a father would want to stay near his young offspring is interesting. The social expectation of active paternal involvement reached the highest level: King Alfred was highly active and evident in the rearing of most of his children, and there is the remarkable law giving a thane leave to take his child's nurse as one of his three permitted servants when he travelled. Thanes did not, apparently, expect to be separated from their families when they went away on business if the law was a reflection of social reality. Alternatively, if this law is interpreted as an incentive to thanes to take more active responsibility for the care of their children, then the lawmakers at least felt that males in the upper echelons of Anglo-Saxon society should always have their children near them.

God the Father embraces Christ the Son. (British Library, Harley 603, f. 1r)

The Anglo-Saxon father was legally responsible for the nuclear family unit, and was answerable for the crimes of his under-age children, but there is little hint in the documentary sources that the Anglo-Saxon father exercised any tyrannical or despotic legal control over the lives of his sons and daughters in the Roman manner, and once a son had married and set up his own household, a father could only hope to influence the son, without having any legal rights over the married son. Daughters may have remained much more closely tied to their fathers: in the early seventh-century law of Æthelbert of Kent, when a childless woman left her husband her portion of the marriage settlement, the property and goods she owned had to go to her father's relatives. The implication of the law seems to be that the childless woman had to return to the care of (and return to the responsiblity of) her father's family. In the same set of laws, a mother seems to have had a choice over whether or not to take her children with her if she left her husband: fathers in seventh-century Anglo-Saxon England did not have absolute authority over their children.

Grandparents

The documentary sources do not suggest that grandparents were involved in the care of their grandchildren, or even that grandparents were a typical part of the Anglo-Saxon household. Exceptions to this rule do occur: the Ætheling Æthelstan was reared by his grandmother even though his father was still alive, and the relationship appears to have been cordial, because the prince remembered his grandmother in his will. Royal children were particularly liable to be brought up away from their parents at times of instability and political crisis, not least because they were obvious targets for intrigues and assassinations, and this may have been one of the motivations for Æthelstan's placement in his grandmother's household. Normally, however, the grandparent's role was to provide peripheral support: the documentary sources paint a picture of doting grandparents with no responsibility for the grandchild, but much affection to give, not unlike the modern western ideal. King Alfred gave a prized sword to his grandson Æthelred, even though Æthelred was, at the time, far too young to have used it and, if the evidence of the earlier pagan cemeteries was a reflection of society's mores, well before the age at which the princeling was entitled to bear such arms.[36] In the epic late Anglo-Saxon poem *The Battle of Maldon*, Ælfwine called on the name of his respected grandfather Ealhelm – 'wise elder, blessed in the world' (*wis ealdorman, woruldgesaelig*) – before throwing himself into battle. One of Beowulf's prized possessions was his battle-clothing, a legacy of his grandfather Hrethel.[37]

A post-Conquest account of a holy Anglo-Saxon family from Cornwall gives further evidence of ties between children and grandparents which also has interesting ramifications for the earlier cemetery evidence. In this account, drawn from the *Life of St Peter of Cornwall and Launceston*, an old man, Jordan, has recently died and the funeral procession is on its way to the church:

When his body was carried through the town to the church of St Stephen, and passed in front of the house of his son-in-law, behold, suddenly from that house instead of a banner there was carried out to meet him the body of the daughter of his daughter and son-in-law. Truly the soul of this little girl and her body were represented symbolically by the banner. Since she had died in a state of innocence immediately after baptism and still dressed in white, she had triumphed over the world and its prince the devil. In token of the victory of her grandfather Jordan, she hastened to meet him as though to do him some service and led him to St Stephen's church. She was laid to rest in the same tomb as her grandfather, between his legs, where both quietly await the blessed hope and resurrection of the dead and the advent of our Lord Jesus Christ whose banner will be in the sky when he comes in judgement.[38]

Although the child was laid between her grandfather's legs in his tomb, the chronicler attempted to demonstrate that the child's death was symbolic, and that the double burial glorified both the innocent child and the grandfather. This account may also help to elucidate the cases where children are found buried with adult males in both the Christian and pre-Christian Anglo-Saxon cemeteries. The story of Jordan and his granddaughter is a reminder that infants buried with adult males may not have simply been slung into the grave of an adult who had died at the same time as a matter of convenience, but that there may have been family ties between the two.

Uncles (Sister's Son)

An Anglo-Saxon boy could also expect to receive special attention from his maternal uncle. Historians have long recognised the peculiarly strong bond of obligation between a man and his sister's son in Germanic society, and the peculiar ties of affection generated by this relationship are evident in the literary sources. The classic example comes in *The Battle of Maldon*, where the grey-haired earl, Byrhtnoth, was engaged in a doomed pitched battle against the Vikings. In the epic narrative, all those types of warrior closest to the lord and members of his household stepped forward to take their place in battle, including Wulfmaer, Byrhtnoth's sister's son who bravely fought by his uncle's side. The relationship was reciprocal – Byrhtnoth had a place in his household for his nephew, and the nephew returned the care with loyalty and support. In Bishop Theodred of London's will, his sister's son Osgot was the main secular beneficiary, inheriting a number of estates.[39] Uncles were not expected to take an active role in the rearing of their sister's children, but they were typically expected to protect the interests of these children.

Brothers and Sisters

When St Guthlac was close to death, his *Life* recorded that he called on his most faithful servant to go to his sister Pega and to give her instructions about his burial. This was the first time Pega had been mentioned in the *Life*, but her passionate response to her brother's death indicates that they had been close: when Pega heard of Guthlac's death, she fell to the ground as though dead. Even though Guthlac had servants and followers, it was Pega who seems to have promoted the cult and sanctification of her brother. As well as organising his funeral, she also, according to the *Life*, was responsible for the translation of the body, moving it from its original tomb, a year after his death. The *Life* indicates that she stayed on Guthlac's inhospitable island in the fens to tend his body, his shrine and his cult. Not all sisters were so supportive: the young St Kenelm who succeeded to the throne of Mercia in 821 was allegedly brutally murdered by his tutor Æscberht at the instigation of his sister Cwoenthryth, but this story is a post-Conquest fabrication. The historical Kenelm (Cynhelm) did predecease his father, but he was signing charters from 803 to 812, and was the owner of Glastonbury by 789, so he must have been at least twenty-three when he died. He may have been killed in a battle against the Welsh: his 'sister' Cwoenthryth appears in contemporary documentary sources as an abbess.[40] Whatever the situation in post-Conquest England when inheritance based on primogeniture inevitably promoted inequalities between siblings, in Anglo-Saxon England, bonds between siblings were typically warm.

Naming the Child

The Old English documentary sources give little information on when a child received a name, or how the name was chosen. However, in the Christian period it was necessary for the child to have a name before it could be baptised, and the god-parents who answered for the child during the rite of baptism would have to have offered a name. Continental practice indicates that, among the élite, a child might have been named after its grandfather or mother, but there is no evidence to suggest that this was common practice in Anglo-Saxon England. One usual practice among royalty and the aristocracy was an onomastic naming pattern which consisted of modelling the name of the child on part of the mother or father's name, usually the initial syllable or section. King Alfred's brothers were called Æthelred, Æthelberht and Æthelbald; his father was called Æthelwulf. He was succeeded by his son Edward who was in turn succeeded by his sons, the kings Æthelstan, Ælfweard, Edmund and Eadred. Thus, a child's name would place him firmly within his family, and allow him to trace his genealogy back through ancestors bearing the same alliterating syllables.

The heart of the Anglo-Saxon family was the parent–child relationship. Anglo-Saxon children lived in a world where family and kinship bonds were central to their identity and their place in society, but those with immediate responsibility for their welfare and upbringing were their parents. Although the evidence does not give a clear picture, it is not easy to argue for large, extended families all living together in one household as a normal feature of Anglo-Saxon society, although members of an extended family probably lived within one settlement made up of several households in the pre-Christian period. However, although the nuclear family was the 'typical' family, not all children could hope to be reared by both their natural parents, and other forms of family experience, including step-families and fosterage, had a place in Anglo-Saxon society.

Christianity brought with it several changes to the Anglo-Saxon idea of family, not least by extending kinship obligations to include god-parents. The Church also may have had some impact in challenging the traditional bonds of affiliation between more distant members of one family by replacing them with an obligation to the Church instead. The area where the Church most directly challenged traditional Anglo-Saxon family structure, however, was in the practice of fosterage. Fosterage, adoption, and the part of the Church in adapting this aspect of the family will be discussed in the next chapter.

CHAPTER 9

Fosterage, God-parents and Adoption

Professor Boswell, in his important study of the widespread practice of child abandonment in western history, argued that giving up your own child to some other person or institution to rear was a sign of bad parenting, but one for which he could find no condemnation in past societies.[1] The sources for the Anglo-Saxon family portray a close and loving relationship between parents and their children as a common ideal, yet fosterage was integral to Anglo-Saxon childrearing practices, although the extent to which children were brought up by those outside their immediate nuclear family, and the purpose of this, varied widely according to the age and status of the child. The Anglo-Saxons used the word 'foster' to cover a range of nurturing patterns, from the equivalent of a mother's help or live-in nanny to what we might recognise as full-scale adoption outside the biological family.

Broadly interpreted, Anglo-Saxon fosterage fell into three main categories. By far the most common 'foster'-parent was a nurse brought into an élite household

A busy scene from the Harley Psalter. *In the centre a female supervises a child. (British Library, Harley 603, f. 2v)*

to take on some of the burden of raising the child. In such cases, warm ties of affection between the nanny and the child could persist into the child's adult life: the Ætheling Æthelstan, for example, remembered his nurse affectionately in his will, bequeathing his *fostermeder* (foster-mother) an estate at Weston, 'for her great merit'.[2]

Children might also be fostered outside their own homes, and this placement of children in another household, often that of a relative, might happen through necessity in the case of the death of a parent, or might be the equivalent of sending a child to school. The Ætheling Æthelstan's *fostermeder* worked for Æthelstan's grandmother, in whose household the prince was reared. Æthelstan may have been brought up away from his father because the kingdom was troubled by the Vikings, and Æthelstan's father spent some time in exile, but Æthelstan's grandmother, Ælfthryth, was a dominant force in the royal family, and may have taken on the upbringing of Æthelstan and his brothers with the deliberate intention of training them to support her and to be useful future kings. Æthelstan also remembered his grandmother in his will.[3] While a foster-mother who was a nanny might be of low status, a child sent to be trained and to learn good manners in another household would customarily expect to be fostered into a family of equal or greater status than his own. King Alfred, for example, fostered a number of the children of his thanes in his own royal household. In such cases, ties between the foster-parent and child would be cordial, but more importantly perhaps, mutual bonds of obligation, similar to though not as powerful as those set up by marriage alliances, could be established between families.

Finally, there were cases where the child would not simply enter a household as a temporary resident, but would acquire rights of inheritance from his new family, and might even abandon his biological family on a permanent basis. It has to be noted that there is little in the documentary sources to support secular 'adoption' as part of Anglo-Saxon childrearing systems, but oblation, whereby children were donated to the Church, might be interpreted in this way. One case of secular 'adoption' that was perceived to entail rights to inherit property from the adopter can be made for Beowulf, whose 'adoption' as an adult by King Hrothgar did not require Beowulf to give up his own family and ties of kinship, but did seem to have given him a right to inherit from King Hrothgar as a son, and this will be discussed in more detail later. In a second example, Bishop Wilfred forcibly removed a child he had baptised from its pagan parents, apparently with the intention that the boy should abandon his parents and become part of Wilfred's household, because the boy was given the surname 'Bishopson'. Whether Wilfred intended the boy to be as a son to him, with the same rights to inheritance and *wergild* as a son, is not obvious, and it is only safe to argue that Wilfred considered the request for the child to be baptised to be an act of oblation.

Examples of foster-mothers or nannies being brought into élite households are frequent in the documentary sources of the period. That noblemen and their wives gave the task of looking after their children to others as a matter of course is beyond dispute: the *cildfoster* (child nurse/carer) was expressly included in the list of servants indispensable to a man of status in the eighth-century lawcodes of

Ine of Wessex. The nurse was considered an indispensable part of the thane's entourage, emphasising that children of noblemen needed to be kept within the household even when that household was peripatetic, but clearly the duty of looking after the day-to-day care of the child was assumed not to be the business of either of the parents of the élite Anglo-Saxon child.

Other examples from the documentary sources make it clear that the presence of nurses and foster-children within élite families was normal: St Guthlac, the fortunate offspring of perfect parents, had, in accordance with what we know of élite children, nurses to care for him. The text does not specify whether Guthlac was sent away for fosterage or whether the nurse was brought into the household to care for him, though, given Ine's law, it is likely that the latter was the case. Whatever the case, his family circle also included not only his parents and nurses, but also blood siblings and foster-siblings in equal measure. Described as the perfect child (he was, after all, destined to be a saint), his biographer records that he was 'dutiful to his parents, obedient to his elders, and affectionate to his foster-brothers and sisters' .[4] The fostering of Guthlac carries no hint of abandonment of care by his parents, and indeed, in a neat twist, the hagiographer asserted that it was Guthlac who eventually abandoned his parents for the sake of his Christian calling. We do not have any further information on Guthlac's extended family with the exception of a sister, Pega, who is mentioned later in the narrative.

King Alfred and his family showed that there was flexibility within the system of fosterage, perhaps depending on the child and the parental hopes for its future. Alfred himself, the youngest of his brothers, was apparently brought up at home, and Alfred's own youngest son, Æthelweard, was likewise reared at home. Two other children of Alfred's – Edward and Ælfthryth – were also raised at home, but the actual business of caring for them seems not to have been taken on by their parents: 'they were at all times fostered at the royal court under the solicitous care of tutors and nurses, and indeed with the great love of all'.[5] It is not clear what happened to Alfred's other two children. The inference from the childhoods of Guthlac and Alfred's children is that whether you were sent to another household to be reared, or whether you remained at home, your parents took little part in your rearing if you belonged to the élite.

The higher echelons of English society may not provide the best model for Anglo-Saxon childcare, but it is clear from other evidence that it was not just the wealthy who expected to be able to find other carers to look after their children. For practically every close familial term in the Old English dictionary – son, mother, father, brother – there is a 'foster' or 'step' equivalent recorded as having been used somewhere in the corpus of Old English literature. The concept of fosterage was so commonplace in this pre-Conquest society as to be the solution to a riddle:

My father and mother gave me away in this world while I was dead, there was no life in me then, no being. Then a very kindly woman covered me with clothes, kept me and cherished me and canopied me with a protective covering, as fittingly as her own child – until under that sheet, according to the way I was made, I became to my unrelated family a bad spirit. This beautiful wife continued to feed me, until I grew, and could lay out wider paths. She had fewer beloved sons and daughters because she did so.[6]

The answer to the identity of the devastating interloper in the family home is, of course, the cuckoo.

Here, the loving foster-mother gave her energies to her fosterling at the expense of her own children, but the anthropomorphic birds do not offer much firm evidence for the physical and psychological impact of fosterage on either the fostered child or the foster-family. Unfortunately the system of fosterage is given only the most casual of mentions in the documentary sources, presumably because it was commonplace and needed no explanation, nor was it felt in any way necessary to comment negatively on the practice – it was simply taken for granted that this was what happened. Reading between the lines, however, it is possible to see slight glimpses of the physical and psychological impact of fosterage on the child, and to see the mechanics of the process in action. Children in Anglo-Saxon society appear to have been given to fosterers to be reared, either within the home or away from it, at any time during childhood.

At some point, boys in particular were sent away from the home to gain an education or training for their adult lives: this form of 'fosterage' might reasonably be equated with the act of sending a child away to boarding school today, and did not necessarily mean that parents gave up all interest in their child. Literary sources indicate that, for boys, formal commitment to another carer for educative purposes or for training up in the skills of the adult world may have come at about the age of seven or eight. Beowulf was fostered at the age of seven by his mother's father, Hrethel, King of the Geats, who have him food, board and honour; Bede went to the monastery at Jarrow at the age of eight, and at the same age Cuthbert too was fostered away from home. This form of fosterage, which will be discussed again in the context of education, provided a method of creating and strengthening bonds between child and carer.

The social significance of the duties and obligations of foster-parents towards the foster-child are illustrated in *Beowulf*, a poem about (and possibly dating back to) pre-Christian Germanic society, but written down in the later Anglo-Saxon period and given a Christian gloss. The eponymous hero, a young warrior in the prime of life but searching to make a name for himself and to acquire wealth, had rescued the court of King Hrothgar from the menace of the monster Grendel. Hrothgar, naturally, wished to reward the hero, and in a speech declaring his gratitude, he also made Beowulf his son: 'Now, Beowulf, best of warriors, I will love you in my heart as a son: keep our new kinship well from now on: you will not lack anything you want of this world that I have power to give.'[7]

Hrothgar backed up his pledge with gifts of a golden banner and weapons and horses. After feasting and story-telling, Wealhtheow, Hrothgar's wife, entered the hall, and her words make it clear that Hrothgar's 'adoption' of Beowulf is more than a figure of speech. Wealhtheow cautioned her husband to remember their own sons, and to bequeath people and lands to his own children, and as she said this she looked at Beowulf, sitting between her children. She was also anxious about her nephew Hrothulf, who was also present at the court as an adopted child. She hoped that this nephew would 'fully repay our offspring, if he remembers all the favours we both gave him for his pleasure and his honour while he was still a child'.[8] Of course, as the listener to the poem would have known, since Hrothulf would later kill her son Hretheric and usurp the kingdom, her fond hope was doomed to failure.

It may seem odd that Hrothgar's first gift to the soldier who had ridded his kingdom of a vicious monster was to offer himself as a father to the hero, yet the tenor of the anxious Wealhtheow's advice to her husband, and her reminder to Hrothulf of the duties of a foster-child to its adopted parents, indicate that the action of fosterage could be very advantageous to the fostered child.

Behind this public declaration of adoption by Hrothgar, there also lay a complicated political agenda in which bonds of kinship were used to seal peace treaties and to secure borders. Wealhtheow herself came to Hrothgar as a wife to ensure co-operation between the Danes and Frisians after a bloody war. Wealhtheow, commenting on Hrothgar's adoption of Beowulf, emphasised the political aspect of kinship ties. Wealhtheow reminded Hrothgar of the benefits of good relationships between the Danes and Beowulf's people – 'be pleasant towards the Geats, remembering of gifts, near and far'.[9] With Beowulf accepted as his son, contacts between the Geats and the Danes were likely to be secure and friendly – the code of family honour would demand no less. The act of fosterage could be advantageous for the fosterer as well as the child, particularly if the foster-child was higher-born than the fosterer's family: the *Prognostications* advised that the 7th day of the moon was an auspicious one to ask a favour of a lord, and 'if you propose to foster a royal child or a nobleman's, fetch it to your home and household, and so foster it; it will be well for you'.[10]

The evidence for fosterage of girls is less clear, but the literary sources indicate that it was not uncommon for parents to give up their infant daughters from birth to be reared away from the home. King Edwin's daughter Eanflaed, King Edward's daughter Eadberga and King Edgar's daughter Edith were all given to monasteries from birth. This might seem to represent the clearest form of abandonment by parents of their children, but in practice the fathers seem to have continued to take a warm interest in their growing children. Edgar was present when Edith was formally dedicated to the Church, and her mother, as abbess of the convent, was of course always present in the growing girl's life. The *Life of St Eadberga* describes two separate occasions on which King Edward came to see how his daughter was getting on. On one occasion, he came to make discreet enquiries about his daughter's progress – the equivalent of picking up the school report – and on another occasion, he visited Nunnaminster to 'see his beloved child in the holy community'. This time, Edward did see his daughter and asked her to sing for him.[11] Kings did not give their sons to the Church to be reared from infancy, however, and there may be some gender bias in this 'abandonment' of girls. One Old English translator of the *Life of St Margaret* attempted to explain why Margaret was given to a foster-mother even while both her parents were alive. The translator, retelling the story, turned Margaret's father into a king, and specified that Margaret was rejected by her father because she was a girl.[12]

MALTREATMENT BY FOSTER-PARENTS

We do not have to look hard to find documentary evidence of maltreated foster-children in the Anglo-Saxon records. One law of Alfred indicated that the fate of children reared outside the family was a cause for concern: 'if anyone entrusts his helpless ones to another, and that person causes the death of his charge, the one who fed him shall clear himself if anyone accuses him'. This law enlarged on the statutory injunction that orphans and widows should be cared for: the lawmaker perhaps had particular cases in mind, and it is clear that abuse and neglect by foster-parents towards their charges was not uncommon. In this law of King Alfred, there is an implication that the child had been voluntarily fostered by parents who were capable of seeking, and receiving, redress for their abused children, but some children must have been fostered because their own parents had died. Such children were in a more vulnerable position, and fosterage did not necessarily work to their advantage.

Laws advocating that widows and orphans should be properly looked after are commonplace: a law of the Kentish King Æthelbert advocated that, if a father died, his widow should receive half his goods *if she had had a living child*. The implication must be that the heir of the man's estate needed protection, and this would best be ensured by providing its mother with means of sustenance. The early seventh-century law of Hlothhere and Eadric similarly made provision for a man dying, leaving a wife and child: 'it is right that the child should remain with the mother, and one of its father's relatives who is willing to act, shall be given as its guardian to take care of its property, until it is ten years old'. The emphasis on the mother as the right person to care for the child is interesting given the prevalence of fostering in this society. It may be that fostering only worked effectively for the child if its father, its male guardian, were alive to take up its cause in case of maltreatment. An orphaned child, lacking the status and security provided by a living father, was at a disadvantage.

Some of the lawcodes attempt to insist on provision for these orphans. One such lawcode issued by Ine of Wessex in the later eighth century is problematic on several counts. In this case, law 26, the child seems to have neither parent surviving: 'For the maintenance of a foundling 6 shillings shall be given in the first year, 12 in the second, 30 shillings in the third, and afterwards "according to its appearance".' Leaving aside the obscure translation of the final part of this code, any interpretation of this law raises serious questions about the nature of Anglo-Saxon law-making and of society. The law does not specify who was to provide the child with maintenance: perhaps other members of the family were presumed, or perhaps its lord or the King were supposed to offer support. The phrase 'according to its appearance' (*be þam wlite*) remains inscrutable, but the implication is that the age of three represented some form of threshold, either for the growing child or for the need to support it.

A little further on in the same edict, Ine also legislated for the more common legal case of a woman and child surviving a deceased male. Under these circumstances, the provision seems much more generous, although once again the providers of the dole are unspecified and the question of how the law was to be policed and enforced remains open: 'If a man and his wife have a child, and the man dies, the mother will keep and look after her child, she will be given 6 shillings to look after it; a cow in summer and an ox in winter; the kinsmen will look after the property until it comes of age.' By the time of Æthelred, the same concern for widows and orphans was expressed, but the law rather limply stated that 'widows and orphans should not always be unhappy but should be readily cheered'. These lawcodes may have been intended to protect the vulnerable, but they also served as a practical and tangible sign of the King fulfilling one of his functions as a good Christian ruler. This role of the King as protector of the weak and vulnerable was emphasised by the description of the pious King St Edmund, whose panegyric hagiographer included the necessary attribute of being 'kind to widows and children as a father' among his virtues. Ælfric in his homilies emphasised that caring for 'step-children' – in this case probably orphans – was the virtue of the righteous: Ælfric's Job complains to God that he does not deserve his unpleasant fate because he has fulfilled all the duties of a virtuous man – he 'delivered the crying poor, and the step-child, that was without support, I helped, and the heart of the widow was comforted'. Equally, he insisted that he had never '[eaten] my bread alone without the step-child'.[13] Job was a virtuous man, and these are examples of his goodness; the inevitable inference is that less virtuous men would neither help the poor, feed the orphaned nor comfort widows.

The very existence of so many laws dedicated to the protection of orphans is in itself an indication that a parentless child was extremely vulnerable, and lacked any guarantee of protection, and there is evidence from other sources that this was true in practice: Ecgferth gave an estate and title deeds to Archbishop Dunstan in order that the Archbishop should act as guardian to Ecgferth's wife and child. In the event, the King confiscated the estate after Ecgferth's death: Dunstan eventually purchased the estate back, but no comment is made in the charter recording these events as to whether Dunstan fulfilled his obligation to the widow and her son.[14] This grim picture is corroborated elsewhere: it is notable in the *Lives* of the saints that it was rarely a foster-parent who brought a child to the saint for a cure. Either foster-parents were not responsible for sick children, or perhaps it was recognised in Anglo-Saxon society that a foster-parent would never care enough about a foster-child to bother going to such lengths. The most common cases where it was not the child's natural parents but other carers who sought a cure for a sick child were in monastic settings, where the nuns and monks had an important duty of care to the children placed in their establishments. Nonetheless, the only example where a nun pleads for a monastic child with the same fervour as secular parents did for their offspring was the case of the Abbess Hereburh, who pleaded with Bishop John to cure a nun dying from complications following blood letting. John refused to see the nun at first, but the urgent entreaties of the Abbess finally lead him to see and cure the sick nun, whose name was Cwenburh and who was the Abbess's daughter, 'whom she loved greatly and had planned to make abbess in her place'.[15]

FAMILY, KIN AND FOSTERAGE

In the previous chapter, the affectionate bonds between parents and children clearly emerged from the archaeological and documentary sources. If we are to maintain that children were loved by their Anglo-Saxon parents, how then can we explain the apparently callous act of fosterage? One possibility is that, in choosing the foster-family, parents were not relying, as Boswell would have it, on the 'kindness of strangers' at all, but would choose fosterers from among their own kin or neighbours. Kinship brought with it strong legal and moral obligations, but we have already seen that to legislate for protection for a child was one thing, to ensure that the legislation was enacted was another. By putting the child to foster with near kin, those bonds of obligation were reinforced, and Germanic society, built on kinship and loyalty, could continue to function.

Another factor to consider is that settlements in the earlier Anglo-Saxon period were frequently very small, and it is likely that most of the inhabitants of villages like West Stow or Mucking, for example, would have been related. The population in the furnished inhumation cemetery at Berinsfield, Oxfordshire, shared a number of genetic traits which might indicate kinship.[16] These relationships may have been very close indeed, and of a significance that modern western experience cannot assess – the bond between a man and his sister's son, discussed in the previous chapter, is a case in point, and emphasises how important the building of ties of responsibility outside the immediate nuclear family, but still within the kin group, were. It is not known what marriage taboos existed in pagan Anglo-Saxon England, but the later evidence suggests that marriages between close kin were acceptable, if only because the church men spent much time and energy banning marriages between in-laws and brother's wives. The church at York gained land in Northumbria because of 'an illicit union – there were two brothers who had one wife', and Judith of Frankia was married first to Æthelwulf and then, after his death, to his son – and this in the ninth-century Wessex royal household.[17] While Judith's two marriages were not condoned, by the same token there was no absolute barrier in élite secular life to prevent such unions.

Anthropological examples would support the possibility of close marriages in small communities with a kinship-based society. In Middle Eastern communities, Fredrik Barth noted that there existed a positive right of a man to marry his father's brother's daughter, and the frequency of such unions was high – between 10 and 30 per cent of such marriages were of this sort.[18] It is probable, then, that not only were members of rural Anglo-Saxon communities all connected by very close ties of blood, but that they were aware of these relationships, and founded their trust in fosterage on the consequent legal and moral obligations inherent in such consanguinity. In these circumstances, fosterage becomes more explicable within the context of caring attitudes by parents.

The mortality rates indicated by the cemetery studies also offer insights as to why parents felt that sending their children out to become part of other families was in their children's best interests. Given the average adult life expectancy of thirty-three to thirty-five years, it is evident that many children would have suffered the death of one or another parent before they reached maturity. The plight of the unprotected orphan is clear from the lawcodes, but what could parents do to ensure that their children would be cared for and that other adults would protect and defend their rights if the worst happened? The act of taking a child into your own family brought with it serious moral obligations – the child in your family *was* part of your family. By increasing the number of adults who had 'parental' responsibility for their children, parents were creating an insurance policy to guarantee the best possible environment for their children. Exchange of children between families may have had advantages for the parents, in creating useful bonds between kin groups, but the benefits to the child, not only as it grew up, but as an adult when it could call on its foster-family to support it in legal and even physical battles, should not be underrated.

BONDS BETWEEN CHILDREN AND FOSTER-PARENTS

In his account of fosterage and adoption, Boswell asserted that 'almost no ancient writers adduced an inherent obligation of procreator to child', a fact he found astonishing on the grounds that children would suffer if not raised by their natural parents.[19] Before Anglo-Saxon society can be blamed for supporting a system of fosterage, however, this assumption should be tested. It is obvious from the legislation that not all fostered children would experience a pleasant environment, but would a fostered child necessarily have suffered from a diminished experience of love, and would they routinely have been deprived of a secure and happy childhood?

Studies of children raised by adults other than their parents have reached differing conclusions, but Derek Freeman, analysing the problem with respect to modern groups and using documentary sources, concluded as a result of his research that the mother/child bond was as much behavioural as biological.[20] A child fostered from an early age would, he suggested, form a bond as close with his foster-parent as with a real parent, and even where the real parent was living in close proximity, the fostered child would regard the foster-mother as the most important in terms of bonds of love. The example of Winston Churchill, as cited by Freeman, is instructive. He was brought up by his nanny, Mrs Everest, with whom he formed a deeply emotional bond. Of his mother Churchill has written: 'she shone for me like the Evening Star. I loved her dearly – but at a distance. My nurse was my confidante. Mrs Everest it was who looked after me and tended all my wants.' A child will usually form the closest of attachments with one carer only, but this carer does not have to be the mother, and there is, according to Freeman, no sign that the infant suffers unduly if the primary bond is not biological. In cases where a child is lovingly fostered, it may be that only the parent suffers from emotional deprivation.

The Anglo-Saxon documentary record does offer comparable evidence to support this thesis. In his prose *Life of St Cuthbert*, dating to about 730, Bede revealed the potential warmth of the bond between a fostered boy and his carer, even after the child has grown to adulthood: as an adult, Cuthbert continued to visit his foster-mother and called her 'mother', and one of his miraculous deeds was to save her house from being destroyed by fire.[21] Unfortunately, the historian revealed nothing about Cuthbert's own parents, nor of the relationship between the foster-mother and Cuthbert's family, although an anonymous chronicler of Cuthbert's life identified her as 'Kenswith . . . a nun and a widow'.[22] It is worth noting that Cuthbert's eighth year was the year of his conversion to Christianity, the year of his leg injury and the associated miraculous visitation by angels, and the year he went into fosterage to be tended by a woman who was certainly a Christian and possibly a nun. There may be a potential subtext that these event were related.

A comparable tale is related in Old English by Ælfric in his homilies concerning Abbot Benedict.[23] According to this version, Benedict was 'nobly born of pious parents' and was sent to Rome for an education during his childhood. He was obviously sent in the care of a foster-mother, because when he ran away from the school, his foster-mother followed him. They came to a village where the foster-mother borrowed a winnowing sieve which subsequently broke in two, much to her distress. Benedict's reaction is noteworthy, for he: 'grieved for his foster-mother's affliction very affectionately'.[24] Needless to say, he was able to repair the sieve through the power of his prayers: this, Ælfric pointed out, was an example of sanctity emerging in childhood. A little later in the story, in a reversal of Professor Brothwell's assumption that the adult abandons the child, the juvenile Benedict finally gave the foster-mother the slip and fled to a waste land in search of a more ascetic lifestyle.

Celtic accounts of saints' *Lives* have more to say about fosterage than the Anglo-Saxon versions, and it may be that Celtic hagiography records more traditional social practices that the Romanised Anglo-Saxon writers were trying to suppress. The Celtic *Lives* do offer useful parallels, and may indicate by analogy how strong the foster-relationship might have been in the Anglo-Saxon environment. A few examples among the many will suffice to demonstrate that the practice of fosterage was widespread in early medieval Britain. Abban, sent to be fostered at an early age, was later returned by his fosterers to his parents, but not before he had converted to Christianity. It is recorded that his father and mother begged him to remain a pagan and their heir, but to no avail. He was imprisoned for being a Christian, and later returned to his foster-parents.[25] This tale parallels Guthlac's in its motif of the Christian child abandoning its parents, and it may be that we are supposed to read these acts as an enactment by the Saints of Christ's promise that those who left their families for the sake of the kingdom of God would be rewarded in the life to come, and the Irish version emphasises this point by suggesting that Christian foster-parents provided the only 'real' family for the converted Abban.[26] Abban's parents certainly learned to their cost that carers influence the development of the child, and that the simple fact of being a parent will not guarantee the love and loyalty of your offspring. Equally suggestive of the way a fostered child could become wholly a part of the foster-family was St Patrick's blessing to Dobtha – 'pre-eminence of dutiful sons and daughters and foster-children'.[27]

In this context, the riddle of the cuckoo (see pp. 124–5) merits closer examination. The poem draws attention to three specific aspects of the relationship between foster-parent and child:

1. The child was 'dead' to the natural parents, but they did not 'abandon' the egg, as some translators would have it, but they 'gave it up' – a subtle emotional distinction exists between these two concepts.
2. The foster-mother takes every care of the child, and treated it exactly the same as one of her own offspring. There is no hint here of the fostered child receiving abuse or lack of attention, or of it missing its natural parents.
3. It is the foster-family that suffered most from the intrusion. The complacent cuckoo was in no doubt that its parents did the best thing for it. Their best way of caring for their child was to give it to another family.

Semantic evidence always poses problems of interpretation, but it is notable that one of the terms for a foster-child is *wiscbearn* – 'wish child'. This may be an ironic term for fosterlings, but alternatively it may be an expression to be taken at face value. In view of the examples given above, the foster-child may indeed have been a wished-for addition to an Anglo-Saxon family.

Choosing a Foster-parent

In the later medieval period, the importance of fostering among nobility and aristocracy as part of an education in chivalric conduct has been well documented by Nicholas Orme. The documentary sources suggest that what is recognisable in later medieval society as the practice of élite apprenticeship appeared to function in the Anglo-Saxon period too. Alfred maintained children of 'both noble and ignoble birth' in his household, and Orme cited this as an early example of the medieval custom of placing aristocratic boys in the royal retinue.[28] Eodwald Bishopson was forcibly adopted into Bishop Wilfred's household, but there were other children given voluntarily into Wilfred's care, and his hagiographer explained how children and parents might benefit from choosing the powerful prelate to look after their children through the education they would receive and the contacts they would make, which would prepare them for influential roles in later life. Wilfred and other fosterers, whether in families, royal courts or ecclesiastical institutions, offered two main services. They acted as a 'prep' school to train the child in the ways of the adult world (a facet of care that will be discussed in more detail in the next chapter), and they acted as extra kin.

SPIRITUAL KINSHIP

There is little detailed information for Anglo-Saxon spiritual relationships, but much good work has been carried out on Frankish and Gallo-Roman god-parenting and oblation practices.[29] Continental practices, however, were not necessarily identical to those in Anglo-Saxon England: Frankia was a foreign country, and they did things differently there. The few detailed references to Anglo-Saxon practices of god-parenting and oblation indicate that, while these systems broadly matched those on the Continent, there were significant contrasts between what seemed normal to Anglo-Saxon writers and what was legislated for in the Frankish world. To give an example, the Anglo-Saxon missionary

St Boniface, working on the Continent, found himself, to his dismay and bewilderment, being severely reprimanded by his Continental counterparts for allowing a man to marry the widowed mother of the man's god-son, a marriage revolting to the Frankish church, but one that seemed perfectly acceptable to St Boniface. As Joseph Lynch rightly commented in his work on medieval god-parenting, we should beware of making the 'easy assumption' that in the early Middle Ages, all spiritual relationships possessed the same religious and social implications at all places and times.[30]

According to the *Canons of Theodore*, written by a monk of Greek origin who became Archbishop of Canterbury in 668, there were three occasions on which a Christian could gain god-parents: in the *catechumenus*, at baptism and at confirmation, and the candidate could be sponsored by a different god-parent on each occasion.[31] That this is likely to reflect Anglo-Saxon custom is indicated by the laws of Ine of Wessex, where there are different words for a god-son from baptism (*godsunu*) and a god-son from confirmation (*biscepsunu*). It is not clear whether there were any limits on who could sponsor a child: Caesarius of Arles (504–42), an influential writer, had already specifically excluded nuns from acting as god-parents – they were supposed to have divorced themselves from the world – and by 581, following this lead, monks were also prohibited from sponsorship.[32] On the Continent, same-sex sponsorship seems to have been the norm, and was certainly prevalent from the sixth to the early eighth century in Frankia, but there is no firm evidence for similar limits in Anglo-Saxon England. In the middle to late eighth century, Frankish sources show that cross-gender sponsorship was occurring, and the late Anglo-Saxon wills give examples of this in England too: Wulfric Spot bequeathed land and a brooch to his god-daughter in his will, for example.[33]

What was the social impact of god-parenting in Anglo-Saxon England? One consequence of accepting sponsorship of a child (or adult) in Frankia was the imposition of marital constraints: families related by spiritual kinship could not intermarry. This prohibition seems to have been in place already on the Continent before a Frankish council of the eighth century firmly established this impediment to marriage. The possibility of such a prohibition seems to have been far from Anglo-Saxon concepts of spiritual kinship, at least in the first centuries of the Christian Church in England. Spiritual kinship, for the Anglo-Saxon, was another way of cementing bonds of kinship and obligation with other groups, and obligations through spiritual ties could be backed up by marriage alliances, so that, for example, when King Oswald of Northumbria stood as the newly converted West Saxon King Cynegisl's sponsor at baptism, he was establishing his authority over the King (Cynegisl became a son to Oswald as father), and at the same time Oswald took the opportunity of arranging a marriage between himself and Cynegisl's daughter, thus strengthening the alliance between the two royal houses. Marriage between spiritual siblings and between spiritual parents and children was regarded as useful, rather than incestuous.

The distance between the Frankish and Anglo-Saxon view of the matter was encapsulated in the controversy sparked by Boniface's agreement to the marriage between a man and the widowed mother of the man's god-son in about 735. Astonished by the reaction of the Frankish church, Boniface wrote home to eminent Anglo-Saxon prelates, asking for their support or at least for some written authority for the mistake he was accused of having made. In letters to Pechthelm, Bishop of Whithorn, Nothelm, Bishop of Canterbury, and Abbot Duddo, Boniface asked whether they knew of any ecclesiastical texts to support such a prohibition, 'for in no way can I understand why in one place spiritual relationship in marital intercourse should be so great a sin, when we are all known to be the sons and daughters, brothers and sisters of Christ and of the Church in holy baptism'.[34] Boniface's logic was flawless, and his argument that there was no biblical authority for marital taboos between spiritual kin was correct, but, nonetheless, he and other Anglo-Saxon ecclesiastics were out of step with the social mores prevailing on the Continent.

Even though marital relationships between spiritual kin were prohibited by the Frankish church in the eighth century, it has been argued that the spiritual relationship between god-parent and child rarely involved the contraction of an important social bond with the child, and that, in Frankish society, the god-child had no right of inheritance from a god-parent, although god-parents might bequeath small gifts to their god-child.[35] The evidence from Anglo-Saxon England suggests that rather more was expected from a spiritual relationship. There is nothing in the lawcodes to suggest that god-children had any rights of inheritance, although, as on the Continent, god-children could benefit from wills. In one interesting will, Ealdorman Alfheah bequeathed an estate to Ælfthryth, who was the King's wife and his own *gefaedere* (co-god-parent), indicating that ties created by spiritual relationships went beyond the confines of the god-parent/god-child link.[36] More significantly, laws of Ine of Wessex demonstrate that obligations created by spiritual relationships were more than nominal and voluntary, and that god-parents and god-children did have substantial legal rights: 'if anyone kills the god-son or god-father of another, the compensation for the relationship is to be the same as that to the lord'. In the Anonymous *Life of Pope Gregory I*, written by a monk of Whitby, St Paulinus was described as King Edwin's 'father' because he baptised him, and this epithet was more than just a figure of speech, because, beyond any other considerations, god-parents and children had rights to *wergild* or compensation just like blood kin. Two people stood to benefit considerably from this law: the King, who would seek to sponsor many of his noblemen's children to reinforce his secular authority through spiritual kinship, and the bishop, who would inevitably stand as sponsor at confirmations. Two additional laws of Ine confirm this: if a king's god-son was killed, his *wergild* was to be paid to the King 'the same as to the kindred', and if a bishop's son was killed, the compensation was to be half.

What is striking in the Anglo-Saxon system of god-parenting is how closely the system of spiritual kinship seems to mirror the practices and obligations involved in Germanic and pre-Christian fosterage. Joseph Lynch, commenting on the functions of Frankish spiritual kinship, noted that it could 'intensify existing bonds and make a friend or relative even closer. It could also reach out to integrate an outsider within the circle of kin. It could serve a king as a diplomatic tool, and it could also enable socially humble people to create positive bonds with their peers or their social betters.'[37] There is nothing in this description that does not equally apply to the social advantages and functions of fosterage in the Anglo-Saxon world.

Child Oblation

Child oblation, the offering and dedication of a child to a monastic life, was already part of the Christian world by the time Benedict, Abbot of Monte Cassino, wrote his *Rule* for monastic life in the sixth century. The practice of donating children to the Church became as widespread in Christian Anglo-Saxon England as it was on the Continent, and the Frankish sources for oblation have been carefully analysed and interpreted by Mayke de Jong. She argued that, on the Continent, oblates were predominantly aristocratic children who brought their inheritance with them to the monastery, that oblation was to be explained in the context of gift-giving by the parents to the Church, that oblation was irrevocable, and that a dedication ritual involving an altar cloth, bread and wine was performed at the time of oblation, as formulated in the *Rule of St Benedict*. By the early ninth century, oblation in the Carolingian world required a total separation between child and natural parents.[38]

Evidence for oblation in Anglo-Saxon England is far from complete, but, as with spiritual kinship, the documentary sources indicate that although the practice was broadly similar to that on the Continent, there were significant discrepancies between Anglo-Saxon attitudes to oblation and those of their Merovingian and Carolingian counterparts. The question of whether oblation should be permanent or not was one that troubled ecclesiastics on both sides of the Channel, and was brought to a head in the Frankish world when Gottschalk, an intelligent and well-educated Saxon who had been donated to a Frankish monastery as a child, attempted to escape from the confines of his monastery by arguing that he had not chosen the monastic life for himself. After fierce campaigns against him, spearheaded by Abbot Hrabanus, and probably fuelled by personal animosity, Gottschalk lost his case, and the iron rule by which child oblates were committed for life was set out in the Council of Aachen for 817. Late in the ninth century, however, the pious King Alfred of Wessex was still troubled by the idea of involuntary and irrevocable oblation. The Viking depredations had emptied England's monasteries, and there was a shortage of adult recruits to fill the places. Alfred's solution for the monastery at Æthelney was to bring foreign monks into England, but Alfred's biographer Asser also discussed another solution. The children of foreign slaves were dedicated to monasteries as oblates: 'he acquired a number of people of Gallic origin: he ordered that certain of their children be educated in the monastery and at a later time be raised to the monastic order. In that monastery too I saw someone of Viking parentage who had been brought up there and who, as quite a young man, was living there in the monastic habit – and he was assuredly not the last of them to do so.' Some of these 'Gallic people' may have been victims of Viking attacks – the *Annals of St Vaast* for 982 recorded that some people were 'sold across the sea', and these may well have been Alfred's oblates and their parents.[39] Press-ganging slave children into monasteries may not have been as callous as it sounds. The children were given shelter and education, and were not bound irrevocably to the monastic life, because Alfred had severe reservations about the morality of child oblation. He recognised that children 'could not yet choose good or reject evil because of the tenderness of their infant years', and allowed older boys to choose whether they wished to remain in the monastery or not.[40]

Further evidence that oblation was not irrevocable in the Anglo-Saxon Church comes in some of the revisions of the *Canons of Theodore*. Theodore probably wrote these canons in England, and they were used, copied and reused by the Anglo-Saxon Church. With each copy, reinterpretations and slight amendments were made by the copyist, so that one copy, version D, allowed oblate boys the right to marry before their sixteenth year, although another version added that a young monk entering into marriage before his sixteenth year was guilty of bigamy and had to do a year's penance.[41]

The Anglo-Saxon sources do not give specific information on whether there were any parallels to the insistence in ninth-century Carolingian documents that oblates committed their inheritance to the Church at the time of donation, so that the gentle suggestion of Benedict's that oblates should be donated with a gift had turned into an injunction that oblates could only be donated if they came with money. King Alfred's slave oblates could not have brought any personal wealth to their monasteries, but circumstances were exceptional.

Details about the oblation ritual itself within the Anglo-Saxon world are sketchy. In the Frankish world, the act of oblation adhered, with some modifications over time, to a simple ritual. The parents would present the child at the altar, with its hand wrapped in an altar cloth, accompanied by a document 'agreeing' to oblation, and with bread and wine. The parents would answer for the child. The one useful description we have of an Anglo-Saxon oblation made no mention of altar cloths, bread and wine, but did indicate that complex negotiations had to take place between the child's immediate family, wider kin and the monastery prior to oblation. There is no evidence for this in the Frankish documents, so this practice may have been peculiarly Anglo-Saxon. The oblate was St Willibald, who seems to have been the first-hand source for his relative Hugeberc's *Life of St Willibald*. According to the account, Willibald fell ill at three years of age, and was taken to an open-air cross by his parents, who promised to dedicate him to the Church if he were cured. Willibald duly recovered, and when he was five years of age, his parents made the arrangements for his entry into the monastery. First, they consulted all their relatives, and then asked the 'honourable and trustworthy' Theodred to accompany the child to the monastery, perhaps to act as a negotiator for the parents. Theodred, Willibald and Willibald's parents then went to Bishop's Waltham to give the child to Abbot Egwald, and Abbot Egwald sought permission for Willibald to enter the monastic community from the other monks.[42]

The complex negotiations surrounding Willibald's oblation, involving full consultation with the relatives of the child and the spiritual relatives of the household the child was to enter, and including the services of a trustworthy intermediary between the two kin groups, one secular and one spiritual, may hint at the delicate contractual arrangements that might have taken place in the secular world too, when a child was formally fostered into another family by its parents. The ties that an alliance through fosterage might impose on all members of a kin group could not be taken on without careful thought. Equally, if oblation involved the donation of an inheritance to the Church, it was important that all members of the family should agree to this loss of their ancestral property to prevent arguments and court cases at a later date. We do not know much about Bede's entry into the monastery, but he did reveal that he was dedicated to the Church by his relatives. This may mean that he was an orphan, or that his oblation, like Willibald's, was a matter for all the relatives to decide, not just the parents.

Oblation, according to the *Rule of Benedict*, demanded a dramatic break between child and parent, and this seems to have been the ideal in Frankish society too. At the important monastery of Fleury, parents in the tenth century were forbidden to see their children even if they were sick, and they were not permitted to bury a child who had died.[43] Oblation in Anglo-Saxon England seems to have been much less severe. St Eadberga's father came to visit his daughter at her convent on at least two separate occasions, but there can be no question that some child oblates must have experienced a considerable sense of loss and homesickness. However, this does not mean that they were necessarily deprived of a loving and affectionate environment. Alcuin grew up in the minster at York, and considered himself to have been nurtured with a mother's love by the monks there, according to his early ninth-century hagiographer. Hugeburc of Heidenheim described St Willibald's relationship to the young boys in his charge at the monastery as that of a father to his adopted children. Alcuin, in his turn, formed a very close bond with the Frisian oblate Luidger: Luidger had defied his own father to train with Alcuin at York, and according to Altfrid, Luidger's

An illustration to Psalm 27: 'for my father and my mother have forsaken me, but the Lord will take me up'. (British Library, Harley 603, f. 15r)

biographer, Alcuin risked his own life to smuggle Luidger out of York during a period of violence towards Frisians in the city: 'he would rather die himself than allow his beloved son to come to any harm'.[44]

What is more interesting is that, in practice, Anglo-Saxon monasteries were family affairs, and a noble child raised in a monastery might well find him or herself surrounded by blood relatives. Edith had just been born when her mother Wulfthryth, third wife (or possibly concubine) of King Edgar, retired from royal life to become Abbess of Wilton nunnery, and it is likely that Edith, reared in the monastery from early infancy, remained in close contact with her mother. Edith's oblation did not cut her off from her father either; he and the royal retinue were present when Edith confirmed her vocation to the Church at the precocious age of 2, and there was a huge royal presence at the funeral of the 23-year-old nun and princess. It could be beneficial to the monastery to ensure that royal parents kept in touch with their children: King Edward's visit to the convent at Winchester to see his daughter led to Eadberga's successful request for grants of land from her father to the convent.[45]

Anglo-Saxon kinsmen could, and did, enter the same monastery in surprising numbers. When Lioba entered a convent as a child oblate in the eighth century, her religious relatives included Boniface, the brothers Wynnebald and Willibald and their sister Walburga, and Hugeburc, Willibald's biographer. Other prominent ecclesiastical members of the same kin group included Beorhtgyth, who followed Boniface as a nun to Germany, and her mother Cynehild, who was also the aunt of Lull, originally trained at Malmesbury, who became Boniface's successor as Archbishop of Mainz. When Lull went on pilgrimage to Rome, he is recorded as having taken his entire kindred with him, and when Wynnebald was looking for fellow Anglo-Saxons to help him undertake his mission to the Continent, he was able to select his team entirely from his friends and family.[46]

CONCLUSIONS AND IMPLICATIONS

Not all children in Anglo-Saxon England were fostered, and not all parents were happy to send their children away from home. Asser explained the fact that King Alfred was never sent away from home (beyond his trip to Rome), but instead was brought up at the royal court, as a consequence of the great love his parents felt for him – parents, it has to be noted, who both died before their youngest son Alfred was nine years of age. The simple fact that Asser felt moved to comment on Alfred's unusual upbringing at home emphasises that fostering, even for loving parents, was the custom in Anglo-Saxon society of the ninth century.[47] The important functions of fosterage, god-parenting and the dedication of children to the Church as oblates meant that no Anglo-Saxon parent could afford not to consider one or more of these options for their children. All offered methods of promoting alliances either between families or between families and the Church, but these benefits to the parents worked for the children too. All these systems provided the child with opportunities and contacts outside the narrow limits of the nuclear family, and ensured that a child could expect protection and care from other adults, especially in the event of the death of parents.

CHAPTER 10

Play and Education

Notwithstanding the economic and physical hardships of pre-industrial life, the concept of play was embedded in adult Anglo-Saxon culture. The 'play' element in place names such as Plaistow in Essex indicates a pre-Christian name for an adult theatre or amphitheatre, while Gamfield Hundred in Berkshire takes its name from the Anglo-Saxon 'game-field'.[1] Entertainments were a significant part of Anglo-Saxon life at most social levels, as the popularity of the manifestly secular, and frequently vulgar, Old English riddles testifies. The idea of the *scop*, the community poet and newsmonger, is understood, but other varieties of professional entertainers could provide amusement for adults, and were recorded in the later Anglo-Saxon period: words survive for male and female players, dancers and singers.[2] If adults could find time for games, there is no reason to think that children were deprived of play.

There is little in the documentary sources to give us a clue about children's playtimes, but occasionally their games form a backdrop to a narrative, observing a natural exuberance in the children. The anonymous writer of St Cuthbert's *Life* gave us a snapshot of Cuthbert as a boisterous playground child:

> When he was a boy of eight years old, he surpassed all of his age in agility and high spirits, so that often after the others had gone to rest their weary limbs, he, standing triumphantly in the playground as though he were in the arena, would still wait for someone to play with him. At that time many youths were gathered together one day on a piece of level ground and he too was found among them. They began thereupon to indulge in a variety of games and tricks: some stood naked, with their legs stretched out and pivoted skywards, and some did one thing and some another.[3]

For the writer, this scene marked a key dramatic point in the narrative, when Cuthbert was given his calling and passed in a spiritual sense from the carefree times of childhood to the serious business of serving God, and there is a hint of true life in the description because Bede, describing the same scene, carefully omitted the reference to the children's nakedness. The playground scene, for the writer, was a typical representation of boisterous Anglo-Saxon childhood, and while it may seem strikingly banal, it is worth noting that Anglo-Saxon childhood *did* include times of play – children were by no means regarded as miniature adults and as economic units, made to work as soon as there was a job they could do. Some historians have portrayed pre-industrial society as a harsh world with no time for play, still less for adults to take an interest in observing and describing such play for an adult audience. Ariès allowed that there might have been play, but that this would have been centred around adults because 'there was simply no place for childhood in the medieval world', a contention that the description of an unsupervised Cuthbert and his friends at their rowdy games overturns.[4]

These noisy groups of children are also mentioned in the *Life of St Guthlac*, who, according to the hagiographer, was never troublesome to others, including the 'bands of children of his own age'. The hagiographer of Guthlac's life gives a damning account of the high spirits of these bands of boys, disliking their 'impudence' and the way they imitated the 'different cries of the various kinds of birds'.[5]

Robust wrestling by boys appears to have been considered a particular characteristic of Anglo-Saxon childhood by post-Conquest writers, because an early attempt to derive the place name of Barnwell in Cambridgeshire from the Old English 'well of the children' (*bearne wyll*) associated the well with games played by the children of the neighbourhood on the Nativity of John the Baptist: '. . . according to the custom of the English, boys and youths . . . assembled there, and practised wrestling and other boyish games, and mutually applauded one another with songs and musical instruments; whence, on account of the multitude of boys and girls who gathered there, it grew a custom for a crowd of sellers and buyers to assemble there on the same day for the purpose of commerce'. [6]

Unaccompanied groups of children seem to have been free to gang together and play noisy games in the Anglo-Saxon period, and such scenes must have been a backdrop to everyday life; in an Old English translation, a town bishop, sitting in the church, saw through the window 'a great throng of boys playing by the sea shore'.[7] The description of a horde of children romping in the waves at the seaside may seem trivial, but it is a refreshing reminder that Anglo-Saxon life was not simply a dusty round of lawcodes and burial ritual; Anglo-Saxon documents occasionally give us a glimpse of real children at play.

In the *Harley Psalter*, children are depicted both in groups on their own and with adults. When they are shown with adults, they have a passive function, being held by the hand or carried in the arms of an adult. Groups of children, however, show more interest in each other. In the illustration to Psalm 102, a number of children are making their way up a hill. All the children look up to the angel on the hill, except one who is turning with arms stretched out as if to help the slowest child up the slope. This type of adult observation of children's patterns of play was also exhibited by Ælfric, who captured the concentration of a child in its games and, in this case, the tragic consequences: 'a child was playing heedlessly, and ran under a running wheel and was crushed to death'.[8] Fortunately the child was miraculously healed when its sorrowing mother carried it to the church of St Stephen.

TOYS

There is even less evidence of toys than of play in the Anglo-Saxon world. There are few grave goods with children that could be interpreted as 'toys' in the usual sense of artefacts specially designed to amuse a child – there is a pottery bottle with a fragment of glass within it from the rich burial of the little girl from Finglesham (grave 7), which could be construed as a rattle, but this is a notable exception if that interpretation is accurate. Some children were buried with items that might be interpreted as their own personal favourite possessions – the little girl in grave 23 from a cemetery in Sarre, Kent, was buried with an amulet of 'a little nautilus-shaped ornament of green stone or porcelain'.[9] Within the cremation cemetery at Caistor-by-Norwich, children's burial urns included artefacts that might possibly be toys – a translucent pebble, pieces of iron pyrites and the base of a Samian ware cup.[10]

Such objects are also found in inhumation burials: a two-year-old from Worthy Park was buried with a single nail; a three-year-old from Buckland was buried with a fossil, and a six-year-old from Sewerby was buried with the rim of a pot, but it is much more difficult to distinguish deliberately placed artefacts from residual objects in the grave fill in inhumation burials, whereas all the contents of a cremation urn must be assumed to have been intentionally included in the pot. In earlier chapters, it was suggested that the broken or worn items buried with some children indicated that it was the symbolic presence of the artefact within the adult burial ritual that was important, but there may be an alternative interpretation. Children value items regardless of their adult significance and 'proper' function; as a child, Alfred coveted his mother's book, not because of its written contents but because of its decorated pages. Artefacts such as the worn and broken brooch buried with the twelve-year-old in grave 21 at Winnall should perhaps be regarded in the same light: the brooch was made of gilt bronze, garnet, shell and silver, and while it was redundant from an adult perspective, a child might have coveted it simply for its beauty.

'Toys' are, in fact, mentioned in several cemetery reports, particularly with reference to cremations, but these are miniature items such as tweezers and knives, and are found in adult graves. The automatic modern assumption that miniature items must be children's toys in earlier times is a misconception, and there is no need to propagate the myth for the Anglo-Saxon period. Some recognisable games have survived in the archaeological record; in particular, playing pieces for board games are known in pagan burial contexts. The high-status adult male graves at Sutton Hoo and Taplow, for example, both contained sets of playing counters, and they are found in a few lower-status contexts too. However, as Julian Richards noted in his study of cremations, playing pieces are positively linked to older adults.[11] The burial evidence indicates that the playing of 'formal' games was an activity associated with older men rather than with children.

Of course, the likely materials for children's toys – scraps of cloth, animal hair and wood – are precisely the organic materials that stand the least chance of surviving in the archaeological record. Documents from the post-Conquest period describe children creating houses and hobby horses out of sticks, a sailing ship from bread, a sword from sedge, and a doll from cloth and flowers.[12] None of these simple springboards for a child's imagination would have survived in the archaeological record. However, in the Anglo-Saxon documentary sources, references to toys are as scarce as evidence for them in the archaeological record. The children in the *Harley Psalter* are seen with adults, but are not depicted playing at games with toys. When children are described at play in the documentary sources, they are borrowing their playthings from the adult world. King Alfred added to his translation of Gregory's *Pastoral Care* the image of children playing with their parents' coins: 'we even warn our children from playing with our money'.[13] The young saint Cuthbert and his friends were engaged in athletic play, but no toys were included in their pastimes. Artefacts built by adults for children seem not to have been part of the childhood world: children found their games out of their own resources. Alfred noted this in one of his personal additions to his translation of Boethius: 'the children ride on their sticks and play many games in imitation of adults'.[14]

What is clear from the texts and illustrations is that children lived and played alongside adults, and that, unremarkably, some of their play took the form of imitating or 'helping' adults – the most effective form of learning and preparation for the adult life. The monk describing the early childhood of the saintly Guthlac was at pains to show that, for this saint-to-be, wise before his time, there was no need for the usual boyish behaviour, which the hagiographer characterised as consisting of imitations: 'He did not imitate . . . the nonsensical chatter of the matrons, nor the empty tales of the common people, nor the foolish shouts of the rustics, nor the lying triflings of flatterers . . . as children of that age are wont to do.'[15]

In the *Harley Psalter*, children are usually shown with adults, often holding the hands of women, but never playing with toys. In a few scenes, however, children are seen playing a helping role with them, rather than simply being nurtured or cared for by adults. The illustration to Psalm 41 shows the psalmist, sitting, instructing a smaller figure – perhaps a servant, but also a child – to feed the needy from a table. A less ambiguous case comes in the illustration to Psalm 25,

A family feed the poor and needy and offer comfort to the weak; the children help the adults. (British Library, Harley 603, f. 14r)

where a woman and man offer food to the poor and sick. The woman comforts three children standing beside her, but the man is being helped in his task by the diminutive figure of a boy. A particularly interesting example comes as a footnote to the illustration of Psalm 116, where, in the bottom left-hand corner, beneath the warriors on horseback and all the other scenes, there is a diminutive naked figure of a boy who appears to be helping a seated cowled figure to pluck a bird.

One possible example of a child with a hoop and a stick may be found in the *Harley Psalter*. The vignette shows a seated woman handing a ring to a male who is holding a stick. This scene has been variously interpreted as a mother giving a blessing to a departing son, or as a mother giving a weaning child a ring. The scene illustrates part of Psalm 131, and Christine Fell has suggested that it depicts the phrase 'as a child that is weaned of its mother'.[16] The Harley artists made consistent efforts to differentiate between babies, small children and older children, and the child seen here is far too mature to represent a toddler. However, verse 1 of Psalm 131 contains the phrase 'I do not occupy myself with things too great and marvellous for me.' A child occupying itself with a hoop and stick would seem an appropriate illustration of this sentiment.

The theme of children preparing for the adult world by playing with adult artefacts rather than purpose-built toys is reiterated in the archaeological record. Boys needed to be able to fight when they grew up, and a number of children were buried with small spears. Abingdon (grave 21), Buckland (graves 137 and 139) and Portway (grave 40), all have undersized spears which may have been the Anglo-Saxon equivalent of the modern boy's toy gun, though with far more serious adult application. Similarly, girls were buried with a variety of artefacts associated with women's activities: chatelaines, weaving battens and spindlewhorls, while by no means common, make sporadic appearances in the graves of girls. If these do represent the possessions of the children rather than the symbols of adult burial ritual, then girls were playing/working alongside their mothers, keeping their personal possessions in their own boxes, and learning the techniques of textile production, vital to the welfare of the community, from an early age – just as children today are taught the rudiments of sewing and knitting. Teaching a child the skills for adult life should not be equated with forcing a child to work as if it were an adult.

It is noticeable that, while younger girls are buried with a single key and girls from the age of six may have two keys, burial with sets of three or more keys is the preserve of adult burials. Women in Anglo-Saxon England had autonomy over a certain amount of personal wealth. These possessions were theirs alone, and were outside the power of their husbands. Women apparently kept their treasures in locked boxes to which they alone had access; in one Anglo-Saxon lawcode, a woman is innocent of complicity in her husband's theft if no stolen goods are found in her own box.[17] Adult women, if the number of keys in the burial ritual is anything to go by, accumulated wealth and boxes to put it in. The single keys buried with the youngest girls may represent their first box in which to put their treasures – broken brooches, pretty pebbles and single beads – partly in play, and partly to begin to learn the importance of ownership and the skills of personal responsibility.

A cowled seated figure and a small naked child appear to be plucking a bird in the corner of the scene, oblivious to the busy people above. (British Library, Harley 603, f. 59v)

A child carrying a stick is given a hoop by its mother in an illustration to Psalm 131: 'I do not occupy myself with things too great and too marvellous for me'. (British Library, Harley 603, f. 67v)

EDUCATION

'How a society selects, classifies, distributes, transmits and evaluates the educational knowledge it considers to be public reflects both the distribution of power and the principles of social control. From this point of view, differences within and changes in the organisation, transmission and evaluation of educational knowledge should be a major area of sociological interest.'[18] Education has been seen to have an impact on childhood, both in terms of prolonging the period before a child takes its place in the workforce, and being a factor in distinguishing between those societies for whom there is a 'concept' of childhood, and those for whom such a concept has no meaning. According to Neil Postman, writing about the disappearance of childhood, literacy 'creates childhood' because reading demands a process of conceptualisation, and brings access to secrets which are beyond the knowledge of children.[19] For Postman, these secrets define the adult world, and in a society without literature (and therefore, in Postman's terms, without schooling), there is nothing to separate the child's world from that of the adult. For Postman, the medieval period represented just such a time, when childhood was invisible: 'What we can say, then, with certainty, is that in the medieval world there was no conception of child development, no conception of prerequisites or sequential learning, no conception of schooling as a preparation for an adult world.'[20]

Secular Education

To an extent, the evidence seems to corroborate Postman's view that there was no formalised period of education for children, particularly in secular life. In the later medieval period up to the twelfth century, a literary education was not considered a necessary part of the training of a noble, and children of more humble origins would have had no more access to learning than their parents did. The famous knight William Marshall was, notwithstanding his status and achievements, illiterate.[21] The sketchy evidence available from the Anglo-Saxon period suggests that the same mentality prevailed. The early education of Guthlac, born of noble Christian parents, appeared to consist entirely of listening to the recitation of heroic poetry in the hall, with, according to the disapproving hagiographer, the inevitable inappropriate influence on an impressionable young mind: remembering the 'valiant deeds of old', the teenage Guthlac took up a career as a warrior.[22] Alfred, for all his interest in literacy, did not learn to read until he was twelve or later, even though he was reared with his parents at the royal court. Asser, a monk and Alfred's biographer, was shocked at Alfred's lack of schooling – 'by the shameful negligence of his parents and tutors he remained ignorant of letters' – and Alfred, too, keenly felt the lack of a scholarly education when he grew up. His efforts to improve literacy among his people included obliging mature noblemen and experienced soldiers to join their children at the school bench, much to their discomfort.

Asser's description of Alfred's childhood education provides some interesting insights into what royal children did learn, even if they were not taught to write.

Alfred may not have had scholarly teachers, but Asser says he did have tutors – so what learning were these tutors supposed to be imparting? We are told that Alfred, like Guthlac, heard and learnt by heart many English poems. Such poems contained within them not only teaching on the proper character and behaviour of a nobleman, but also the history of the people. In a society that was still largely illiterate, the important skills to develop for adulthood were a retentive memory, and a thorough knowledge of the history of feuds, kinships and land claims. Alfred, like other young noble boys, also learnt how to hunt – a skill for life, as Asser confirmed: 'an enthusiastic huntsman, he strives continually in every branch of hunting, and not in vain, for no one else could approach him in skill and success in that activity'.[23] To know the history of your people, how to lead in battle, how to chase a quarry and how to handle weapons, and to have a good memory – these were the skills boys had to develop. It has to be stressed that the lack of an education in reading and writing must have been a *choice* for Alfred's parents, since there were evidently people with reading and writing skills accessible to their son. This is Asser's famous account of Alfred's first contact with books:

> One day, when his mother was showing him and his brothers a book of English poetry which she held in her hand, she said: 'I shall give this book to whichever one of you can learn it the fastest'. Spurred on by these words, or rather by divine inspiration, and attracted by the beauty of the initial letter in this book, Alfred spoke as follows in reply to his mother, forestalling his brothers (ahead in years though not in ability): 'Will you really give this book to the one who can understand it the soonest and recite it to you?' Whereupon, smiling with pleasure, she reassured him, saying: 'Yes I will.' He immediately took the book from her hand, went to his teacher and learnt it. When it was learnt, he took it back to his mother and recited it.[24]

What is most noticeable about the story is not that Alfred was encouraged to read, but conversely, that he was encouraged to *memorise*. We cannot be sure that his mother could read, although it was she who owned a book and offered it to her sons, but clearly one of his teachers had the requisite skills. Osburh's challenge to her boys was not to read the book, but to learn its contents.

It is also worth noting that, in spite of his apparent obsession with education, Alfred did not educate all his own children in the same way. One, the youngest, was singled out for special attention: 'Æthelweard, the youngest of all . . . was given over to training in reading and writing under the attentive care of teachers, and it was around this child that Alfred's famous school was created, because Æthelweard was not taught privately by a personal tutor, but "in company with all the nobly born children of virtually the entire area, and a good many of lesser birth as well"'.[25] Asser's description of Æthelweard's education gives further examples of what a scholarly education actually consisted of: 'In this school books in both languages – that is to say in Latin and English – were carefully read; they also devoted themselves to writing to such an extent that, even before they had the requisite strength for manly skills (hunting, that is, and other skills appropriate to noblemen), they were seen to be devoted and intelligent students of the liberal arts.'[26]

Two more of Alfred's children lived at the court, but do not seem to have been given the schooling of Æthelweard. The education of Edward and Ælfthryth, Alfred's eldest son and second daughter, consisted of learning the Psalms and books in English, 'and especially English poems'. Asser was at pains to assert that these two 'frequently made use of books', but their lives seem to have focussed more around 'other pursuits of this present life which are appropriate to the nobility'.[27]

Boys, as in the later medieval period, must have learnt how to behave in company as part of their education. Children, noble and otherwise, crop up in the sources as servants of noblemen, although one aristocratic child placed in service with Abbot Benedict objected to this method of education: 'A noble born child held light before [Benedict's] table, and began to take offence that he had to serve him in such mean things. The saint, through God's Spirit, soon perceived his pride, and, severely reproving him, said, "Brother, bless thy heart", and ordered the light to be taken from him, and him to sit; and he related to his brothers the pride of the child in detail.'[28] Even Alfred, champion of schooling and literacy, taught 'virtuous behaviour' as well as literacy to the sons of his household and visitors.[29] As in the later Middle Ages, learning the skills of service and noble behaviour were of paramount importance in the education of the nobility.

The picture of secular élite illiteracy should not be taken as a rule. Sigeberht of East Anglia was taught Latin at school and came unexpectedly to the throne in 631, as did Aldfrith of Northumberland, who was also learned in Latin and was crowned in 685. Nicholas Orme described Aldfrith as 'the first clear English example of a literate layman' but the fact that neither Sigeberht nor Aldfrith expected to be kings might indicate that their Latin education was intended to prepare them for a monastic life.[30] Sigeberht, however, seems to have felt that literacy was a useful skill, and he is credited with founding the first school in East Anglia, while Aldfrith, educated in Ireland, had already gained a reputation as a scholar in Bede's estimation, and we have to suspect that he fully intended to join the Irish Church had politics not intervened.

Monastic Education

In the ideal later medieval monastery, 'arduous physical and emotional effort were demanded of . . . children in a highly disciplined way of life in which there was no room for childish diversions and innocent amusements'.[31] This may have been the Anglo-Saxon ideal too: an Anglo-Saxon scribe copied the *Rule of Chrodegang* into Old English, which stated that the adults of the monastery had to keep a strict eye on the children and youths in their care, and to maintain strict discipline, so that 'playful youth, which loves to sing' should find no outlet for their exuberance.[32] The *Rule* further stated that wherever a priestly community had children or youths, they should all live in one strict house, so that their unsteady youth should not be passed in idle frivolity, but according to the teaching of the Church.[33] Play and a monastic upbringing and education were mutually exclusive. The monk Herebald, looking back on his youth and education under the tutelage of Bishop John in the seventh century, was well aware of the conflict between a boy's exuberance and the gravity required of an oblate. He recounted that one day, as Bishop John was travelling with Herebald and several youths on horseback, they came to a level plain where the other young men (mostly belonging to the laity) began to race their horses. Herebald was, in his words, 'not free of youthful impulses', and begged to be allowed to join in the games. Bishop John forbade Herebald, but Herebald, unable to resist, dashed away to race with the others, and soon had a disastrous fall, just as Bishop John had foreseen.[34] Here, youthful impetuousness is contrasted with monastic restraint, but there is no dramatic narrative pressure to point to a moral, suggesting that this is a genuine reminiscence of an event, rather than a homily. Herebald recovered from his fall, and the 'moral' of the story, if there is one, is that even when a good monk like Herebald is being guided by the wisdom of a respected teacher, youth is heedless.

In the Anglo-Saxon period, it appears that education in a monastic milieu was considered appropriate for noble children destined for the secular as well as the religious world. Bishop Wilfred seems to have run the equivalent of a modern boarding preparatory school for the élite: 'Secular chief men too, men of noble birth, gave him their sons to be instructed, so that, if they chose, they might devote themselves to the service of God, or that, if they preferred, he might give them into the king's charge as warriors when they were grown up.'[35] A similar arrangement seems to have been practised by Bishop John of Beverley. When Herebald had his riding accident, the bishop was travelling in the company of a mixed group of boys, both oblates and laity. Herebald himself was given to the bishop 'in his earliest years of his youth', to be educated in music and book learning.[36]

Ælfric, writing in the tenth century, described Aidan's mission to convert the Northumbrians in the seventh. As well as preaching and baptising, Aidan taught 'young men', so that wherever Aidan went, his young pupils recited the Psalms and read passages of scripture.[37] For Ælfric, a Christian education was the province of young boys; the teacher was a monk, the classroom was wherever the monk was, and initial stages of education were focussed on memorising material rather than learning to read and write. In 752, Boniface, nearing death and seeking some reassurance about the fate of his English helpers working in Germany, wrote to Fulrad, Abbot of St Denis, describing his companions: 'some are priests . . . some are monks . . . and children set to learn to read, and some are older men . . .'.[38]

Schools were established in Anglo-Saxon England after the conversion to Christianity – first, St Augustine's school at Canterbury, then Sigeberht of East Anglia's school under Bishop Felix, where 'boys and young men' were taught and educated on the same model as the Canterbury school.[39]

Within the monastic environment, the treatment of children was distinguished from that of adults. According to the oblate describing his monastic life in Ælfric's early eleventh-century *Colloquy*, boys were distinguished from the older brethren by not being allowed to drink wine: 'I am not lucky enough to be allowed to drink wine, and wine is not a drink for children nor fools, but for the older and wiser.'[40] It may not be appropriate to interpret this as a sensible gesture towards keeping children from intoxicating drink: the child tells his schoolmaster that he is allowed to drink ale or water – wine had to be imported into Anglo-Saxon England, and was probably too much of a luxury to give to the oblates. By the later Anglo-Saxon period, one monk was in charge of teaching, and presumably specialised in overseeing the education of the boys. One surviving Old English charter is in the name of 'the monk Edwin, child master at the New Minster'.[41]

Secular Literacy

The great champion of education for all in the Anglo-Saxon period was, of course, King Alfred. According to Asser's *Life* of the King, he forced old men to take up book learning, he gave money to schools, and the sons of all the visitors and residents at Alfred's court, including foreigners, clergy and ealdormen, received a personal education, as Asser records: 'nor, in the midst of other affairs, did [Alfred] cease from personally giving, by day and night, instruction in all virtuous behaviour and tutelage in literacy to their sons, who were being brought up in the royal household, and whom he loved no less than his own children'. Alfred's policy recorded in his preface to his book *Pastoral Care* was clear: that every boy of free birth, whether destined for the Church or for the active life of a warrior, should learn to read and write: 'All the youth of England's free men who have the means so that they may apply themselves to it, be set to learning as long as they can not be set to any other employment, until such time as they know how to read English writing well. Afterwards let those chosen for further education to be brought to higher office be taught Latin as well.'

Alfred may have been a pedagogue ahead of his time, but nonetheless it is worth noting that he believed childhood to be the appropriate time to learn, and that adults found it much harder to do so: 'he used to affirm, with repeated complaints and sighing from the depths of his heart, that among all the difficulties and burdens of his present life this had become the greatest; namely, that at the time when he was of the right age and had the leisure and the capacity for learning, he did not have the teachers'.[42] This may be a simple observation of fact, but it is also the expression of a belief that certain skills and qualities belonged to childhood – 'the right age' – and were lost later, rather than an assumption that the child was an unformed adult.

Donald Bullough noted that there is an 'almost total lack' of direct evidence for schools and schooling in the first half of the tenth century.[43] There is more information after the reforms of Dunstan, Æthelwold and Oswald, when we have evidence for monastic schools catering especially for children of the cloister. Children were taught English and Latin, and a number of glosses and study books survive from the late tenth and eleventh centuries showing that young monks were expected to study a range of classical and patristic texts, including Priscian, Sergius, Cato and Bede.[44]

In the late tenth century, the greatest of teachers was undoubtedly Ælfric (born *c.* 950), who, according to his own writings, was poorly educated as a child by a rural priest who barely understood Latin. Ælfric was determined to be a better teacher himself, and among his ground-breaking achievements, even within a European context, was the creation of a *Grammar* for children in which he not only had to wrestle with his own educational shortcomings to explain Latin grammar, but also in the process formulated a grammar of Old English too, thus creating 'the first grammar in any vernacular'.[45] Ælfric also constructed a latin *Glossary* and a *Colloquy*, consisting of a series of conversational exercises for boys to help them learn Latin. The emphasis within the *Colloquy* is on familiar, every-day Anglo-Saxon life, so we read of fishermen, shepherd boys, young monks and other children in training for adult professions. The content of the *Colloquy* has been taken to indicate that some, at least, of the pupils at Ælfric's monastic school were destined for secular life. What is true is that, reading the *Colloquy*, we feel, as Bullough wrote, that 'we have personally entered some Anglo-Saxon school-house, and are listening to the voice of the master, to the voices, too of some of the pupils'.[46] The *Colloquy* opens with a chant from pupils: 'We children ask you, oh teacher, to teach us to speak [in Latin], because we are uneducated and speak ungrammatically.'[47]

Most of the documentary sources give the impression that the education of boys was of more importance than that of girls, and to an extent, within a Christian context, this was inevitably true. The missionaries to Anglo-Saxon England needed to train Anglo-Saxons to become priests, and only males could fulfil this role. The first schools were training schools for priests and monks, and again, inevitably, they were for boys. However, in spite of the bias enforced by the purpose of a Christian education, there does not appear to have been any underlying assumption on the part of the Anglo-Saxons that girls should be excluded from an education. It is true, as Bede claims, the early missionaries from the Continent and Ireland set up selective schools, but that simply meant that the girls of noble and royal families had to be sent abroad for an education, to France and Gaul. King Anna of the East Angles sent both his step-daughter Sæthryth and his own daughter Æthelberg to the monastery at Brie for their education.[48]

The earliest Christian and literary curriculum in the south of England for which we have any details was set by Abbot Adrian – sent by the Pope from Naples to the episcopate at Canterbury – and Theodore, born in Tarsus. They were both, according to Bede, conversant with the ways of the Mediterranean Church: 'well trained in the sacred writings and in monastic and ecclesiastical discipline, and duly instructed both in the Latin and Greek languages'. Adrian and Theodore passed on this education to their new English pupils, 'and along with the holy books and ecclesiastical discipline, they taught and instructed them in metre and astronomy, and in grammar'.[49] Latin and Greek were also taught. Dunstan, placed in the monastery at Glastonbury where he passed his youth and adolescence, learnt writing, harp-playing and painting.[50] Æthelwold, having demonstrated his sanctity in earliest childhood, was set 'in his very boyhood' (according to Ælfric, his hagiographer) to studying the sacred writings.[51] Leoba, a girl destined to be consecrated as a nun even before her conception, was brought up by her parents and educated 'from early infancy', presumably with her ecclesiastical vocation in mind, in 'grammar and the study of the other liberal arts.' She had a particular facility for memorising large quantities of text.[52]

We know little about Anglo-Saxon educational methods. Thrupp, writing in 1862, felt that he had a good grasp of the sound educational methods employed by the Anglo-Saxon pedagogues: 'The Anglo-Saxon had but one mode of tuition, and that was the simplest in the world. They told a child to learn, and if he did not, they beat him. A stiff rod and a strong arm were all that a teacher needed.'[53]

Thrupp's views may reveal more about his own Victorian upbringing, spiced by a little wishful thinking, because there is actually little in the Anglo-Saxon documentary record to support this theory. Some corroboration might be drawn from the *Life* of the post-Conquest St Anselm: 'On one occasion, a certain abbot, who was considered to be a sufficiently religious man, was talking with him about matters of monastic discipline, and among other things he said something about the boys brought up in the cloister, adding "What, I ask you, is to be done with them? They are incorrigible ruffians. We never give over beating them day and night and they only get worse and worse."'[54]

Anselm offered the reasonable suggestion that kindness may be more effective than brutality, but is violence or gentleness more typical of Anglo-Saxon methods? The story was intended to show Anselm's saintly qualities, and the contrast between the beatings and the mildness may be deliberately exaggerated. More importantly, Anselm, though living in post-Conquest England, was not English, and neither, by the time of his hagiography, were its writers. What new approaches to education might have been introduced by the Normans is not clear. In the tenth century St Æthelwold had an approach to education as humane as Anselm's, according to Ælfric, Æthelwold's hagiographer. 'It was always a pleasure to him to teach young men and boys, and to explain books to them in English, and with kindly exhortations to encourage them to better things.'[55] The monks of Anglo-Saxon England were Benedictines, and if children were beaten, then this punishment was within the *Rule* – Benedict's *Rule* prescribes 'fasting or sharp blows for naughty boys or youths'.[56]

It does appear from other records of saints that beatings may have been a common method of discipline within monasteries, both for adults and children. St Eadberga, daughter of King Edward, was dedicated to the convent at Nunnaminster from an early age, and as a child in the convent was beaten by one of the nuns because she was reading in solitude, although the nun apologised as soon as she discovered Eadberga's royal identity.[57] In marginal notes to Anglo-Saxon manuscripts, masters note instructions to their pupils, and threaten a good hiding if their instructions are not obeyed. On the top margin of the Oxford copy of the *Liber Pastoralis* are written the words: 'Willimot, write like this or better . . . or lose your skin.' Another marginal note, this time in Harleian MS 55, fol. 4b, offers a similar threat: 'write like this or better ride away: Alfnar Pattafox will beat you, child Alfric'.[58] Alfric is in for trouble, but the epithet 'child' could have been applied to any pupil up to young adulthood.

Abbot Ælfric noted that Solomon in the Hebrew Bible suggested that children should be beaten for their own good: 'Correct your child and strike it with the rod, and so shall you redeem its soul from death. He who spareth his rod hateth his child; and he who loveth it, teacheth it soundly.' Ælfric agreed with this principle; he added his own comment: 'Children require vigorous correction and good heed to good morals, that wisdom may be dwelling in them.'[59] Ælfric cited the example of Eli, whose children led to his death, and the example of a child who was not properly chastised by his father and was taken by devils. Finally, he pointed out (erroneously) that those children who were brought up properly and 'thoroughly corrected against all vices' were the children Christ was referring to when he said to his disciples 'of such is the kingdom of God'. Punishing children by beating seemed to have been to the forefront of Ælfric's pedagogic mind, for when he was compiling his *Grammar* and searching for illustrations, the punishment of children was the example that came naturally to his pen: '*ACCUSSATIVO: hos pueros flagello* – *þas cild ic swinge* [I am beating the child], *VOCATIVO o pueri, cantate bene* – *eala ge cild, singað well* [O child, sing well]: *flagellaistum puerum* – *beswing ðis cild* [beat this child].'[60]

An educated society may appear to be a civilised and free-thinking society, but it is clear from the documentary record that not all education was entered into voluntarily by students. Continental examples indicate that taking children into schools could be an effective political weapon in pacifying an antagonistic population and converting them to Christianity. In the thirteenth century, the Danish Archbishop of Lund took children of the Livonian aristocracy as hostages and sent priests out to preach in exchange. Charlemagne, in his attempts to quell the rebellious pagan Saxons, obliged the sons of Saxon noblemen to be brought up in Frankish monasteries, and the Spaniards epitomised this technique in the sixteenth century in Latin America by taking local children to be brought up by the Franciscans.[61]

Ælfric described Bishop Aidan as having educated young men in the scriptures and Psalms, but the Old English version of Bede adds further information about where these young men came from: Aidan gave money to redeem men from slavery and 'many of those whom he redeemed with a price he took as his disciples, and by his zeal in training and instructing them, raised them after a time to the priesthood'.[62] Bishop Wilfred, as we have already seen, forcibly abducted the son of non-Christian parents and had him raised in his monastery. Not all of Alfred's schoolboys necessarily wanted to be part of his grand project to provide England with literate monks. The presence of a Viking child in Alfred's monastery, discussed in the chapter on fosterage, also hints at a policy of assimilation through the Church, practised by medieval and later kings. Both Wilfred – attempting to control and convert the native British population in the Midlands – and Alfred – attempting to subdue and assimilate the Danish population in England – might have been adopting similar tactics to those of Charlemagne in pressing children into monasteries.

The documentary sources and archaeological evidence combine to suggest that Anglo-Saxon children enjoyed a relatively prolonged period of childhood, during which adults recognised that they could play to give outlet to their acknowledged childish wilfulness and exuberance, and they were educated according to their own needs for social integration as adults. For most children, that education appears to have been relatively informal and consisted of a combination of play and adult imitation. Young boys learnt to wield weapons, and girls learnt to fill the adult female roles. As previously mentioned, toys specifically designed for children were rare, but it may be that, in a society where children were allowed to play/participate in adult activities, toys were a redundant concept, and children had all the entertainment they needed in their own games and in games with adults.

Schooling for the élite consisted of a combination of literary education and learning the arts of the aristocrats – hunting, recitation of poetry and leadership.

Formal schools did exist in Anglo-Saxon England, but for the majority of élite boys schooling took place within families or under the tutorship of an important individual such as Wilfred or John of Beverley; the concepts of fosterage and education were closely intertwined – the Anglo-Saxon *Prognostications* stated that the eighteenth day of a lunar cycle was good to 'put out children to foster or to school'. A steady supply of boys educated in Latin was important for the Church, but aristocratic girls were by no means excluded from a literary education, as Boniface's female correspondents attest. The education of boys and girls was a commonplace among the élite rather than an exception: the *Prognostications* assume that a boy will be 'booklearned' if he is born on the first moon of a lunar month, a child born on the seventh moon will have a good memory and be learned and literate, a child born on the seventeenth moon will be booklearned if male and learned in words if female, and that the fourth, tenth, fourteenth, seventeenth and eighteenth days of the moon are useful to put a child to school.[63]

Above all, the sources indicate that the Anglo-Saxon parent allowed children the time to play, and recognised that a child's good memory meant that childhood was inextricably linked to education.

CHAPTER 11

Adolescence

A chapter on Anglo-Saxon childhood entitled 'adolescence' could be seen as anachronistic, and might suggest to sociologists of childhood that the writer is attempting to fit a view of the past into a modern and ethnocentric interpretation of childhood. If 'childhood' was the invention of the seventeenth century, as Ariès claimed, then the sociological phenomenon of the 'teenager' has an even shorter history.[1] Jenks recently stated that 'adolescents' or 'teenagers' or 'youths' are an invention post-dating the Second World War, and defined them as a 'quite clearly distinguishable group of people within our society (albeit only within the western world) who occupy a now firmly established twilight zone of the quasi-child or crypto-adult'.[2]

Not all commentators insist that the modern western world should be credited with recognising that children do not pass immediately from childhood to adulthood. Fox claimed that adolescence *can* be traced before the modern period: 'adolescent years were seen as a period of transition to adulthood well before the modern era', but Kleijwegt has argued that a period of transition is not synonymous with 'adolescence' as we use the term today. Kleijwegt suggested that to categorise a group as 'adolescent', that group had to manifest the following: a limited age range; rebellion against the prevailing norms and traditional values of adulthood; exclusion from adult society; personal crisis. According to Kleijwegt, pre-industrial adolescence (from the post-Conquest period) failed to fulfil any of these criteria. Pre-industrial youth embraced a wide age range, from ten up to thirty, and the older and younger members were not differentiated. Pre-industrial youth organisations such as the *charivari* worked to uphold and enforce sexual values and traditional practices. Furthermore, pre-industrial youth frequently worked as servants, and thus were partly integrated into adult society. Kleijwegt concluded that 'adolescence' was missing from the past, but an ambiguous period of 'youth' was part of the development from childhood to adulthood.[3]

Kleijwegt was right to try to define modern adolescence before assessing youth in past cultures, but some of his assertions could be challenged. According to Kleijwegt, medieval youth never fulfilled the criteria for 'adolescents' because they worked as servants and apprentices, and this meant that they could not belong to a discrete, non-child, non-adult group: 'it was considered normal that they [youths] would perform tasks from an early age on, whether they remained at home or were sent away. In performing these tasks, they became equal to

An illustration to Psalm 127: 'Like arrows in the hand of a warrior are the sons of one's youth – happy is the man who has a quiver full of them'. The sons are waiting on their father, who clutches arrows in his hand, at table. (British Library, Harley 603, f. 66v)

adults.'[4] As we have seen, Anglo-Saxon children were sent away to other households, and part of their training for adult life included serving. Such servants were usually termed *cnapa*: in the Old English version of Genesis, when Abraham was preparing to sacrifice his son, he gave orders to his servant – his *cnapa* – to stay behind with the ass.[5] We have already seen, however, that the developmental stages of the male child went from *cild* to *cnapa* to *cniht* before reaching *ylde*. Kleijwegt may be overlooking the possibility that some tasks in the medieval world, particularly those of fetching, carrying and errand-running which he himself draws attention to, were not 'adult' jobs but tasks for the youth, just as today certain paid work, such as delivering newspapers, is customarily work for boys and girls rather than adults. The function of the *cnapa* is considered later in this chapter.

Just as childhood was present in the past as a sociologically structured and determined experience, so too was the transitional period between childhood and adulthood. According to the evidence of the Anglo-Saxon lawcodes, there was a recognised age, culturally established and subject to alteration in subsequent laws – about ten to twelve years old – when children took on adult responsibilities for their actions. In many senses, childhood had ceased at this point, and adulthood had started. However, an 'adulthood' stretching from ten to old age encompasses many stages in human development, not least the continued evolution of the child into the adult. The very fact that the age of legal transition fluctuated from ten to fifteen in the surviving lawcodes is the clearest indicator that Anglo-Saxon lawmakers were uneasily aware that identifying a specific age at which childhood should be thought to have ceased was a difficult problem. Furthermore, the semantic evidence shows that Anglo-Saxons were well aware that 'youth' and 'adulthood' were not synonymous, and a category of 'youth' existed, not perfectly defined but recognised as overlapping with earlier childhood and extending beyond the age of ten into greater maturity. The length of this period of 'adolescence' seems to have been flexible, as one might expect, depending on the maturity of the individual. Adolescence was a phase of life, to which particular characteristics – and, possibly, distinct tasks – were applied.

This interim period between childhood and maturity is most clearly seen in the sources in relation to boys, and the concept of 'adolescence' is most fully explored by the Anglo-Saxon writers in relation to males, perhaps because the duties of a full adult male within Anglo-Saxon society depended upon a level of experience, judgement and economic status that boys just into their teens could not be expected to have.

MALES – *CNAPA* AND *CNIHT*

The terms *cnapa* and *cniht* were usually associated in Anglo-Saxon usage with younger males . In modern English, these translate simply as 'knave' and 'knight', words now carrying a thousand years' worth of semantic meaning, but one still carries the sense of servant from the lowest-ranking court card, and the other bears military overtones. In the following discussion, the functions of the *cnapa* and *cniht* within Anglo-Saxon society are considered, beginning with the idea of the child or adolescent as a warrior.

There are no definite age categories to which the terms *cnapa* and *cniht* were firmly applied, and they clearly had a wide spectrum of meanings, ranging from 'male child' to 'servant' and 'warrior'. As we have seen, where the two terms are used together, the *cnapa* is younger than the *cniht*. There are examples where *cniht* was clearly intended to carry the sense of 'boy' or 'child'. In the Old English *Orosius*, Philippus was sent as a hostage to the Thebans 'although he was a *cniht*'; Hannibal was described as a nine-year-old *cniht*, and Scipio was sent to Spain with an army even though he was a *cniht*.[6] In each of these cases the boy was caught up in warfare, and the point was that, in spite of their extreme youth, they were required to play the part of an adult of military age. The same argument might be made when *cniht* was used as the term to describe the ten-year-old who could be considered a thief in the law of Ine, or the young Osred whom Bede described as an eight-year-old *cniht* when he unexpectedly came to the throne of Northumbria. The use of these terms in Old English to translate Latin texts is instructive. In one homily, *servus* (servant) was translated by *cniht*, and the sense of servitude and junior status is reinforced by the Old English term *leorningcnihta* (learning servant) to translate 'disciple'.[7] The Latin *miles* (soldier) was also translated as *cniht*, and a person of this status was assumed to carry a sword.[8] Furthermore, Ælfric translated *pubis* (adult) by *cniht oðe cnihthad*, in contrast to *inpubis*, translated by an Old English term meaning 'beardless'.[9]

The later Old English texts indicate that, by the eleventh century, there had been some semantic narrowing in the meaning of *cniht*, and its use was being restricted to what was to become its more common meaning in early middle and modern English, that of a warrior with high status. Anglo-Saxon charters were witnessed by men individually identified as *cniht*, and the king called on armies made up of *cnihtas* in the *Anglo-Saxon Chronicle* entry for AD 1094. When William the Conqueror wanted to gather all the powerful men in the land together, the *Chronicle* for AD 1086 listed those men as 'archbishops, bishops, abbots and earls, thanes and *cnihtas*'.[10]

In his investigation into the meaning and context of early Anglo-Saxon weapon burials, Heinrich Harke argued that the inclusion of weapons as part of the grave furniture was symbolic rather than indicating the death of a warrior, since children were buried with weapons. 'Children', in this context, meant juveniles below the age of fifteen. As a corroboration, his database statistics showed that children were buried with 'weapons' from the age of two.[11] It is possible, however, to draw different conclusions from this evidence. Documentary sources suggest that 'childhood' may have been short in the Anglo-Saxon period, and this same archaeological evidence is a strong indicator that 'children' may also have been 'warriors'. It is inconceivable that a two-year-old could have wielded weapons to any good effect, but the only 'weapons' buried with children under seven years of age with any frequency are knives and, less frequently, small- or medium-sized spears. It is doubtful whether knives should be classed as 'weapons' and associated with warriors. Women, too, are buried with knives; they are among the most common of recoverable grave goods, and a more plausible explanation for their presence with children is that they are domestic items, intended for everyday use by everybody. Between the ages of about seven and twelve, weapons are still not a typical male artefact, although single spears, often shorter than the usual adult length, begin to occur with a little more frequency.

The weapons commonly associated with burials between the ages of about twelve to twenty are spears and shields. Harke considers these to represent incomplete weapon sets, not appropriate to the weaponry of a true fighting man. It is only into the twenties that 'full' weapon burials including swords occur, and these are relatively uncommon. It is indeed highly unlikely that these few 'complete' weapon sets represent all the Anglo-Saxon warriors, as Harke argues. There is differentiation in the weapon burial ritual. Boys over the age of about ten or twelve were, according to the lawcodes, legally entitled to adult rights and status. However, throughout the teenage years, male burials, where they include weapons, do not have the full weapon kit. The weapon burial ritual is not 'childlike' for these teenagers, but neither are they accorded full 'adult' status, although it is worth noting that not all males over the age of twenty were buried with full weapon kits either. As we have already seen, part of the child's education for its adult life consisted in learning appropriate skills, and the spears associated with smaller boys might quite reasonably be assumed to be the weapons they were using to hone and refine their spearmanship: they were not symbolic but a relevant and useful training artefact for the boy who would have to be prepared to fight for his lord as an adult.

If we are to argue that the burial ritual represents status in life in some way, and if we also argue that in early Anglo-Saxon England warfare was more or less endemic, then we must further assume that the burial ritual does tell us something about who the warriors were in Anglo-Saxon society, but that we have not found the right model to interpret the evidence. The ritual evidence tells us that 'children' were buried with weapons, but that few men were buried with enough weapons to qualify as warriors. This poses awkward questions as to the nature of burial ritual in Anglo-Saxon England, and Harke bravely wrestles with his statistics to answer the conundrum, deciding in the end that weapon burials do not represent warriors, a conclusion that suggests a wonderful lack of logic on the part of the Anglo-Saxons.

What happens to this equation if we suppose instead that the Anglo-Saxons did bury weapons with the people who used them in life? We must then shift our ground, and redefine our terms. Children appear to have been buried with weapons, but do we know that the Anglo-Saxons prohibited 'children' from fighting? Only a few people were buried with a full variety of weapons, but do we know how many weapons an Anglo-Saxon needed to carry to qualify as a 'warrior'?

Part of the problem – the need to create an explanation for the appearance of weapons with the burials of children – may be, once more, self-created by the inability of archaeologists to define their terms. The case of the analysis of the cemetery at Berinsfield, Oxfordshire, is an instructive example of how misleading and ethnocentric terminology may confuse interpretation of the data and create unnecessary complications. In the Berinsfield site report the reader's attention is drawn to the fact that both male children and adults were buried with weapons. In one table the results of calculating spear-shaft length by measuring from the recorded position of the spear to the foot end of the grave are presented. Attention is specifically drawn to the presence of two 'child burials' with spears, burials 61 and 128. Elsewhere in the report a possible household group, where the key specifically differentiates between 'male adult with weapons' and 'juvenile with weapons'. The juvenile graves are burials 29 and 61. The ages at death of these non-adults is given elsewhere in the report as eleven to twelve years old for grave 61, around nine for grave 128, and about sixteen for grave 29.[12]

So what are these tables supposed to tell us about Anglo-Saxon weapon burial practice? The point seems to be that both children and adults were buried with weapons, the inference being that weapon burial was symbolic rather than indicative of any ability to carry and use weapons. For this hypothesis to be tenable, the writer must be able to demonstrate that 'children' are identified according to the Anglo-Saxon interpretation of the concept, and it must also be demonstrable that Anglo-Saxon culture insisted that their concept of childhood precluded the participation of this group in battle. It is absolutely clear from the Anglo-Saxon lawcodes that none of the burials identified by Harke as 'children' were unequivocally children in Anglo-Saxon terms. A case might just be argued for burial 128, who, at about nine years of age, was on the cusp of being under-age by the limit set in the earliest lawcodes, and the small size of the spear with this burial indicates that this individual might still have been regarded as a *cnapa*, but there is no such excuse for grave 29, whose occupant, even by Æthelstan's generous measure, was definitely an Anglo-Saxon adult. As for the assumption that boys would not have been included in battles, it may fit laudable modern western ideals, but recent wars make it undeniable that many cultures are happy to send armies of boys into war.[13]

The attempt by Æthelstan and his *witan* or counsellors to raise the age of culpability for crime is interesting in view of the assumptions it makes about the potential threat posed by a 'child' under the age of fifteen. The various clauses to the law state that the under-age offender will incur the adult punishment if he 'tries to defend himself or tries to run away and refuses to give himself up. Then, he shall be struck down whether his offence is great or small.' The lawmakers apparently expected some 'children' under the age of fifteen to attempt to defend themselves, presumably with weapons, but does the ritual distinction in weapon burial between those under the age of ten to twelve (buried with small spears) and those over that threshold (buried with adult-sized shield and spear, but not swords) reflect attitudes in life: were children over the age of ten to twelve expected to fight like, or with, older Anglo-Saxon males?

Historical parallels suggest that the possibility that this did happen is very real. The *Chronicle* of Thomas de Wykes noted that the fighting supporters of the barons in the wars against Henry II were young men 'who truly deserve the epithet boys, and whom the barons could mould, like soft wax, however they wished'.[14] In the same vein, Walter of Guisborough described the students at Oxford, who were unlikely to have been over fifteen years of age, taking part in the Battle of Northampton in April 1264: 'They wrought greater havoc against the attackers than the barons themselves, with slings and bows and arrows.'[15]

In times past, it was standard practice for young boys to be trained to fight at an early age, and to be expected to participate in action as soon as they had the physical strength. In the medieval period, children were sent away for education at around the age of six, and that education included teaching a boy how to ride and bear himself as a knight.[16] This age of education tallies neatly with the age threshold for burial with small spears in Anglo-Saxon graves. After six years of training, there is little reason to suppose that twelve-year-olds were unable to use full-sized spears. Later medieval boys in training for knighthood knew how to ride by the time they were seven, and had received partial military training by the time they were twelve. Full military training began at twelve, and by fifteen it was complete.[17]

Stephanus's *Life of Wilfred* described how, at the age of fourteen, the young lad 'obtained arms and horses and garments for himself and left the parental home to fit himself for the royal court, there to petition the queen for her patronage' to enable him to enter a monastery.[18] It is unlikely that this was the first time that Wilfred had picked up his weapons – his training must have started earlier. The hagiographer does not note this as a case of startling precocity, which may imply that he expected his audience to receive this detail as a commonplace.

Wilfred is not an isolated example of a teenager carrying weapons. Guthlac left his home to become a warrior at the age of fifteen: 'A noble desire for command burned in his young breast, he remembered the valiant deeds of heroes of old, and as though awakening from sleep, he changed his disposition and gathering bands of followers took up arms.'[19] Although his chronicler mentions nothing of it in his education, Guthlac must have been trained as a warrior competent in the use of arms years before this phase of actual fighting. Furthermore, not only did Guthlac set out to fight, but he actually led a warband. Who were his followers? Is it likely that seasoned 'adult' warriors would have followed this 'child' into battle, regardless of his noble status, unless he had previously shown his abilities as a fighter? If older men were not the followers of this young soldier, were his companions then of a similar age, or even younger? Gangs of intimidating teenagers were implied in other contexts. The Old English translation of Matthew 11:16 turned children sitting in the market place calling to their playmates into 'youths [*cnapa*] sitting in the porch calling to their peers'.[20] The choice of the word *cnapa*, rather than *cild*, suggests that the translator was not envisaging children playing with their noisy friends, but had in mind older boys, wasting time in their gangs in the fashion familiar on street corners today.

Guthlac's successful career as leader of a warband came to an abrupt halt when he underwent a change of heart and renounced his buccaneering life in favour of the Church. Perhaps his renunciation was connected with a defeat that the chronicler does not care to mention, for when 'British hosts' approached Guthlac in his hermitage at a later date, Guthlac was able to understand their speech, 'for in years gone by he had been an exile [hostage?] among them'.[21] Alternatively, Guthlac may have decided he was now too old for that kind of lifestyle and so gave up arms, a possibility that will be returned to.

In spite of Bede's efforts to gloss over episodes in Cuthbert's early life it seems that Cuthbert, too, spent some part of his childhood familiarising himself with the use of weapons. An anonymous chronicler suggested that Cuthbert entered a monastery in the year Aidan died, giving an age for Cuthbert of around seventeen. He may have seen some kind of military service before this time because he arrived at the monastery riding a horse and carrying a travelling spear, much to the consternation of the monks, who assumed he was a warrior. It is noteworthy that the carrying of a spear alone was enough to mark Cuthbert as a warrior and potential threat to the members of the monastery. Bede omitted this material altogether, perhaps not wishing to associate his hero with the activities that the anonymous writer took for granted as an accepted part of a youth's upbringing, though even the anonymous writer sensed the inappropriate nature of such behaviour in a saint, because he, too, glossed over any further episodes: 'the rest of the abundant works of the flower of his youth I pass over in silence . . . how when dwelling in a camp with the army in the face of the enemy he yet lived abundantly all the time'.[22] At seventeen, Cuthbert had apparently already spent some time on the front line of fighting, was assumed to be a warrior by monks, and was ready to give up his previous activities within an army in favour of the Church.

Turning to the semantic evidence, far from drawing distinctions between 'child' and 'warrior', the difficulty lies in disentangling these concepts. Although *cild* was frequently used to mean 'child', it also had the connotation of 'young warrior', a confusion of terms that can hardly be coincidental; it is this second usage that survived into the Middle Ages in such appellations as 'Childe Roland' and 'Childe Horn', two knights of medieval romance. In the same way, *cniht* could mean a young male, or in a more specific sense it could mean a 'servant', 'retainer' or 'henchman' (cf. the German *knecht*), or even 'ruffian' in the sense of 'lad' – this was certainly an eleventh-century usage. The direction to a cemetery 'where the *cnihtas* lie' in the Witney charter-bounds of 1044 may refer to an execution cemetery of a gang of young offenders, with the modern sense of 'the lads' or 'the boys', and may actually identify the nearby cemetery within the Roman villa at Shakenoak where excavation revealed a group of thirteen graves. All but one were certainly male and four showed signs of weapon injury to their heads and bodies, although most were aged in their early thirties rather than late teens.[23] Other place names with *cnapa* and *cniht* might fall into the same category.[24] One might also consider the use of *puer* in the Bayeux tapestry: Odo of Bayeux *comfortat pueros* – that is, 'urges on the lads'.[25] The dual meaning of the words *cild* and *cniht* may reflect an actual blurring of the roles of young teenagers, still children in many senses, but having adult responsibilities. The dual meaning is exemplified in the *Exeter Book*, Riddle 26, where the anthropomorphic sword laments that: 'I dare not hope that a child will avenge me with the life of my murderer if some enemy assails me in war, nor will a family be augmented by the children I beget afterwards.'[26] Here the word for 'child' is *bearn*, a word that embraces concepts of progeny and of one who will fight in battle to avenge a death. The concepts of 'child-as-immature-offspring' and 'child-as-avenging-fighter' are inextricably interwoven.

The late Old English poem *The Battle of Maldon*, written with the immediacy of first-hand observation and certainly devised shortly after the disastrous Anglo-Saxon encounter with the Vikings in 991, describes the types of warrior bravely fighting alongside their ageing leader Byrhtnoth, Ealdorman of Essex. Byrhtnoth's entourage included the old faithful retainer, the low-status churl, and a valuable member of the warband called Wulfmaer: 'By his side a youth not grown to manhood was standing, a boy in battle, the son of Wulfstan, young Wulfmaer, who very bravely plucked the bloody spear out of [Byrhtnoth]. He threw the hard spear back again. The point penetrated so that he who had just now severely struck his lord lay dead on the ground.'[27] Here, there can be no equivocation about the meaning of *cniht* – he is a boy, specifically stated as not being fully grown to adulthood even by Anglo-Saxon terms, yet the writer has no doubt that his audience will accept his presence in the thick of battle, fighting by the side of the war leader. Wulfmaer may be a boy, but he is no novice. He is a seasoned warrior, fully capable of seizing the spear thrown by the enemy and hurling it back to deadly effect. Nor does the format of the epic suggest that Wulfmaer is unusual: he takes his place in the list of combatants as an example of a type.

Another youth is given a place among Byrhtnoth's personal soldiers: 'The son of Ælfric urged them forward, a soldier young in years, with these words, Ælfwine then spoke: he spoke bravely . . .'.[28] This youth Ælfwine is presented as a young warrior, yet old enough to have supped at the mead table with the other warriors. He boasts that he is of good Mercian stock, and that he will not shame his people, and this boast of a foreigner to fight for their lord stings other warriors around him into braver action. It may be stretching a point, but the situation of Ælfwine, a youthful warrior fighting under the lordship of a famous foreign earl, bears distinct parallels with the youthful exploits of Guthlac or Cuthbert, leaving home to seek excitement and fame by the use of their weapons, perhaps in the service of a foreign lord.

The participation of boys just into their teens in battle seems, then, to have been an acceptable possibility to the Anglo-Saxons, and it could be argued that this was an anticipated step on the path to becoming a full adult; that it was in fact not the end of, but a part of the rites of passage. Fascinating parallels are suggested by the evidence for juvenile behaviour in early medieval Ireland, revealed by the documentary sources. Ireland suffered from the activities of gangs of lawless young warriors, operating outside the boundaries of the community (the *tuath*). Fosterage for freeborn males in Ireland would finish at about fourteen years old, but thereafter the boys were in social limbo. They lacked the wealth to establish their own families, so they joined the *fian*, 'an independent organisation of predominantly landless, unmarried, unsettled, and young men given to hunting, warfare, and sexual licence outside the *tuath*'.[29] At around twenty years of age, often on the acquisition of an inheritance through the death of older male relatives, a young man would finally join the group of married property owners.

This pattern of behaviour by young, underemployed men – of forming gangs, of being sexually active and irresponsible and of behaving in an antisocial manner outside the control of their parents – is a familiar modern picture, but one that was also described in the Anglo-Saxon era. Bede, in a letter to Archbishop Egbert dated 734, complained that too much land was being given to monasteries for no good purpose. The result of this, he pointed out, was that less land was now owned by thanes and other noblemen, and the tracts of wasted monastic land could not be used to levy an army. Worse, there was now 'a complete lack of places where the sons of nobles or of veteran thegns can receive an estate; and thus [they are] unoccupied and unmarried, though the time of puberty is over'. As in the case of the Irish youth, true adulthood and marriage could not be achieved without wealth, and the landless, idle and prospectless adolescents of Bede's time were spending their energies in going abroad, causing trouble or sleeping around, even with nuns.[30] The worst case of such wanton adolescent behaviour on record is surely that of Osred. Osred came to the throne of Deira and Bernicia on the death of his father in 705 when he was aged about eight years old. Although Bede welcomed him to the throne by likening him to Josiah of the Old Testament, Osred's reign of eleven years until his untimely death was not without blemish. In a letter from Boniface to King Æthelbald of about 746/7, Osred was described as 'driven by the spirit of wantonness, fornicating, and in his frenzy debauching throughout the nunneries virgins consecrated to God, until with a contemptible and despicable death he lost his glorious kingdom, his young life and his lascivious soul'.[31]

The military dress of the early medieval Irish juveniles may also shed light on the Anglo-Saxon evidence. Young Irish warriors travelled light, with spears and perhaps shields. There are further parallels in the panels on the Gundestrup cauldron, where again the warriors are shown as lightly clad and lightly armed. Tacitus's *Germania* and Caesar's *De Bello Gallico* laid considerable emphasis upon bands of lightly clad or naked young footsoldiers devoted to war and brigandage and who were initiated by being presented with spear and shield.[32] A courageous soldier, in the Anglo-Saxon heroic tradition, demonstrated his bravery by his lack of armour and weapons. Christ on the cross became, in the Old English poem *The Dream of the Rood*, an Anglo-Saxon warrior stripped naked for the battle. Beowulf famously fought his successful battle with the monster Grendel in hand-to-hand combat, ignoring the shields, swords and spears scattered around the hall. The enigmatic figure on a belt buckle from the cemetery at Finglesham was also clearly naked except for a belt, and his weaponry consisted only of a pair of spears and a totemic helmet – no armour, no shield and no sword.

The light weaponry of young Celtic warriors exactly tallies with the kinds of weapons usually associated with 'children' over the age of ten at the time of death in the Anglo-Saxon mortuary ritual, and with the weaponry associated with the young Anglo-Saxon saints and recognised as the emblem of warrior status. When Guthlac, a semi-orphan with no prospects of immediate inheritance – his father had remarried – set out for adventure, his motivation appears remarkably like that of his Celtic counterparts. He gathered a band of followers and proceeded to amass a sizeable fortune through pillage and plunder; more than enough on which to retire to a respectable married adult life. Equally, the later chivalric parallels are irresistible; for those raised in a milieu of epic heroes and battles for treasure, youth was essentially a time to do battle and win fame.[33] The writer of Guthlac's *Life* may have been drawing a significant parallel when he noted that Guthlac, arriving at his island retreat at twenty-six, came 'as though to a home inherited from his father'.[34] In the secular world, Guthlac at this age might well have expected, after a youth of violence, to arrive at manhood and an inheritance, but within the world of the Church, his hermit's island has become his kingdom and inheritance.

The presence of shields and spears in the graves of Anglo-Saxon teenagers cannot be taken as an empty token in the burial ritual, nor as a sign of adult imposition of non-child-related symbols, nor may these burials be taken as proof that weapons were not necessarily buried with warriors. The small spears buried with boys under the age of ten to twelve are best interpreted as practice weapons, and combinations of spears and shields found in the graves of teenagers represent the full, functional weapon complement of these young warriors. Weapon burials with 'children' are simply explicable as functional items, indicative of the fact that for their possessors, the natural progression from juvenile to adult involved a period of trial by battle.

Although boys from the age of six were buried with small spears, and from twelve would have had spears and shields, the most prized weapon, the sword, was not as a rule buried with teenagers. This seems to imply a contradiction: legally a boy held adult responsibility by the age of ten, and was expected to behave as an adult in battle at least by seventeen, but did not, in some respects, achieve full integration into male adult society until a later date. The same phenomenon was witnessed in the later medieval period, when young men

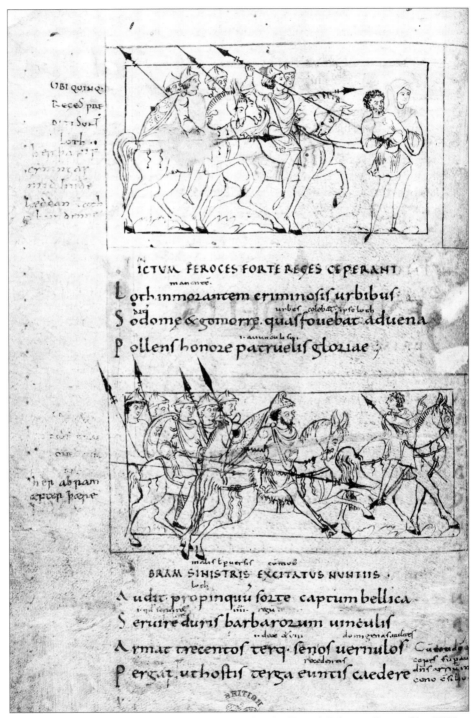

A lightly armed young soldier leads Abraham into battle. (British Library, Cotton Cleo VIII, f. 4v)

became warriors at a majority of fifteen, but could not own a fief without a guardian (and therefore effectively could not marry) until twenty-one years old. The discrepancy between the social expectation that young noblemen would participate in battle and their actual emotional development has been identified as the explanation for older knights referring to the younger warriors as 'child'.[35]

The documentary sources indicate that occasionally the 'rules' of weapon-bearing could be bent to confer special honour on élite children who were outside the 'normal' social rules. Asser recorded that Alfred was given a sword by the Pope at the age of four, and Asser interpreted this as conferring the status of heir to the throne on Alfred – in ritual terms, the sword was not given to a child but to a future king. This also appears to have been the motive when Alfred recognised Æthelstan as his heir by a sword-giving when Æthelstan was not much older than Alfred had been when he had received his own sword.[36]

Some corroborative evidence for the concept of a flexible interim period between childhood and adulthood, sharing characteristics of both, may also be gleaned from the illustrations in Anglo-Saxon manuscripts. In the *Harley Psalter*, the illustration to Psalm 102 shows a group of children making their way up a hill. One, who is the same size as his companions, and therefore certainly a child, is alone in not looking up the hill – he has turned back to help the slowest child. It may be significant that this helpful child is the only one not wearing the distinctive short tunic of children in the *Harley Psalter*. Instead, he wears the adult cloak. This child, presented in a caring role within the group rather than in the passive, nurtured role more usually shown for children in the *Psalter*, has been given an adult dress to represent different status to the other children – perhaps élite, and therefore with greater 'adult' attributes than the others, or perhaps this is one of the older children, still younger than the age of transition but verging on adulthood in his dress and behaviour.

Earlier in this chapter the way in which young males developed their warrior skills from boyhood onwards was discussed. Part of their secular education included the acquirement of these skills, and secular adolescent males, like their later medieval counterparts, learnt some of the required skills for noble adult life by serving in the courts of the nobility. Lower-status males may also have trained as servants in the households of the richer families, partly to improve their chances of survival in the world – once they had joined an élite household they were under the protection of their lord – but also because they had neither the resources nor the experience, and probably could not look forward to a sufficiently significant inheritance, to start a household of their own. Kussmaul, in a study of servants in early modern England, suggested that 'the institution of servants and apprentices helped solve the problem of what to do with children between puberty and marriage'.[37] Young male servants are depicted in the manuscript illustrations: 'Nebuchadnezzar at dinner' from the *Winchester Bible* shows three Hebrew children waiting on the king. One carries a cup and cover, while the other two boys clutch the tablecloth, ready to spring into action when called upon. From the *Biblioteca Apostolica* in the Vatican comes a clear example: a young man offers service to a seated man with a sword. The caption reads:

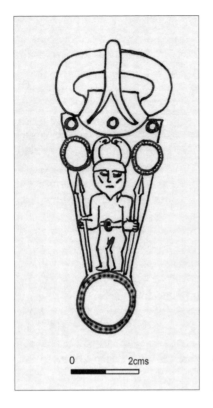

0   2cms

A lightly armed man, carrying two spears and wearing only a belt and helmet, shown on a gold buckle from Finglesham, Kent.

'*Saulus adolescens*'. Service within a household, as already discussed, was a career step in learning courtly behaviour not confined only to the post-Conquest period, and was one which extended the period before full admission to adulthood.

FEMALES

Tracing the transition of girls from childhood to adulthood is significantly more problematic than for boys, and may indicate that girls had a much shorter period of adjustment between the two states. In part, this may be because girls, from an early age, started to engage in 'adult' female tasks. In addition to childbearing, women in Anglo-Saxon England appear to have had one overriding function – the production of cloth. Spinning, weaving and sewing were the activities that defined the gender. The neutral Old English *man* was given masculine gender by the addition of a weapon to *weapman*, while the female compound was created by the addition of weaving: *wifman*. Girls probably took up some aspect of textile craft from an early age, and by the time they were adolescent, they must have been as fully active as weavers as adult women. In the Old English *Life of St Margaret*, the translator stayed faithful to the Latin version of the text, but to the story that Margaret went out tending sheep with the other girls when she was fifteen, one Old English version adds that she was also spinning. Looking after sheep was not, in the eyes of the translator, a full-time occupation for a teenage girl, and there were more important tasks she ought to be undertaking at the same time.[38]

Female children were sometimes referred to as *cild* (occasionally *wifcild*), *maeden* (maiden) or *faemne*. Both *mæden* and *fæmne* were used to translate the Latin *virgo*, and both Old English terms are used specifically in the context of virginity. The Old English Bede translated the Latin for 'the immaculate virgin Mary' (*semperque virginis Mariae*) as '*ðaere unmælan fæmnan Sancte Mariam*', while in a comparable context, Ælfric uses the term *mæden* specifically to mean 'virgin' in a discussion of the vexed question of Mary, the virgin mother: '*mæden* [virgin] she was before the pregnancy . . . and *mæden* [virgin] she was afterwards'.[39] Ælfric also showed that, as far as he was concerned, even the distinctions in life stages for girls offered by Latin vocabulary did not translate into English: in his *Grammar*, he translated both *puella* and *virgo* as *mæden*, while *mulier* translated into *wif*.[40] For Ælfric, 'girl' and 'virgin' were synonymous, indicating that for the Anglo-Saxon girl, the transition into adulthood was abrupt and signalled not by gradual change or even by any chronological achievement, but by the act of sex or marriage. There may be some ambiguity here: 'marriage', or at least, leaving your father's household for the household of another man, might have been of more importance in the distinction between *mæden* and *wif* than the presence or absence of virginity, because in the lawcodes, a girl who had been raped was still not classed as a *wif*.

For girls, the transition from childhood to adulthood took place without great impact on the documentary sources, perhaps because the movement of a girl from the home of her parents to the home of her husband had little political impact. The problem for Anglo-Saxon society, as for many others, was how to deal with young adolescent men, too young or poor to establish their own families, but full of youthful energy and too self-confident to be governed by their parents. Many of the problems were overcome by sending boys to learn service in a household or to join the Church, but the Anglo-Saxon record reveals that the tendency of adolescent males to gang together in aggressive, unlawful, excessive and intimidating groups is a teenage phenomenon not restricted to the modern western world.

Conclusion

'In the Middle Ages, children were generally ignored until they were no longer children.'[1]

In the final analysis, what may be said of the position of children within Anglo-Saxon society? Does Anita Schorsch's comment above that children were 'generally ignored' hold true, or did Anglo-Saxon parents have a 'concept' of childhood? Were children regarded callously as economic commodities; were they sentimentalised; were they regarded with superstition as being in touch with the spirit world because of their liminal place on the threshold of the adult world? When were they considered to 'count' as human beings, and did the mysteries and horrors of childbirth and child death lead to better or worse treatment of the child?

The documentary and archaeological sources provide some evidence that parents did invest love and care in their children, although their ideas about nurturing children were not necessarily in accordance with our views on best practice. The child þryþyyfu, an only child, was intended for the Church even before conception. However, the knowledge that their child was destined to leave their care for the monastery at a relatively early age did not prevent her parents from lavishing care and love on the girl, to the extent that she became known by her nickname Leoba (the dear one).[2] When John of Beverley cured a young man of scurvy, baldness, deafness and dumbness, he generously offered to let the man remain with his entourage, but the youth preferred to return home to his family village; in this case, his affection for the parents who had reared him in spite of his infirmities and deformities far outweighed the opportunity to be part of the prestigious household of the bishop.[3]

Anglo-Saxon parents seem to have recognised and assimilated the fact that their children would inevitably have to leave the family at some point and make their own fortunes outside their control and care, but this knowledge only served to emphasise that, however lovingly you reared a child, the purpose of your care was to produce an adult whose future was not yours to protect. This poignant message is clearly enunciated in one of the few pieces of Anglo-Saxon literature to evaluate the relationships between parents and children:

It very often happens through God's powers that a man and wife bring a child into the world, and dress him in colours and train him and teach him until the time comes, as it does with the passing of the years, that the young and lively limbs and members are mature. In this way his father and mother lead him along and guide his footsteps and provide for him and clothe him – but God knows what the years will bring him as he grows up. For an unfortunate one, it happens that he dies tragically in his youthful prime. He shall be eaten by the wolf, the grizzled hunter of the wasteland; then his mother will mourn his going hence. Such things are not man's to control.'[4]

Many historians of childhood have followed the dogma that high mortality rates among children would lead to parents having a lower emotional investment in their offspring.[5] But not all historians agree, and the sources indicate that the Anglo-Saxons themselves would not have perceived their reactions as callous or unfeeling.[6] King Alfred, in his translation of Gregory's *Pastoral Care*, was moved to add the comment 'what sight is more intolerable than the death of a child before its father's eyes?' as the worst possible pain he could imagine, and one with which he must have been certain his Anglo-Saxon readers would have sympathised.[7]

In both the inhumation and the cremation rituals of the pagan period, children are buried with fewer grave goods than adults. Some of the grave goods are found only with adults and are unlikely to be found with children, such as weaponry, scales and multiples of brooches or keys in inhumations, or iron tweezers, bronze sheet and ivory in cremations.[8] Children are not buried with their own specific range of grave goods. Within the burial ritual in the pagan period, in both inhumation and cremation contexts, they were treated as low-status adults, or even, as Richards suggested, as 'small adults'.[9] This poses problems for the interpretation of a child's status in the burial ritual. If children were buried as adults, with the same types of grave goods as adults, then, as Richards noted, status must have been ascribed at birth, to the extent that a young child could be granted the same range of grave goods as an adult.[10] There are problems with this interpretation. Children were much more likely to be buried in the lower-status range of the cemetery, but some infants are in higher-status groups – are we therefore to suppose that more infants belonging to low-status families died in infancy than higher-status babies?

At the same time it is clear that children were not simply buried as adults; they could never be ascribed the highest adult status while they were young, because some grave goods – horse and cow bone in cremations, or swords in inhumations, for example – were never buried with infants and younger children. There are correlations between age and grave goods in the inhumation ritual, but in terms of children it is a negative correlation based on artefacts not included in the graves of certain juvenile age categories. In the cremation ritual, there is a correlation between the size of urn and the age of the person placed in it – the smallest vessels for infants, the tallest for old adults – but in terms of grave goods, children are again differentiated by the goods they do not have.[11] Family status is not the whole answer in studying children's graves – they may have been buried within an adult-centred ritual, but age had a part to play in the choice of size and range of adult artefacts buried with children.

Although it is hard to argue for child-specific grave goods or artefacts associated only with children, nonetheless there are indications that some of the adult grave goods were considered more appropriate for children than others. Audrey Meaney noted that pots can be found associated with children in cemeteries where ceramics were otherwise not included.[12] At the cemetery of Castledyke, Barton-on-Humber, it was noted that the most likely person to be buried with a pot in the sixth and seventh centuries was a small child, and the least likely was an adult male, and this link, it was suggested, was indicative of the functional relationship between the parent and child: pottery vessels were used as containers for food and drink, so 'in the case of infants and children, the association of pottery vessels in general may be with the whole concept of "the hearth", for one of the obvious characteristics of a child is its dependence on adults for its food and general nurture'.[13] The burial ritual defined the child by the function or social role in which adults engaged in relation to the child; the ritual reflected the adult as nurturer.

Although a 'concept' of childhood, as a particular state requiring special treatment, may have existed in the Anglo-Saxon period, the evidence provides no clear indication of strict and coherent rites of passage for the Anglo-Saxon child. Baptism was certainly a rite with associated legislation to demand that it be carried out within a specified period after the birth, but it marked a change in spiritual state, not an age threshold, and adults could receive baptism as well as children. It could be argued that the lack of any 'official' token or act to mark a rite of passage might mean that there was no clear idea of when one stage in life ended and another began, and therefore there was no clear recognition of any stage – childhood blended into adolescence, and adolescence into adulthood in a seamless and unremarkable flow; unremarkable, because one state was not significantly different from another. To argue this, however, is to demand that past societies should fit themselves into neat categories for our benefit, whereas in reality, a concept of life stages and a lack of definitive rites of passage are not mutually exclusive ideas. In real life, people mature at different ages, and the type of society they have to prepare for in childhood may be more or less complex depending on a number of factors, including status and environment. Shulamith Shahar has rightly stressed that all societies are obliged, by a biological imperative, to recognise that children, unlike adults, need nurturing, but the point at which that nurturing needs to cease varies according to the individual.[14] In fact, for the individual, many moments go into marking the shift from childhood to adulthood. For Anglo-Saxon boys, it may have been the time they were given their first weapons, or the time they moved out of the short tunic and received adult cloaks. For the teenager Wilfred, the moment when he left his father's house must have marked a personal turning point. As Barbara Hanawalt emphasised, 'not one ceremony but a whole range of changes defines a life stage'.[15]

There may not have been clearly marked threshold ages and rites of passage associated with children, but the documentary sources do indicate a persistent belief that children were not like adults in their behaviour or temperament, exhibiting a recognisable set of characteristics peculiarly their own. The ideal child, in Asser's view, was exemplified by King Alfred's children. As they grew up, Asser noted that Edward and Ælfthryth continued to show 'humility, friendliness and gentleness to all compatriots and foreigners, and . . . great obedience to their father'.[16] The documentary sources indicate that normal children were very different and were considered naturally uncontrolled in their emotions. Guthlac's chronicler had little time for the games of children – their whistling like birds and imitating the behaviour of others – and there is a sense of patient understanding of the rowdy and exaggerated behaviour of their young pupils among the bishops and abbesses. Rudolf of Fulda's *Life of St Leofgyth* recounted that at the monastery of Wimborne, a certain nun who was made prioress had such a zealous enthusiasm for discipline and a strict life that she was hated by the nuns, especially the young. When the prioress died, the young nuns vented their anger by jumping on the mound of earth over the grave and cursing the woman. When Tette, the mother of the community, discovered this, she restrained the unreasonable behaviour of the young nuns with 'strong reproof'.[17] Uncontrolled passions, even within an ecclesiastical setting, were considered to be part of the state of youth. Even when these uncontrolled passions became a form of violent madness – as with the youth Hwaetred, brought to St Guthlac by Hwaetred's wretched parents in hope of a cure – the parents continued to look after and care about their demoniac and outrageous children.

Incidents such as the case of Hwaetred in the *Lives* of the saints, coupled with the archaeological evidence, make it clear that Anglo-Saxon children were not merely cared for in a perfunctory way but were actively loved and supported by their parents and by other members of their family and community. The mortuary evidence demonstrates that even children suffering from chronic and debilitating illnesses were given every care, and similar cases occur in the miracle stories. Parents, both mother and father, are usually the ones to visit the saint in search of a miracle for sons and daughters, but not always. In one instance in the life of John of Beverley, a mason's child suffered a crushing fall, and it was the concerned workmates who rushed to the saint for help. The desperation of parents in the documentary sources when their children are sick is a constant theme. St Wilfred only raised a dead infant to life because the mother created such a fuss in front of an audience of pagans that Wilfred was left with no choice but to perform the miracle. In the case of the abbess's daughter who was healed by John of Beverley, John at first refused to intervene: the child was going to die, and that was the end of the story. It was only because the mother absolutely insisted that John do something that the child was cured. In terms of the literary narrative, John's refusal to heal the child and his eventual agreement because of the mother's pleas emphasised how impossible the cure was, how modest John was, and how great was the faith of the abbess in his powers, but nonetheless if mothers in the Anglo-Saxon world in general invested little emotional care in their offspring, this tale could not have been told.

These are examples of parents caring for their children, but the case of the mad youth Hwaetred implied that the sick child and his family were allowed a certain amount of indulgence by the community as a whole. Hwaetred, we are told, was still living at home under the care of his parents. This would not be so astonishing

An adult female cradles a child in her arms, part of a mass burial from Lechlade, Gloucestershire.

if the child had not already murdered three men in his madness. It is not simply that the parents were able to protect the mad child from vengeful kin – was there perhaps some waiving of the blood feud in view of Hwaetred's age and sickness? – but that they continued to look after him even though he appeared to be subject to violent and uncontrollable bouts of temper. The parents' hope was that Hwaetred would die or be cured rather than continue as he was, but given the devastating consequences of Hwaetred's illness and their continued care of their child, their wish for his death cannot be seen as callous, and their joy at the child's cure cannot be in doubt.

Within the literary construct of the *Lives*, parents cared deeply even about their sick children; they expressed grief at the illnesses and sufferings of their children, and even people who were not immediate members of the family would rush to help a child in pain. The lawcodes, too, corroborate the implications of the archaeological and hagiographical evidence that parents would naturally take on long-term care of their sick children rather than abandon them. A law of Alfred's demanded that: 'If anyone is born dumb or deaf, so that he cannot deny or confess his sins, his father shall pay compensation for his misdeeds.' Since a child was not considered culpable for his crimes until he reached the age of twelve, one has to assume that the lawcode legislated for parents who had raised a handicapped child from birth to adulthood, and were still looking after that child. This may give an insight into Anglo-Saxon definitions of what differentiated a child from an adult, and may hint that the distinction rested on questions of intellectual, as well as biological maturity. Writing in the seventeenth century, Locke argued for the first time that children were not born with innate knowledge, and that adulthood should be equated with full rationality, so that the achievement of adulthood depended on a state of mind rather than on chronological age. Locke followed through this argument to concede that in these terms some adults – 'innocents' and 'madmen' – remained in a state that naturally defined childhood.[18] The Anglo-Saxon legislators and the community at large may never have articulated this view, but the practical result of the legislation, and the hints given by the story of Hwaetred, give indisputable evidence that the Anglo-Saxon approach to childhood was based on more than crude observations of age or sexual maturity, and that, in turn, there was more to joining adult society than being physically fit for labour and ready to procreate.

Anglo-Saxon society, from the pre-Christian period onward, demanded intellectual competence and personal responsibility and accountability from its members. Children were excluded from this adult group because they were not intellectually competent to join it. There was no clearly fixed age for joining adult society, because, as exemplified by the lawcode of Æthelstan, who desperately tried to legislate to protect teenage boys whose crimes would earn an adult the death penalty, there was an acute understanding that individuals reached a point of intellectual readiness for the complexities of Anglo-Saxon society at different ages, and that for some – the mad, or the physically disabled – the point at which they could take a full and responsible part in the adult world would never come, and their caretakers or parents would always be guardians and representatives of their welfare and actions.

Not all children had a happy or nurtured childhood in the Anglo-Saxon period, any more than they do today, and for some their childhood experiences could be grim. A number of children, like adults, were sold into slavery: the most famous slaves in English history were the young Deiran boys found in the market place in Rome by Pope Gregory the Great, who were recorded as being the inspiration for the Augustinian mission to convert the Anglo-Saxons to Christianity. Slavery was endemic in early medieval society, and men, women and children could be captured as part of war booty and sold into slavery. On occasion, it appears that children and adults were sold into slavery by unscrupulous characters for the revenue they could raise: Wulfstan in his *Sermon of the Wolf to the English* written in about 1014 complained that '. . . poor men are deceived and cruelly defrauded and sold far and wide out of this country into the power of foreigners, although quite innocent, and children in the cradle are enslaved for petty theft by cruel injustice widely throughout this people'.[19] Wulfstan was haranguing the populace at a time when, he felt, good, Christian values were being compromised and would lead inevitably to the wrath of God, or at least the arrival of more Vikings from the north, so his comments that babies in their cradles were accused of theft might be taken with a pinch of salt, were it not for a similar statement in the laws of King Canute: 'It has been the custom until now for grasping persons to treat a child which lay in the cradle, even though it had never tasted food, as though it were fully intelligent: but I strictly forbid such a thing henceforth.' Wulfstan had great political influence over Canute, but there is no reason to suppose that Canute's law was an empty echo of Wulfstan's polemic.

Balthilde, another famous Anglo-Saxon slave whose servitude in the Merovingian court led to her royal marriage, was only about fourteen when Erchinoald, Neustrian mayor of the palace, married her to Clovis II in about 650, so she must have become a slave when she was still a child. An earlier law of King Ine of Kent stated that, if a man stole with the knowledge of his household, all were to go into slavery, and it may be that Canute's law reflected an unscrupulous or overzealous application of this law.

Not all children sold into slavery lost touch with their family or were abandoned by their relations. In about 718, Brihtwold, Archbishop of Canterbury, was engaged in a lengthy correspondence with Forthhere, Bishop of Sherbourne, in an attempt to redeem a captive: 'Since my petition, which I made in your presence to the venerable Abbot Beorwold about the ransoming of a captive girl, who has kinsmen among us, has contrary to my expectation, proved in vain, and I am importuned afresh by their entreaties, I have considered it best to send this letter to you by the brother of the girl, Eppa by name.' Three hundred shillings, equivalent to the highest class of *wergild*, were offered in payment, so that 'she can pass the remainder of her life with her relations, not in the sadness of servitude, but in the joy of liberty'.[20]

Any idea that Anglo-Saxon childhood 'did not exist' or that children were given little time to be children in the period cannot be sustained. Both girls and boys were loved by their families and were educated during their childhood to prepare them for their lives as adults. Girls seem to have entered life more abruptly than boys: for a girl the main rite of passage from childhood to adulthood was marriage. Children were recognised as different from adults, but childhood was never sentimentalised. Children had their own characteristics and their own games, but it was not a world apart from adulthood. Just as in the burial ritual age led to the acquisition of more adult grave goods, so childhood was assumed to be a time during which the child learnt and acquired adult attributes. The ultimate goal of childhood was to grow to a better state: that of a fully functional adult. Ælfric's view of what would happen when people who died as children were resurrected in the afterlife is an instructive commentary on the function of childhood in Anglo-Saxon society. Instead of being brought back to life at the age they died, children would be resurrected 'as great as they would have been if they had fully grown into wonderful adulthood'.[21] Childhood was not a perfect state, nor a complete state. It was a step on the way to achieving adulthood, and was made up of negatives – children were defined by the ways in which they were not adults. For Ælfric, there were no children in Anglo-Saxon heaven.

Appendix

ANGLO-SAXON LAWCODES RELATING TO CHILDREN

Æthelbert of Kent (c. 595–616)

25: If a man's bread eater (dependant) is killed, 6 shillings in compensation.

78: If a wife bears a living child, she shall have half the property left by her husband, if he dies first.

79: If she wishes to depart with her children, she shall have half the goods.

80: If the husband wishes to keep the child, she shall have a share of the goods equal to a child's.

81: If she does not have a child, her father's relatives shall have her goods, and her bridal gift.

Hlothhere and Eadric of Kent (–686)

6: If a man dies leaving a wife and child, it is right that the child should remain with the mother, and one of its father's relatives who is willing to act shall be given it as its guardian to take care of its property, until it is ten years old.

Ine of Wessex (–726)

2: A child must be baptised within thirty days: if this is not done, 30 shillings to be paid in compensation.
   If, however, it dies without being baptised, he shall pay as compensation all he possesses.

7: If anyone steals without the knowledge of his wife and children, he shall pay a fine of 60 shillings.
   If he steals with the knowledge of all his household, they shall all go into slavery.
   A ten-year-old child may be regarded as an accessory to theft.

23: The *wergild* of a Welsh taxpayer is 120 shillings, of his son 100 shillings.

26: For the maintenance of a foundling up to three years: 6 shillings shall be given in the first year, 12 in the second, 30 shillings in the third, and afterwards according to its appearance.

27: He who secretly has a child and disowns it, does not get his *wergild*, but his lord and the king do.

38: If a man and his wife have a child between them, and the man dies, the mother will keep and rear the child: she will be given 6 shillings to maintain it, a cow in summer and an ox in winter. The kinsman will look after the property until it comes of age.

63: If a thane travels, he may take with him his reeve, his smith and his children's nurse.

76: If anyone kills someone's god-son or his god-father, the sum to be paid to them equal to the amount paid to the dead man's lord.

Alfred the Great (871–99)

8: If anyone takes a nun from a monastery without the permission of the King or bishop, he shall pay 120 shillings, half to the King, and half to the bishop and lord of the church to which the nun belongs.
   If she lives longer than the man who abducted her, she shall inherit nothing of his property.
   If she bears his child, it shall inherit no more than the mother.
   If her child is slain, the share of *wergild* due to the mother's family shall be paid to the King, but the father's family shall be paid the share due to them.

9: If anyone kills a pregnant woman, while the child is in her womb, he shall pay the full compensation for the woman, and half the compensation for the child, in accordance with the *wergild* of the father's kindred.

14: If anyone is born dumb or deaf, so that he cannot deny or confess his sins, his father shall pay compensation for his crimes.

17: If anyone fosters out his dependants to another, and that person causes the death of the fosterling, then the one who fed it shall clear himself if anyone accuses him.

29: If anyone rapes an under-age girl, the same compensation shall be paid to her as to an adult.

65: If a man is so badly wounded in the genitals that he cannot have children, 80 shillings compensation.

Edward and Guthrum (–890)

4: If siblings marry, the *witan* has decreed that the King shall take the one and the bishop the other . . . unless they atone in any way the bishop prescribes.

If two brothers or two near kinsmen lie with one woman . . .

Æthelstan (924–39)

Laws 2
1: First, no thief shall be spared who is caught in the act, if he is over twelve years old and if the value is more than 8 pence.

Laws 4
3: and if anyone is so rich or belongs to so powerful a kindred that he cannot be restrained from crime or from protecting and harbouring criminals, he shall be led out of his native district with his wife and children, and all his goods . . .

Laws 6
1: No thief shall be spared for stealing more than 12 pence, who is over twelve years old. If we find him guilty according to the public law, and he cannot deny it in any way, we shall put him to death and take all he possesses . . .

12: Now the King has been talking to his *witan* [councillors] at Whittlebury again, and commanded word to be sent to Archbishop Theodred that he thinks it cruel that such young men are executed and for so little, as he has learnt happens everywhere. He declares that he, and those with whom he has spoken, think that no one should be executed who is under fifteen years old, unless he tries to defend himself, or tries to run away and refuses to give himself up.

Æthelred (978–1016)

5: Of priests having two or more wives, and some, though they put by those that they had before, they take them back or take more in a way improper to any Christian man.

47: . . . and that widows and step-children should not always be unhappy but should be readily gladdened.

Canute (1016–35)

20: Every freeman, over twelve years of age . . . shall be brought within a hundred and a tithing . . .

21: We wish that everyone over twelve years shall swear the oath that he will not be a thief nor a thief's accomplice.

Notes

Introduction

1. See, for example, Wiedemann 1988, Shahar 1990 and Hanawalt 1993.
2. Ariès 1962, p. 125.
3. Thrupp 1862, p. 117.
4. Schorsch 1979, p. 14.
5. Postman 1983, p. 10.
6. See, for example, the seminal works of Shahar 1990, Pollock 1983 and Hanawalt 1993. For some attempts to interpret Anglo-Saxon childhood, see Kuefler 1991 for an analysis of the written sources relating to the later Anglo-Saxon period and Crawford 1991b for a study of the archaeological evidence for the earlier Anglo-Saxon period.
7. Boswell 1989, Somerville 1987, p. 60.
8. See Chapter 3 for further discussion of the semantic evidence.
9. Cook and Dacre 1985.
10. Source: Attenborough 1922 and Robertson 1925 – see Appendix 1.
11. Jenks 1996, p. 7.
12. Turner 1979.
13. Schultz 1995, p. 1.
14. Keynes and Lapidge 1983.

1. Anglo-Saxon Childhood and the Social History of Children

1. Ariès 1960, p. 125.
2. Pollock 1983, p. 59.
3. Ibid.
4. De Mause 1974, p. 5.
5. Ibid., p. 10.
6. Ibid., p. 51.
7. Shorter 1976; Lyman 1974.
8. Firestone 1972, pp. 4–44.
9. McLaughlin 1974.
10. Pollock 1983, p. viii.
11. Ibid., p. 41.
12. Ibid., p. 61.
13. Ibid., p. 65.
14. Opie 1959.
15. James and Prout 1990, pp. 8–9.
16. Jenks 1996, p. 3.
17. Archard 1993, p. 161.
18. See, for example, Sennett 1970.
19. Filmer is discussed in Laslett 1972, p. 10; see also Ariès 1960, Stone 1979, Boswell 1989.
20. Van Es 1967; Waterbalk 1973; Hameror 1987.
21. Laslett 1972, p. 73.
22. Crawford 1991b, Appendix I.
23. Hough, C. 1999, p. 272, in Keynes and Lapidge 1983.
24. Goody 1972.
25. Wall 1972.
26. Beresford 1987.
27. Keynes and Lapidge 1983, p. 178; Robertson 1939, p. 151.

2. Archaeological Sources

1. Meaney 1964.
2. Richards 1987.
3. An archaeological database derived from a range of Anglo-Saxon inhumation cemeteries was used to provide information in this book. The cemeteries used are: Abingdon, Berkshire (Leeds and Harden 1936), Alton, Hampshire (Evison 1988), Berinsfield, Oxfordshire (Boyle, Dodd, Miles and Mudd 1996), Buckland I, Dover (Evison 1987), Finglesham, Kent (Chadwick 1958), Lechlade, Gloucestershire (Boyle 1998), Monkton, Kent (Chadwick Hawkes and Hogarth, 1974), Morning Thorpe, Norfolk (Green, Rogerson and White 1987), Polhill, Kent (Philp 1973), Portway, Andover, Hampshire (Cook and Dacre 1985),

Sewerby, East Yorkshire (Hirst 1985),
Swaffham, Norfolk (Wade-Martins 1976),
Westgarth Gardens, Suffolk (West 1988),
Winnall, Hampshire (Meaney and Hawkes
1970), Worthy Park, Kingsworthy,
Hampshire (Hawkes 1983, main site report
unpublished; I am grateful to Sonia
Hawkes for allowing access to the site
information).
4. See, for example, Brothwell 1972 and 1981
and Workshop of European
Anthropologists 1980 for further details of
these methods.
5. Brothwell 1981, p. 69.
6. Ferembach, Schwidetzky and Stloukal
1980.
7. Brothwell 1981, p. 60.
8. But see Rösing 1983 for a discussion of
methods of sexing immature human
skeletons and Henderson 1989 for a
discussion of the problems of sexing by
grave goods and bones in Anglo-Saxon
cemeteries.
9. See, for example, Tainter 1978, Binford
1972, Saxe 1970, Pader 1982.
10. Filmer-Sankey 1992.
11. Wilkinson 1980.
12. Gittings 1984.
13. Crawford 1991a for a discussion of this
issue.
14. For example, Lechlade (Boyle 1998) and
Berinsfield and Didcot (Boyle 1996) show a
consciousness of the problem, and give
clear guidelines to the reader as to how the
age categories were determined and on
what basis. However, even very recent
publications continue to ignore the
problem.
15. Evison 1987.
16. See Brothwell 1987 for a discussion of the
problems of reconstructing child mortality
patterns on the basis of archaeological
evidence and Waldron 1994, p. 12 for the
influence of cultural determinants on a
mortuary population. See Waldron also for
aspects of analysis of a mortuary
population and its relationship to a living
population.
17. See Waldron 1994 and Orton 1980 for a
discussion of archaeological statistics.
18. Crawford 1991b.
19. Larick 1980; Bernadi 1985.
20. Cook and Dacre 1985.
21. Timby 1996, p. 93.
22. Davies 1985.

23. As observed by Pader 1982, p. 155.
24. See Hodges 1989 for a discussion of the
workings of the Anglo-Saxon economy.
25. See White 1988 for the reuse of Roman
coins in the Anglo-Saxon burial ritual, and
Meaney 1981 for coins as amulets.
26. Alexandre-Bidon and Lett 1998, p. 23.
27. Boyle 1998, p. 41.

3. Documentary Sources

1. Bradley 1980, p. 175.
2. Colgrave 1940, 1956.
3. Davies 1980, p. 83.
4. Colgrave 1956, p. 4.
5. Ridyard 1988, pp. 61, 234.
6. See Bullough 1983 for a discussion of the
application of hagiographical material to
archaeological data.
7. Colgrave 1940, p. 3 for Bede's authorial
directions on how to read Cuthbert's
conversion as an eight-year-old.
8. Granger-Taylor 1989.
9. Whitelock 1967, p. 23.
10. Ælfric, from *The Life of King Edmund*, my
translation of text in Needham (ed.) 1976,
p. 58.
11. Colgrave 1940, p. 1.
12. My translation of the opening of *The Life
of St Edmund* in Needham (ed.) 1976, p. 43.
13. Colgrave 1956, p. 127.
14. For a discussion of the rejection of
biological parents in favour of the spiritual
parent in a Continental context, see
Alexandre-Bidon and Lett 1998,
pp. 18–20. For Wilfred, see Colgrave 1927.
15. Keynes and Lapidge 1983, p. 69.
16. *EHD*, p. 219.
17. Keynes and Lapidge 1983, p. 69.
18. Lawcodes relating to children or the family
are listed in Appendix 1, and are derived
from the laws collected by Attenborough
1922, Robertson 1925, Richardson 1966
and Whitelock 1972.
19. *Ecc. Hist*. II, Chapter 5.
20. Cameron 1983a, 1983b for a discussion of
Anglo-Saxon medicine and its sources.
21. Useful commentary on the sources and
compilation of the medical texts may be
found in Grattan and Singer 1952, Rubin
1974, and more recently, Cameron 1993.
22. My translation of 'From the Moon's Age'
in Cockayne 1866 (Vol. III), p. 190 ff.
23. Collections of charters and wills translated
into modern English may be found in

Robertson 1939, Whitelock 1930 and
Harmer 1914.
24. *Ecc. Hist.* II, Chapter 12.
25. Nelson 1994, p. 81.

4. Age Thresholds and Rites of Passage

1. Hirst 1985, p. 101.
2. Colgrave 1940.
3. Talbot 1954.
4. Cook and Dacre 1985.
5. Leeds and Harden 1936.
6. Schultz 1995, p. 29.
7. AS *Ecc. Hist.* 187/21 (cneohtwerendum), 209/9 (cneohtas and geonge menn), 242/29 (cildhade oððe cneohthad), 285/30 (cneohtcild).
8. Venezky and Healey 1980: 'Seo gastlice acennednyss is ungeswenlic, and þæs lichaman acennednyss is gesewenlic eall, þonne þæt cild wyxt, and gewyrð eft cnapa, and eft syððan cniht, oþþæt he swa becymð to þære ylde þe him geann his Scyppend'.
9. All vocabulary listed in Venezky and Healey 1980.
10. Ibid.: 'Fæmne oð þæt heo sy sxtynewintre oððe seofontynewintre sy heo in hire eldrena mihtum'.
11. Shephard 1979, p. 67.
12. Schultz 1995, p. 39.
13. Venezky and Healey 1980.
14. Ibid.: 'cildra 7 milcdeondra'.
15. Extracted from Ælfric's *The Life of St Æthelwold* in *EHD*, p. 904.
16. Colgrave 1956, Chapter 10.
17. Cockayne III, p. 145.
18. Keynes and Lapidge 1983, pp. 94–5.
19. Davidson 1962, p. 109.

5. Conception, Birth and Babies

1. Mensch 1985, p. 310.
2. Cockayne I, p. 339.
3. Ibid., p. 345.
4. Ibid., p. 347.
5. Cockayne III, p. 64.
6. Cockayne I, p. 393.
7. Hagen 1993, p. 109.
8. Cameron 1993, p. 182.
9. Cockayne I, p. 343.
10. Cockayne II, p. 331.
11. Cockayne I, p. 392.
12. Cockayne III, p. 67.

13. Ibid., p. 69.
14. Miles 1986, 45.
15. Wedlake 1958.
16. Meaney 1981, pp. 123–8.
17. Boyle 1996; see following chapter for a discussion of infant and child burials.
18. Venezky and Healey 1980: 'for þam þe hit sceall eft of deaþe arisan on domes dæg gif hit ær cwicu wæs innan þære modor 7 hæfð þonne helle wite gif hit hæþan acwylð.'
19. Cockayne III, p. 147.
20. Cockayne I, p. 87.
21. Smith 1992, p. 947.
22. Cockayne I, p. 167.
23. Woodward 1971, p. 184.
24. Mills 1989, p. 165.
25. Cockayne I, p. 363.
26. Cockayne II, p. 331; I, p. 267.
27. Wells 1980, p. 254 and Wells, 'The Human Bones', in Evison and Hill 1996, p. 23.
28. Boddington 1996, p. 114.
29. Evison 1994.
30. Mays 1995, p. 8.
31. Mattingly and Handford 1948.
32. *EHD*, p. 735 ff.
33. *Ecc. Hist.* III, Chapter 25.
34. Clark Hall 1984 and Clunies Ross 1985.
35. Venezky and Healey 1980: 'Nu cweþað sume men, hwi god gescyppan wylle of þam dyrnum forligrum ænig lybbende cild.'
36. Hawkes and Wells 1975, p. 120.
37. Crawford 1993.
38. Miles 1986 (Barton Court Farm) and Cocks 1921 (Hambledon).
39. Mays 1995, p. 8.
40. Evison 1994, p. 31.
41. Clunies Ross 1985.
42. Skeat 1881, Chapter 17:
'sume hi acwellað heora cild aerðam þe hi acenned beon
oððe aefter acennednysse þaet he cuðe ne beon
ne heora manfullu forligr ameldod nwurde
ac heora yfel is egeslec and endeleaslic morð
þaer losað þaet cilð ladlice hæðen
and seo arleasa modor butan heo his æfre gebete.'
43. Cockayne I, p. 305 (sea holly); Cockayne II, p. 331 (to stop periods).
44. Thorpe 1840, p. 368.
45. Cockayne I, p. 295.
46. Fell 1981, p. 51.

47. See Cockayne I, pp. 287, 293, 295, 305; II, p. 331.
48. Venezky and Healey 1980: 'heo hine baðode, 7 beðede, 7 smerede, 7 bær, 7 frefrede, 7 swaðede, 7 roccode.'
49. Ibid.
50. *Ecc. Hist*. I, Chapter 27.
51. Cockayne I, pp. 113, 289.
52. Ine, Law 63: 'Gif gesiðcund mon fare, þonne mot he habban his gerefan mid him 7 his smið 7 his childfestran.'
53. Hawkes and Wells 1983.
54. Venezky and Healey 1980: 'Ærest man fet þæt cild mid meolce, and syððan mid hlafe.'
55. Garmonsway 1978, pp. 36–7: 'Ic heortan mannes gestrangie, ic mægen wera 7 furþon littlincgas nellaþ forbicgean me.'
56. Hagen 1992, pp. 18–19.
57. Harke 1989, for example, suggests that knife blade lengths increase with age, but his large category of 'juveniles' is not given a specific age range, and his sample of 'juveniles' buried with knives is much smaller than his comparative female adult set, which in turn is considerably smaller than his male adult sample. Harke also chose to include knives with blade lengths in excess of 25 cm in his sample; such knives might more reasonably be described as single-edged seaxes, and are a weapon associated with males, a very different artefact from the quotidian knives found with men, women and children. To include such artefacts in a database sample will inevitably influence the outcome of any calculations to suggest that male knife blades are slightly longer than female knife blades.
58. Cockayne I, p. 117: 'Gif hwyc cyld ahwaened sy þonne genim þu þar ylcan wyrte 7 smoca hit mid þonne gedest ðu hit ðe gelaedre.'
59. Trease and Evans 1978, p. 577.
60. Southern 1979, p. 13.
61. Habicht 1985, p. 213.

6. *Infancy, Baptism and the Afterlife*

1. Mensch 1985.
2. Shahar 1990, p. 149.
3. See e.g. Evison 1987 in the Buckland cemetery report, who comments on the lack of infants in Kentish cemeteries. See also Crawford 1993. An exception seems to be the site of Great Chesterford, Essex (Evison 1994, p. 31) where there were eighty-six non-adults (aged fifteen or less), including seventeen foetuses. This appears to be a cemetery 'where all the dead of the community were buried without exception'. For cremation cemeteries, see Richards 1987, p. 124.
4. Collis 1977.
5. Sherlock and Welch 1992, p. 109.
6. Ayres 1979.
7. Boddington 1987 and Kjolbye-Biddle 1975.
8. Boyle 1998
9. Hills 1977; Myres and Green 1973.
10. Kinsley 1989.
11. Timby 1996, Leeds 1944.
12. Miles 1986 (Barton Court Farm) and Cocks 1921 (Hambledon).
13. Leeds 1947, p. 86.
14. Bradley, Chambers and Halpin 1984. See also West Stow (West 1985), where fragments of infant bones were recovered from layers associated with both sunken featured and post-built structures.
15. Ivens 1995, pp. 33, 431.
16. Keynes and Lapidge 1983, p. 90.
17. Powlesland 1997, p. 164.
18. For a mortuary population derived from a selection of Anglo-Saxon cemetery sites, consisting of burials where it was possible to assign an age, 73 per cent were buried with grave goods (931 out of 1,271 burials). Of those aged five or under, 41 per cent were buried with grave goods (54 out of 130 burials). Of the total population, 17 per cent were buried with only one grave good (210 out of 1,271 burials), while 27 per cent were buried with five or more grave goods (339 out of 1,271 burials). Of those aged five or under, 22 per cent (29 out of 130 burials) were buried with only one grave good, while only 4 per cent were buried with five or more grave goods (5 out of 130 burials).
19. Timby 1996.
20. Remarked upon by Wilson 1992, p. 57.
21. Matthews 1962.
22. Boyle et al. 1995, p. 242.
23. Myres and Green 1973.
24. Lethbridge 1951.
25. Meaney and Hawkes 1970.
26. Timby 1996, p. 17.
27. Hirst 1985, p. 41.
28. Evison 1994, p. 30.
29. Magnusson and Palsson 1960. There is a strong tradition of superstitious attitudes towards children in Scandinavian sources:

see particularly Pentikainen 1968, *The Nordic Dead Child Tradition*, for a summary.

30. See, for example, Gregory's reply to Augustine's question on the issue of infant baptism, *Ecc. Hist.* I, Chapter 27.
31. Hawkes and Wells 1975.
32. Parikh 1979, p. 159.
33. I am indebted to Mrs Anne Marshall for this suggestion.
34. Cockayne III, p. 67.
35. Thorpe 1844–6, p. 175. The story was told by St Gregory in his *Dialogues*, and was also repeated in the Irish collection *De Cura Pro Mortuis*. I am most grateful to Dr E. O'Brien for drawing my attention to these references.
36. Barber 1988.
37. *Ecc. Hist.* IV, Chapter 8: 'Erat in eodem monasterio puer trium circiter non amplius annorum, Æsica nomine, qui propter infantilem adhuc aetatem in virginum Deo dedicatarum solebat cella nutriri ibique meditari. Hic praefata pestilentia tactus, ubi ad extrema pervenit, clamavit tertio unam de consecratis Christo virginibus, proprio eam nomine quasi praesentum alloquens 'Eadgyd, Eadgyd, Eadgyd', et sic terminans temporalem vitam intravit aeternum. At virgo illa, quam moriens vocobat, mox in loco quo erat eadem adtacta infirmitate, ipso, quo vocitata est, die de hac luce subtracta et illum, qui se vocavit, ad regnum caeleste secuta est.'
38. Thorpe 1844–6: St Augustine, Sermon 334, Patrologie Latine 38, col. 1447.
39. *Ecc. Hist.* I, Chapter 27.
40. Thorpe 1840.
41. Colgrave 1956 and *Ecc. Hist.* II, Chapter 24.
42. Hull and Sharpe 1986.
43. Colgrave 1927.
44. Alexandre-Bidon and Lett 1998, p. 53.
45. Suggested by R. Daniels in his paper 'The Anglo-Saxon Monastery at Hartlepool, England', presented to the International Conference of Medieval Archaeology, York, 1992.
46. Watts 1989, p. 372.
47. Alexandre-Bidon and Lett 1998, p. 56.
48. Hill 1997, p. 45.
49. Barber 1988, p. 75.
50. Görlach 1994.
51. Nelson 1994.
52. See Doran 1994, p. 128.
53. Venezky and Healey 1980.
54. Ibid.: 'Hi settað heora fingras innan þæs cildes earan mid heora spatle, 7 on þæs cildes nosu.'
55. Skeat 1881, p. 375: 'Eac sum gewitlease wif farað to wega gelætum and teoðheora cild ðurh ða eorðan and swa deofle betæcað hi sylfe and heora bearn.'
56. Venezky and Healey 1980: 'And þæt nan man ne sece to nanre wellan, ne to nanum stane, ne to nanum treowe, ne nan man his cild þurh þa eorþan ne teo, for ðam se ðe þæt ðeð, he betæcð þæt cild eallum deoflan and seo modor forð mid.'
57. Ibid.: 'þa wifman þe berað hyre cild to wegelætum 7 teoð þurh þa eorþan ne begytað hi næfre godes miltsa.'
58. Venezky and Healey 1980: 'Wifman beo þæs ylcan wyrðe hif heo tilað hire cilde mid aenigum wiccecræfte oððe æt wega gelætan þurh þa eorþan tyhð, forþam þæt is micel hæþenscype.'
59. Ibid.: 'And riht is þat preosta gehwylc . . . forbeode wyllweorðunga, 7 licwigeluge, and hwata, 7 galdra, 7 treowurðunga, 7 stanwurðunga, 7 ðone deoflæs cræft þe man dryhð pær man þa cild þurh þa eorþan tihð, and ða gemearr þe man drigd on geares niht on mislicum wigelungun 7 on friðsplotum 7 on ellenum, and on manegum mislicum gedwimerum.'
60. Eliade 1959, p. 38: 'Le passage du monde profane au monde sacré implique d'une manière ou d'une autre l'expérience de la Mort: on meurt à une certaine existence pour accéder à une autre . . . on meurt à l'enfance et à l'irresponsabilité de l'existence enfantine, c'est-à-dire profane, pour pouvoir accéder à une existence supérieure; celle où est rendue possible la participation au sacré'. See also K. Dowden in *Death and the Maiden*, 1989, who explores the connections between the symbolisation of death at times of transition or rites of passage. His fascinating discussion is based on the rites of passage of girls in Ancient Greece.

7. Health and Childcare

1. Thrupp 1862, p. 79.
2. *Ecc. Hist.* III, Chapter 27.
3. *Ecc. Hist.* IV, Chapter 13.
4. Colgrave and Mynors 1991, p. 577.
5. *Ecc. Hist.* II, Chapter 20.
6. *Ecc. Hist.* II, Chapter 14.
7. *Ecc. Hist.* II, Chapter 20.

8. Thorpe 1840: 'Mater, si juxta focum infantem suum posuerit, et homo aquam in caldarium miserit, et ebullita aqua infans superfusus morluus fuerit; pro negligentia mater pœniteat, et ille homo securus sit.'

9. Venezky and Healey 1980: 'Nu is eft oðer þing þe dysige wif doþ lecgaþ heora cild betwux him 7 of licgaþ hit þonne he on slæpe beoð forðan þe se slæpenda man nat hwet he dæþ' and '7 we secgað þæt seo modor gif heo to þam unwær bið mid hire breoste mæg þæt cild acwellan gif heo hit læt sucan 7 wurþ þonne on slep þonne of lið þæt breost þæs cildes fnæst oð þæt hit bið forsmorod for þan þe hit ne cann hit aweig don þonne bið heo hier agenes cild bana.'

10. Hanawalt 1977.

11. Colgrave 1940, Chapter 1.

12. Brothwell 1981, plate 9.

13. Drinkall and Foreman 1998, p. 10. The teat on the pot is much abraded, and the report speculates that the bottle may have been used by an animal rather than a human baby: its actual function may become clearer when its contents have been analysed.

14. Ethelberg 1986, p. 176.

15. Manchester 1983, p. 50.

16. Meaney 1981, pp. 135–8.

17. Timby 1996, p. 29.

18. Mays in Timby 1996, p. 25.

19. Manchester 1983.

20. Hill 1997, p. 172.

21. Boddington 1996, p. 123.

22. Cockayne II, p. 85.

23. Cockayne I, pp. 367 (matter in neck), 121 (children's worms), 123 (water sickness); III, p. 87 (scabby head).

24. Cockayne I, pp. 227, 363, 347; II, p. 241.

25. Manchester 1983, p. 50.

26. Cockayne II, p. 241.

27. Keynes and Lapidge 1983, p. 89.

28. Cockayne, II, p. 145.

29. *Ecc. Hist.* I, Chapter 21.

30. Colgrave 1940, Chapter 4.

31. *Ecc. Hist.* V, Chapter 3.

32. My thanks to Dr A.A.S. Randall who suggested this explanation.

33. *Ecc. Hist.* V, Chapter 2.

34. Cockayne I, pp. 347, 363; III, p. 87.

8. *The Family*

1. Herlihy 1985, p. 112.

2. Parker 1965 and Van Es 1967.

3. West 1985.

4. Bell 1977.

5. West 1985; Hamerow 1993.

6. Scull 1993.

7. Matthews and Hawkes 1985.

8. Gardiner 1986.

9. Boyle et al. 1995.

10. Drinkall and Foreman 1998.

11. Timby 1996, p. 27.

12. Harden and Treweeks 1945.

13. Hooke 1981, p. 298.

14. See, for example, Robertson 1939, pp. 6, 9, 13, 26, 27, 42.

15. Lancaster 1957.

16. Shahar 1990, p. 248.

17. Leeds and Harden 1936.

18. Ullrich 1975.

19. Colgrave 1956, p. 75.

20. Venezky and Healey 1980.

21. Smith 1980, p. 22.

22. Keynes and Lapidge 1983, pp. 74, 89.

23. Wells 1980, p. 309.

24. Hassan 1981.

25. Keynes and Lapidge 1983.

26. Goody 1972, p. 148.

27. Robertson 1938, p. 41.

28. Freeman 1973, p. 119.

29. Schorsch 1979, p. 16.

30. Bradley 1982, p. 1043.

31. Robertson 1939, p. 68.

32. Timby 1996, p. 17; Leeds 1944; Chambers 1973.

33. Robertson 1939, p. 151.

34. Bradley 1982, p. 341.

35. Whitelock 1930, p. 46.

36. *EHD* I, p. 279.

37. Swanton 1978, p. 55, line 454.

38. Hull and Sharpe 1986, p. 27.

39. Whitelock 1930, p. 4.

40. Farmer 1996, p. 280.

9. *Fosterage, God-parents and Adoption*

1. Boswell 1989, p. 429.

2. Whitelock 1930, p. 60.

3. Ibid.

4. Colgrave 1956.

5. Keynes and Lapidge 1988, p. 90.

6. ASPR, Riddle, p. ix.

7. Swanton 1986, p. 79: 'Nu ic Beowulf, þec secg betsta me for sunu wylle/freogan on ferhþe heald forð tela/niwe sibbe ne bið þe aenigra gad/worulde wilna þe ic geweald haebbe'.

8. Ibid., p. 91: 'wene ic þæt he mid gode gyldan wille/uncran eaferan gif he þæt eal gemon/hwaet wit to willan and to worðmyndum/umbor wesendum ær arna gefremedon'.
9. Ibid.: 'beo wið Geatas glæd geofena gemyndig/nean and feorran'.
10. Cockayne III, p. 179.
11. Ridyard 1988, p. 100.
12. Clayton and Magennis 1994, p. 152.
13. Thorpe 1846, p. 449: 'Ic alysde hrymende þearfan, and ðam steop bearne, þe buton fultume waes, ic geheolp, and wydewan heortan ic gefrefrode . . . ne ic ne aet ana minne hlaf buton steop-bearne'.
14. Robertson 1939, p. 93.
15. *Ecc. Hist.* V, Chapter 3.
16. Boyle 1996.
17. Robertson 1925, p. 54; Keynes and Lapidge 1983.
18. Barth 1973.
19. Boswell 1989, p. 429.
20. Freeman 1973.
21. Colgrave 1940.
22. Ibid.
23. Venezky and Healey 1980.
24. Ibid.: 'besargode his fostor-modor sarnysse swiðe arfæstlice'.
25. Plummer 1968.
26. Luke 18:29: 'there is no man who has left house or wife or brothers or parents or children, for the sake of the kingdom of God, who will not receive manifold more in this time, and in the age to come eternal life'.
27. Plummer 1968, from *The Life of Berach*.
28. Orme 1984.
29. See especially De Jong 1996 and Doran 1994 for western European oblation, and Lynch 1986 for a discussion of god-parents and kinship in early medieval Europe.
30. Lynch 1986, p. 143.
31. Ibid., p. 213.
32. Ibid., p. 153.
33. Whitelock 1930, p. 60.
34. Lynch 1986, p. 246.
35. Ibid., pp. 168, 190.
36. Whitelock 1930, p. 23.
37. Lynch 1986, p. 337.
38. De Jong 1996.
39. Keynes and Lapidge 1988.
40. Ibid., p. 103.
41. De Jong 1996, p. 52.
42. Ibid., p. 54.
43. Ibid., p. 216.
44. Ibid., pp. 50–5, 220.
45. Ridyard 1988.
46. De Jong 1996, p. 222. Some details survive concerning the oblation ritual of Lioba, who eventually became Abbess of Tauberbischofsheim until her death in 782, but the *Life* containing these details was commissioned by the same Hrabanus who had been so fierce in his defence of oblation in the Gottschalk case, so Lioba's recorded oblation is more likely to be a reflection of conservative Frankish practice than an actual representation of the events in Anglo-Saxon England.
47. Keynes and Lapidge 1988.

10. Play and Education

1. Gelling 1982.
2. Fell 1984, p. 64.
3. Colgrave 1940.
4. Ariès 1960, pp. 31, 65 ff.
5. Colgrave 1940, Chapter 12.
6. Wright, 1862, from Harley 3601 cited: 'Pueri et adolescentes . . . illic convenientes, more Anglorum luctamina et alia ludicra exercebant puerilia, et cantilenis et musicis instrumentis sibi invicem applaudebant, unde propter turbam puerorum et puellarum illic concurrentium, mos inolevit ut in eodem die illic conveniret negotiandi gratia turba vendentium et ementium'.
7. Cockayne 1864, p. 78.
8. Thorpe 1846, p. 27.
9. Brent 1866.
10. Myres and Green 1973.
11. Richards 1987, p. 130.
12. Girvan 1939, pp. 32–3.
13. Sweet 1871, p. 391: 'Hwæt we eac wiernað urum cildum', but note in Vol. 50 this is translated as 'we even give our children' – why change his mind? The earlier version makes more sense.
14. Sedgefield 1899, p. 108: 'þa cild ridað on hiora stafum 7 manigfealds plegan plegiað ðaer hi hyriað ealdum monnum.'
15. Colgrave 1940, Chapter 12.
16. Fell 1984, p. 77.
17. Ibid., p. 60.
18. Bernstein 1972, p. 47.
19. Postman 1983, p. 13.
20. Ibid., p. 15.
21. Shahar 1990, p. 209.
22. Colgrave 1956, Chapters 9 and 16.

23. Keynes and Lapidge 1983, p. 75.
24. Ibid.
25. Ibid., p. 90.
26. Ibid.
27. Ibid.
28. Thorpe 1844, p. 171.
29. Keynes and Lapidge 1983, p. 91.
30. Orme 1984, p. 143.
31. Shahar 1990, p. 195.
32. Venezky and Healey 1980: 'Geornlice þæs mynstres ealdrum gedafenað to gymenne þæet cild 7 þa geonglingas þe man fet 7 lærð on geferrædene beon swa fæstlice be healdene mid mynsterlicum larum and steorum þæt seo plegonle geogoð, þe byð hraed to singienne, ne mage nane stow aredian þe heo an mage ænigne gylt befeallan.'
33. Ibid.: 'Swa hwilce swa an preosthirede cild bið oððe geonglingas, wunion ealls þa an anre fæstre wnunge, þaet þa gear þæs slyporan geogoðhades ne beon adrgene an ydelum gaelsan, ac an ciriclicum larum.'
34. OE Ecc. Hist. V, Chapter 6.
35. Colgrave 1927.
36. OE Ecc. Hist. V, Chapter 6.
37. Needham 1976, p. 31.
38. EHD, p. 825.
39. OE Ecc. Hist. III, Chapter 18.
40. Garmonsway 1966, p. 47: 'Ic ne eom swa spedig þæt ic mæge bicgean me win: 7 win nys drenc cilda ne dysgra, ac ealdra 7 wisra.'
41. Venezky and Healey 1980: 'Ic Eadwine munuk cilda mastere an Niwan mynstre'.
42. Keynes and Lapidge 1983, p. 23.
43. Bullough 1972, p. 465.
44. Ibid., p. 489.
45. Garmonsway 1966, Preface.
46. Bullough 1972, p. 473.
47. Garmonsway 1966, p. 18: 'We cildra biddaþ þe, eala lareow, þæt þu tæce us sprecan forþam ungelærede we syndon 7 gewæmmodlice we sprecaþ.'
48. OE Ecc. Hist. III, Chapter 7.
49. OE Ecc. Hist. IV, 2: 'heo betweoh halige bec 7 ciriclicne þeodscipe in metercræft 7 in tungolcræft 7 in grammaticcræft tydon 7 lærdon'.
50. EHD, p. 897.
51. Ibid., p. 904.
52. Ibid., p. 785.
53. Thrupp 1862, p. 105.
54. Southern 1962.
55. EHD, p. 909.
56. McCann 1969: 'pueri vel adolescientiores aetate'.
57. Ridyard 1988, p. 98.
58. Cockayne II, p. xxii: 'Willimot writ þus oððe bet . . . writ þus oððe bet oððe þine hyde forlet' and 'writ þus oððe bet ride aweg ælfnærpattafox þu wilt swingan ælfric cild.'
59. Thorpe 1844, p. 325: 'Cildru behofiað swiðlicere steore and godre gymene to godum ðeawum, þaet se wisdom mage on him wunigende beon.'
60. Venezky and Healey 1980.
61. Hanawalt 1993, p. 98.
62. OE Ecc. Hist. III, Chapter 5, 'Ond he monige þaro þe he mid weorþe alysde, him to chicipulum genom, þa aefter faece to sacerhade'.
63. Cockayne III, pp. 185 ff.

11. Adolescence

1. Ariès 1973, p. 48: 'on n'avait pas l'idée de ce que nous apelons adolescence, et cette idée sera longue à former'.
2. Jenks 1996, p. 63.
3. Fox 1977, p. 8; Kleijwegt 1991, p. xii.
4. Kleijwegt 1991, p. 22.
5. Venezky and Healey 1980: 'Da cwaeð Abraham to þam cnapum ðus: anbidiað eow her mid þam assum sume hwile.'
6. Ibid.
7. Ibid.
8. Ibid.: 'ne byrð na se cniht butan intingan his swurd.'
9. Ibid.
10. Ibid.
11. Harke 1990 includes a shield burial with a six-year-old among his weapon burials, but this seeming anomaly is misplaced. The burial is grave 50 at Westgarth Gardens (West 1998), and a close analysis of the remaining teeth indicate that this is actually the burial of a ten- to twelve-year-old (Crawford 1991).
12. Harke's comments in Boyle 1996.
13. See, for example, Cohn 1994.
14. Luard 1865–9.
15. Rothwell 1957, p. 190.
16. Gue 1983, p. 42.
17. Shahar 1990, p. 210.
18. Colgrave 1927, II.
19. Colgrave 1956, p. 16.
20. Venezky and Healey 1980: 'Sittendum cnapun on foretige þa hrymað to hra efengelicon'.

21. Colgrave 1956, p. 34.
22. Colgrave 1940, I, p. 7.
23. Suggested by Patrick Wormald and enlarged on by Blair 1994, p. 17.
24. For example, the charter place name 'cnapwelle' (Venezky and Healey 1980) or the possible 'Knightsbridge' in Shirburn and Shifford, Oxfordshire (Blair 1994, p. 17).
25. I am grateful to Dr W.J. Blair for drawing my attention to this parallel.
26. ASPR: 'Ic me þenen ne þearf/þaet me bearn wraece on banan feore/Gif me gromra hwylc guþe genaegeð/ne weorþed sio maeg-burg gemicledu/earoran minum þe ic aefter woc.'
27. Whitelock 1979, p. 121: 'Him be healfe stod hyse unweaxen/cniht on gecampe, se full caflice/braed of þam beorne, Wulfmaer se geonga/forlet forgeardne faran eft ongean/ord in gewod, þaet se on eorþan laeg, þe his þeoden aer þearle geraehte.'
28. Ibid., p. 123: 'Swa hi bylde forð bearn Ælfrices/wiga wintrum geong, wordum maelde/Ælfwine þa cwaeð (he on ellen spraec) . . .'.
29. McCome 1986, p. 13.
30. EHD, p. 804.
31. Ibid., p. 821.
32. See McCome 1986, p. 19.
33. Gransden 1972.
34. Colgrave 1956, Chapter 26.
35. Shahar 1990, p. 213.
36. Davidson 1962, p. 109.
37. Kussmaul 1981, p. 3.
38. Clayton and Magennis 1994, p. 154.
39. OE Ecc. Hist. V, Chapter 19 and Thorpe 1846, p. 75: 'heo waesbeþran ðaere

40. cenninge . . . and maeden aefter ðaere cenninge'.
Venezky and Healey 1980.

Conclusion

1. Schorsch 1979, p. 14.
2. EHD, p. 784.
3. Ecc. Hist. V, Chapter 2.
4. From The Fates of Man; my translation but see ASPR III.
5. Postman 1983, p. 17.
6. Pollock 1983, p. 51; Shahar 1990, p. 155.
7. Sweet 1871, p. 342: 'Hwæt bið ðonne unaberendlicre togesionne ðonne ðæs bearnes cwalu beforan ðæs fæder eagum?'
8. Crawford 1991a; Richards 1987, p. 130.
9. Richards 1987, p. 124.
10. Ibid., p. 130.
11. Ibid., p. 136.
12. Meaney 1964, p. 20.
13. Didsbury 1998, p. 314.
14. Shahar 1990, p. 1.
15. Hanawalt 1993, p. 11.
16. Keynes and Lapidge 1983.
17. EHD, p. 783.
18. Locke 1689.
19. Whitelock 1976, pp. 51–2: '7 earme men syndan sare beswicene 7 hreowlice besyrwde 7 ut of þysan earde wide gesealde swyþe unforworhte fremdum to gewealde: 7 cradolcild geþeowede þurh wælhreowe unlage for lytelre þyf þe wide gynd þas þeode'.
20. EHD, p. 794.
21. Venezky and Healey 1980: 'Swa miccle menn swa swa hi mihton beon, gif hi fulweoxon on gewunlicre ylde.'

Bibliography

Abbreviations

ASPR – Krapp, G. and Dobbie, E. (eds). *The Anglo-Saxon Poetic Records: A Collective Edition, Vol. III, The Exeter Book*, New York, Columbia University Press/London, Routledge & Kegan Paul, 1936

Cockayne – Cockayne, O. *Leechdoms, Wortcunning and Starcraft of Early England*, 3 vols, Rolls Series, London, 1864–70

Ecc. Hist. – Colgrave, B. and Mynors, R.A.B. (eds report). *Bede: Ecclesiastical History of the English People*, Oxford, Oxford University Press, 1991

OE Ecc. Hist. – Miller, T. *The Old English Version of Bede's Ecclesiastical History of the English People*, London, Early English Text Society, 1890

EHD – Whitelock, D. (ed.). *English Historical Documents I c. 500–1042*, 2nd edn, London, Eyre Methuen, 1979

Alexandre-Bidon, D. and Lett, D. *Les Enfants au Moyen Age: Ve–XVe Siècles*, France, Hachette Littératures, 1998

Archard, D. *Children: Rights and Childhood*, London, Routledge, 1993

Ariès, P. *L'enfant et la Vie Famille sous l'ancien Régime* Paris, Plon, 1960 (trans. Baldick, R. as *Centuries of Childhood; a Social History of Family Life*, London, Penguin, 1962)

Arnold, C. *The Archaeology of the Early Anglo-Saxon Kingdoms*, London, Routledge, 1988

Attenborough, F.L. *The Laws of the Earliest English Kings*, Cambridge, CUP, 1922

Ayers, B. *Excavations within the North-East Bailey of Norwich Castle, 1973*, East Anglian Archaeology 28, Dereham, Norfolk, Norfolk Archaeological Unit, Norfolk Museums Service, 1985

Barber, P. *Vampires, Burial and Death: Folklore and Reality*, New Haven, London, Yale University Press, 1988

Bell, M. 'Excavations at Bishopstone: the Anglo-Saxon Period', *Sussex Archaeological Collections* 115, (1977), 193 ff.

Beresford, G. *Goltho: the Development of an Early Medieval Manor c. 850–1150*, English Heritage Archaeological Report 4: London, Historic Buildings and Monuments Commission for England, 1987

Bernadi, B. *Age Class Systems*, trans. D.I. Kertzer, Cambridge, CUP, 1985

Bernstein, B. 'On the Classification and Framing of Educational Knowledge', in M.F.D. Young (ed.), *Knowledge and Control*, London, Collier-Macmillan, 1972

Binford, L. *An Archaeological Perspective*, London, Seminar Press, 1972

Boddington, A. *Raunds Furnells: the Anglo-Saxon Church and Churchyard: Raunds Area Project*, English Heritage Archaeological Report 7, London, English Heritage, 1996

Boswell, J. *The Kindness of Strangers: the Abandonment of Children in Western Europe from Late Antiquity to the Renaissance*, London, Allen Lane, the Penguin Press, 1989

Boyle, A., Dodd, A., Miles, D. and Mudd, A. *Two Oxfordshire Anglo-Saxon Cemeteries: Berinsfield and Didcot*, Thames Valley Landscapes Monograph 8, Oxford, Oxford Archaeological Unit, 1996

Boyle, A. *The Anglo-Saxon Cemetery at Butler's Field, Lechlade, Gloucestershire: Vol. 1, Prehistoric and Roman Activity and Anglo-Saxon Grave Catalogue*, Thames Valley Landscapes Monograph 10, Oxford, Oxford Archaeological Unit, 1998

Bradley, R. 'Anglo-Saxon Cemeteries; Some Suggestions for Research', in P. Rahtz, T. Dickinson and L. Watts (eds), *Anglo-Saxon Cemeteries 1979: the Fourth Anglo-Saxon Symposium at Oxford*, pp. 171–8

Bradley, R., Chambers, R.A. and Halpin, C. *Barrow Hills, Radley 1983–4: Excavations: an Interim Report*, Oxford, Oxford Archaeological Unit, 1984

Bradley, S.A.J. *Anglo-Saxon Poetry*, London, Everyman, 1982

Brent, J. 'Account of the Society's Researches in the Anglo-Saxon Cemetery at Sarre', *Archaeologia Cantiana* 6 (1866), 157–85

Brothwell, D.R. *Digging up Bones*, 2nd edn, Oxford, Oxford University Press, 1972

——. *Digging up Bones*, 3rd edn, Oxford, Oxford University Press, 1981

——. 'The Problem of the Interpretation of Child Mortality in Earlier Populations', *Antropologia Portiguesa* 5 (1987), 143–53

Bullough, D. 'The Educational Tradition in England from Alfred to Aelfric: Teaching "Utriusque linguae"', *Settimane di Studio del Centro Italiano di Studi Sull'Alto Medipevo* XIX (1972), 453–94

——. 'Burial, Community and Belief', in F. Wormald (ed.), *Ideal and Reality in Frankish and Anglo-Saxon Society*, Oxford, Blackwell, 1983, pp. 177–201

Bulwer-Lytton, Lord E. *Harold, or the Last of the Saxon Kings*, George Routledge and Sons, 1848

Cameron, M.L. 'The Sources of Medical Knowledge in Anglo-Saxon England', *Anglo-Saxon England* 11 (1983a), 136–55

——. 'Bald's "Leechbook"': its Sources and their Use in its Compilation', *Anglo-Saxon England* 12 (1983b), 153–82

——. *Anglo-Saxon Medicine*, Cambridge Studies in Anglo-Saxon England 7, Cambridge, Cambridge University Press, 1993

Chadwick, S.E. 'The Anglo-Saxon Cemetery at Finglesham, Kent', *Medieval Archaeology* 2 (1958), 1–71

Chadwick Hawkes, S. and Hogarth, A.C. 'The Anglo-Saxon Cemetery at Monkton, Thanet', *Archaeologia Cantiana* 89 (1974), 49–89

Chadwick Hawkes, S. 'Finglesham. A Cemetery in East Kent', in J. Campbell (ed.), *The Anglo-Saxons*, London, Phaidon Press, 1982, pp. 24–5

Chambers, R.A. 'A Cemetery Site at Beacon Hill, Near Lewknor', *Oxoniensia* 38 (1973), 138–45

Clark Hall, J.R. *A Concise Anglo-Saxon Dictionary*, 4th edn, Toronto/London, Toronto University Press, 1984

Clayton, M. and Magennis, H. (eds). *The Old English Lives of St Margaret*, Cambridge, Cambridge University Press, 1994

Clunies Ross, M. 'Concubinage in Anglo-Saxon England', *Past and Present* 108 (1985), 3–34

Cockayne, T.O. *Leechdoms, Wortcunning and Starcraft of Early England*, 3 vols, Rolls Series, London, Longman, Green/Longman, Roberts and Green, 1864–70

——. *The Shrine: a Collection of Occasional Papers on Dry Subjects*, London, Williams and Norgate, 1864

Cocks, A.H. 'A Romano-British Homestead in the Hambledon Valley, Bucks', *Archaeologia* 71 (1921), 141–98

Cohn, I. *Child Soldiers: the Role of Children in Armed Conflict*, Clarendon Press, 1994

Colgrave, B. *The Life of Bishop Wilfred by Eddius Stephanus*, Cambridge, Cambridge University Press, 1927

——. *Two Lives of Saint Cuthbert*, Cambridge, Cambridge University Press, 1940

——. *Felix's Life of Saint Guthlac*, Cambridge, Cambridge University Press, 1956

Colgrave, B. and Mynors, R.A.B. (eds). *Bede: Ecclesiastical History of the English People*, Oxford, Oxford University Press, 1991

Collis, J. 'Owlesbury, Hants and the Problem of Burials on Rural Settlements', in R. Reece (ed.), *Burial in the Roman World*, Council for British Archaeology Research Report 22 (1977), 26–35

Cook, A.M. and Dacre, M.W. *Excavations at Portway, Andover 1973–75*, Oxford, Oxford University Committee for Archaeology, Monograph 4, 1985.

Crawford, S.E.E. 'When Do Anglo-Saxon Children Count?' *Journal For Theoretical Archaeology* 2 (1991a), 17–24

——. *Age Differentiation and Related Social Status; a Study of Earlier Anglo-Saxon Childhood*, Oxford University unpublished doctoral dissertation (1991b)

——. 'Children, Death and the Afterlife in Anglo-Saxon England', *Anglo-Saxon Studies in Archaeology and History* 6 (1993), 83–92

——. 'Anglo-Saxon Medicine', in R. Arnott and S.E.E. Crawford (eds), *The Roots of Western Medicine*, Stroud, Sutton Publishing (forthcoming)

Davidson, H.R.E. *The Sword in Anglo-Saxon England: its Archaeology and Literature*, Oxford, Clarendon Press, 1962

Davies, S.M. 'The Excavation of an Anglo-Saxon Cemetery (and Some Prehistoric Pits) at Charlton Plantations, near Downton', *Wiltshire Archaeological and Natural History Magazine* 79 (1985), 109–54

Davis, N. (ed.). *Sweet's Anglo-Saxon Primer*, Oxford, Oxford University Press, 1980

de Jong, M. *In Samuel's Image: Child Oblation in the Early Medieval West*, Leiden, E.J. Brill, 1996

de Mause, L. 'The Evolution of Parent-Child Relationships as a Factor in History', in L. de Mause (ed.), *The History of Childhood*, pp. 1–71

——. (ed.). *The History of Childhood*, New York, Psychohistory Press, 1974

Didsbury, P. 'The Pottery', in G. Drinkall and M. Foreman (eds), *The Anglo-Saxon Cemetery at Castledyke South, Barton-on-Humber*, pp. 297–314

Doran, J. 'Oblation or Obligation? A Canonical Ambiguity', in D. Wood (ed.), *The Church and Childhood*, Studies in Church History 31, Oxford, Blackwell, 1994, pp. 127–42

Dowden, K. *Death and the Maiden: Girls' Initiation Rites in Greek Mythology*, London, Routledge, 1989

Drinkall, G. and Foreman, M. *The Anglo-Saxon Cemetery at Castledyke South, Barton-on-Humber*, Humber Archaeology Partnership, Sheffield Excavation Reports 6, 1998

Eliade, M. *Initiation, Rites, Sociétés Secrètes: Naisances Mystiques: Essai sur Quelques Types d'Initiation*, Paris, Gallimard, 1959

Ethelberg, P. *Hjemsted-en gravplads fra 4. & 5. årh.e.Kr.*, Haderslev, 1986

Evison, V.I. *Dover; the Buckland Anglo-Saxon Cemetery*, London, Historic Buildings and Monuments Commission for England Archaeological Report 3, 1987

——. *An Anglo-Saxon Cemetery at Alton, Hampshire*, Hampshire Field Club Monograph 4, Winchester, Hampshire Field Club and Archaeological Society, 1988

——. *An Anglo-Saxon Cemetery at Great Chesterford, Essex*, York, Council for British Archaeology Research Report 91, 1994

Evison, V.I. and Hill, P. *Two Anglo-Saxon Cemeteries at Beckford, Hereford and Worcester*, York, Council for British Archaeology Research Report 103, 1996

Farmer, D. *The Oxford Dictionary of Saints*, Oxford, Oxford University Press, 1996

Ferembach, D., Schwidetzky, I. and Stloukal, M. 'Recommendations for Age and Sex Diagnoses of Skeletons', *Journal of Human Evolution* 9 (1980), 517–49

Filmer-Sankey, W. 'The Snape Anglo-Saxon Cemetery: the Current State of Knowledge', in M.O.H. Carver (ed.), *The Age of Sutton Hoo: the Seventh Century in North-western Europe*, Woodbridge, the Boydell Press, 1992, pp. 39–52

Firestone, S. *The Dialectic of Sex: the Case for Feminist Revolution*, London, Cape, 1971

Fox, V. 'Is Adolescence a Phenomenon of Modern Times?', *History of Childhood Quarterly* 5 (1997–8), 271–90

Freeman, D. 'Kinship, Attachment Behaviour and the Primary Bond', in J. Goody (ed.), *The Character of Kinship*, London, Cambridge University Press, 1973, pp. 109–19

Gardiner, M. *Sussex Archaeological Society Newsletter* 50 (December 1986), 512

Garmonsway, G.N. (ed.). *Ælfric's Colloquy*, New York, Appleton-Century-Crofts, 1966

Gelling, M. 'Some meanings of "Stow"', in S. Pearce (ed.), *The Early Church in Western Britain and Ireland*, British Archaeological Reports 102 (1982), 187–96

Girvan, R. (ed.). *Ratis Raving*, Edinburgh and London, Scottish Text Society, 3rd series 11, 1939

Gittings, C. *Death, Burial and the Individual in Early Modern England*, London, Routledge, 1984

Goody, J. 'The Evolution of the Family', in P. Laslett (ed.), *Household and Family in Past Time*, pp. 103–24

Görlach, M. (ed.). *The Kalendre of the Newe Legende of Englande, from Pynsons Printed Edition, 1516*, Middle English Texts 27, Heidelburg, Winter 1994

Granger-Taylor, H. 'The Weft-Patterned Silks and their Braid; the Remains of an Anglo-Saxon Dalmatic of c800?', in G. Bonner, D. Rollason and C. Stancliffe (eds), *St Cuthbert, His Cult and Community to AD 1200*, Woodbridge, the Boydell Press, 1989, pp. 303–27

Gransden, A. 'Childhood and Youth in Medieval England', *Nottingham Medieval Studies* 16 (1972), 3–19

Grattan, J. and Singer, C. *Anglo-Saxon Magic and Medicine: Illustrated Specially from the Semi-Pagan Text 'Lacnunga'*, London, Oxford University Press for the Wellcome Historical Medicine Museum, 1952

Green, B., Rogerson, A. and White, S. *The Anglo-Saxon Cemetery at Morning Thorpe, Norfolk, Volume 1: Catalogue*, East Anglian Archaeology 36, Dereham, Norfolk, Norfolk Archaeological Unit, Norfolk Museums Service, 1987

Gue, E. *The Education and Literary Interests of the English Lay Nobility c1150–1450*, unpublished D.Phil. thesis, Oxford University (1983)

Hagen, A. *A Handbook of Anglo-Saxon Food: Processing and Consumption*, Middlesex, Anglo-Saxon Books, 1993

Hamerow, H. *Excavations at Mucking Volume 2: The Anglo-Saxon Settlement*, British Museum Press, 1993

Hanawalt, B. 'Childrearing Among the Lower Classes of Late Medieval England', *Journal of Interdisciplinary History* 8, 1 (1977), 1–22

——. *Growing up in Medieval London: the Experience of Childhood in History*, Oxford, Oxford University Press, 1993

Harden, D.B. and Treweeks, R.C. 'Excavations at Stanton Harcourt, Oxon 1940 II', *Oxoniensia* 10 (1945), 16–41

Harke, H. 'Warrior Graves? The Background of the Anglo-Saxon Burial Rite', *Past and Present* (1990), 22–43

Harmer, F. *Anglo-Saxon Writs*, Manchester, Manchester University Press, 1952

Hawkes, S.E. 'The Inhumed Skeletal Material from an Early Anglo-Saxon Cemetery at Worthy Park, Kingsworthy, Hampshire, South England', *Paleobios* 1 (1983), 3–36

Hawkes, S.E. and Wells, C. 'Crime and Punishment in an Anglo-Saxon Cemetery?', *Antiquity* 49 (1975), 118–22

Henderson, J. 'Pagan Saxon Cemeteries: a Study of the Problems of Sexing by Grave-Goods and Bones', in C. Roberts, F. Lee and J. Bintliff (eds), *Burial Archaeology, Current Research, Methods and Developments*, British Archaeological Reports 211, Oxford (1989), 77–83

Herlihy, D. *Medieval Households*, Cambridge, Mass., Harvard University Press, 1985

Hill, P. *Whithorn and St Ninian: the Excavation of a Monastic Town, 1984–91*, Stroud, Sutton Publishing for the Whithorn Trust, 1997

Hills, C. 'The Anglo-Saxon Cemetery at Spong Hill, North Elmham, Part 1: Catalogue of Cremations', Gressenhall, Norfolk Archaeological Unit, East Anglian Archaeological Report 5 (1977)

Hirst, S.M. *An Anglo-Saxon Inhumation Cemetery at Sewerby, East Yorkshire*, Department of Archaeology, York University, York University Archaeological Publications 4, 1985

Hodges, R. *The Origins of Towns and trade AD 600–1000*, London, Duckworth, 2nd edn, 1989

Hooke, D. *Anglo-Saxon Landscapes of the West Midlands; the Charter Evidence*, British Archaeological Reports, British Series 95, 1981

Hull, P. and Sharpe, R. 'Peter of Cornwall and Launceston', *Cornish Studies* 13 (1986), 27

Ivens, R., Basby, P. and Shepherd, N. *Tattenhoe and Westbury: 2 Deserted Medieval Settlements in Milton Keynes*, Aylesbury, Buckinghamshire Archaeological Society Monograph Series 8, 1995

James, A. and Prout, A. (eds). *Constructing and Reconstructing Childhood*, Basingstoke, Falmer, 1990

Jenks, C. *Childhood*, London, Routledge, 1996

Keynes, S. and Lapidge, M. *Alfred the Great, Asser's 'Life of King Alfred' and other Contemporary Sources*, London, Penguin, 1983

Kingsley, C. *The Romans and the Teutons*, London, MacMillan and Company, 1864

Kinsley, A.G. *The Anglo-Saxon Cemetery at Millgate, Newark-on-Trent, Nottinghamshire*, Nottingham Archaeological Monographs 2, 1989

Kleijwegt, M. *Ancient Youth: the Ambiguity of Youth and the Absence of Adolescence in Greco-Roman Society*, Amsterdam, J.C. Gieben, 1991

Kuefler, M. 'A Wryed Existence: Attitudes toward Children in Anglo-Saxon England', *Journal of Social History* 24/4 (1991), 823–30

Kussmaul, A. *Servants and Husbandry in Early Modern England*, Cambridge, Cambridge University Press, 1981

Lancaster, L. 'Kinship in Anglo-Saxon Society', *The British Journal of Sociology*, Vol. 9, nos 3 and 4 (1957), 230–3

Larick, R. 'Age Grading and Ethnicity in the Style of Loikop (Samburu) Spears', *World Archaeology* 18/2 (1986) , 268–82

Laslett, P. (ed.). *Household and Family in Past Time: Comparative Studies in the Size and Structure of the Domestic Group*, London, Cambridge University Press, 1972

Leeds, E.T. 'A Saxon Village at Sutton Courtenay, Berkshire, Third Report', *Archaeologia* 42 (1947), 79–93

Leeds, E.T. and Harden, D.B. *The Anglo-Saxon Cemetery at Abingdon, Berkshire*, Oxford, Ashmolean Museum, 1936

Leeds, E.T. and Atkinson, R.J.C. 'The Anglo-Saxon Cemetery at Nassington', *Northants Antiquaries Journal* 24 (1944), 100–28

Lethbridge, T.C. 'An Anglo-Saxon Cemetery at Lackford, Suffolk', *Cambridge Antiquarian Society*, Quarto Publications 6, Cambridge, Bowes and Bowes, 1951

Locke, J. *An Essay Concerning Human Understanding*, London, printed for Thomas Tegg, 1689

Luard, H.R. (ed.). 'The Chronicle of Thomas de Wykes', in *Annales Monastici*, Rolls Series IV, 1865–9

Lyman, R. 'Barbarism and Religion: Late Roman and Early Medieval Childhood', in L. de Mause (ed.), *The History of Childhood*, pp. 75–100

Lynch, J. *Godparents and Kinship in Early Medieval Europe*, Princeton, Princeton University Press, 1986

McCann, J. (ed. and trans.). *The Rule of St Benedict*, London, Sheed and Ward, 1969

McCome, K.R. 'Werewolves, Cyclops, Diberge and Fianna; Juvenile Delinquency in Early Ireland', *Cambridge Medieval Celtic Studies* 12 (1986), 1–22

McLaughlin, M.M. 'Survivors and Surrogates; Children and Parents from the 9th to the 13th Centuries', in L. de Mause (ed.), *The History of Childhood*, pp. 101–82

Magnusson, M. and Palsson, H. *Njal's Saga*, London, Penguin Books, 1960

Manchester, K. 'Resurrecting the Dead: the Potential of Palaeopathology', in E. Southworth (ed.), *Anglo-Saxon Cemeteries, A Reappraisal*, Stroud, Alan Sutton, 1990, pp. 87–96

Matthews, C.L. 'The Anglo-Saxon Cemetery at Marina Drive, Dunstable', *Bedfordshire Archaeological Journal* 6 (1962), 23–6

Matthews, C. and Hawkes, S. 'Early Saxon Settlements and Burials in Puddlehill, near Dunstable, Bedfordhire', *Anglo-Saxon Studies in Archaeology and History* 4 (1985), 59–115

Mattingly, H. and Handford, S.A. (trans.). *Tacitus Germania*, London, Penguin Books, Harmondsworth, 1970

Mays, S. 'Killing the Unwanted Child', *British Archaeology* March 2 (1995), 8–9

Meaney, A. *A Gazetteer of Early Anglo-Saxon Burial Sites*, London, Allen & Unwin, 1964

———. *Anglo-Saxon Amulets and Curing Stones*, British Archaeological Reports British Series 98 (1981)

Meaney, A. and Hawkes, S.C. *The Anglo-Saxon Cemeteries at Winnall, Winchester, Hampshire*, Society for Medieval Archaeology Monograph 4, 1970

Mensch, B.S. 'The Effect of Child Mortality on Contraceptive Use and Fertility in Colombia, Costa Rica and Korea', *Population Studies* 39 (1985), 309–27

Miles, D. *Archaeology at Barton Court Farm, Abingdon; an Investigation of Late Neolithic, Iron Age, Romano-British and Saxon Settlements*, Council for British Archaeology Research Report 50, 1986

Miller, T. (ed). *The Old English Version of Bede's Ecclesiastical History of the English People*, Part 1, Early English Text Society, London, 1890

Mills, S. *The A–Z of Modern Herbalism: a Comprehensive Guide to Practical Herbal Therapy*, HarperCollins, 1989

Myres, J. and Green, B. *The Anglo-Saxon Cemeteries of Caistor-by-Norwich and Markshall, Norfolk*, London, Society of Antiquaries, Thames & Hudson, 1973

Needham G. *Aelfric: Lives of Three English Saints*, Exeter, University of Exeter, 1976

Nelson, J. 'Parents, Children and the Church in the Earlier Middle Ages', in D. Wood (ed.), *The Church and Childhood*, Studies in Church History 31, Oxford, Blackwell, 1994, pp. 81–114

Opie, I. and P. *The Lore and Language of Schoolchildren*, Oxford, Oxford University Press, 1995

Orme, N. *From Childhood to Chivalry: the Education of the English Kings and Aristocracy 1066–1530*, London, Methuen, 1984

Orton, C. *Mathematics in Archaeology*, London, Collins, 1980

Pader, E-J. *Symbolism, Social Relations and the Interpretation of Mortuary Remains*, British Archaeological Reports International Series 130, 1982

Parikh, C.K. *Parikh Textbook of Medical Jurisprudence and Toxicology*, 3rd edn, Bombay, Medical Publications, 1979

Pentikainen, J. *The Nordic Dead Child Tradition*, Helsinki, Suomalainen Tiedeakatemia, 1968

Philp, B.J. 'The Anglo-Saxon Cemetery at Polhill, Kent', in Philp, B.J. (ed.), *Excavations in West Kent 1960–1970*, Kent, Kent Archaeological Rescue Unit (1973), 164–214

Plummer, C.J. *Vitae Sanctorum Hiberniae Partium Hactenus Ineditiae*, Oxford, Clarendon Press, 1968 (reprint)

Pollock, L. *Forgotton Children: Parent/Child Relations from 1500–1900*, Cambridge, Cambridge University Press, 1983

Postman, N. *The Disappearance of Childhood*, London, W.H. Allen, 1983

Powers, R. 'A Tool for Coping with Juvenile Human Bones from Archaeological Excavations', in W. White, *The Cemetery of St Nicholas Shambles*, London and Middlesex Archaeological Society Monograph, London, 1988, pp. 74–8

Powlesland, D. in J. Hines (ed.), *The Anglo-Saxons from the Migration Period to the 8th Century: an Ethnographic Perspective*, Woodbridge, the Boydell Press, 1997, p. 164

Rahtz, P., Dickinson, T. and Watts, L. *Anglo-Saxon Cemeteries 1979: the Fourth Anglo-Saxon Symposium at Oxford*, British Archaeological Reports British Series 82, 1980

Richards, J. *The Significance of Form and Decoration of Anglo-Saxon Cremation Urns*, British Archaeological Reports British Series 166, 1987

Richardson, H.G. *Law and Legislation from Aethelberht to Magna Carta*, Edinburgh, Edinburgh University Press, 1966

Ridyard, S. *The Royal Saints of Anglo-Saxon England: a Study of West Saxon and East Anglian Cults*, Cambridge, Cambridge University Press, 1988

Robertson, A.J. *The Laws of the Kings of England from Edmund to Henry I*, Cambridge, Cambridge University Press, 1925

——. *Anglo-Saxon Charters*, Cambridge, Cambridge University Press, 1939

Rösing, F.W. 'Sexing Immature Human Skeletons', *Journal of Human Evolution* 12 (1983), 149–55

Rothwell, H. (ed.). *The Chronicle of Walter of Guisborough*, Camden third series, 39, London, Offices of the Society, 1959

Rubin, S. *Medieval English Medicine*, Newton Abbot, David and Charles, 1974

Saxe, A.A. *Social Dimensions of Mortuary Practices*, doctoral dissertation, University Microfilms, Ann Arbor, 1970

Schorsch, A. *Images of Childhood: an Illustrated Social History*, New York, Mayflower Books, 1979

Schultz, J. *The Knowledge of Childhood in the German Middle Ages, 1100–1350*, Philadelphia, University of Pennsylvania Press, 1995

Scull, C. 'Archaeology, Early Anglo-Saxon Society and the Origins of Anglo-Saxon Kingdoms', *Anglo-Saxon Studies in Archaeology and History* 6 (1993), 65–82

Sedgefield, W.J. *King Alfred's Old English Version of Boethius*, Oxford, Oxford University Press, 1899

Sennet, R. *Families Against the City: Middle Class Homes of Industrial Chicago 1872–1890*, Cambridge, Mass., Harvard University Press, 1970

Shahar, S. *Childhood in the Middle Ages*, London and New York, Routledge, 1990

Shephard, J. 'The Social Identity of the Individual in Isolated Barrows and Barrow Cemeteries in Anglo-Saxon England', in B. Burnham and J. Kingsbury (eds), *Space, Hierarchy and Society*, British Archaeological Reports International Series 59 (1979), 47–79

Sherlock, S.J. and Welch, M.G. *An Anglo-Saxon Cemetery at Norton Cleveland*, London, Council for British Archaeology Research Report 82, 1992

Shorter, E. *The Making of the Modern Family*, London, Collins, 1976

Skeat, W.W. (trans.). *Aelfric's Lives of Saints, Being a Set of Sermons on Saints' Days Formerly Observed by the English Church*, Old English Text Society Original Series, London, N. Trubner and Company, 1881

Smith, A.H. (ed.). *The Parker Chronicle 832–900*, Exeter University Press, 1980 (rev. edn)

Smith, T. (ed.). *The British Medical Association Complete Family Health Encyclopedia*, Dorling Kindersley, London, 1992 (reprint)

Somerville, C.J. *The Rise and Fall of Childhood*, Vol. 40, Sage Library of Social Research, Sage Publications Inc, Beverly Hills, Cal., 1987

Southern, R.W. (ed.). *Eadmer: The Life of St Anselm, Archbishop of Canterbury*, London, Nelson, 1962

Stone, L. *The Family, Sex and Marriage in England 1500–1800*, London, Weidenfeld & Nicolson, 1977

Swanton, M. (ed.). *Beowulf*, Manchester, Manchester University Press, 1986

Sweet, H. (ed.). *Kind Alfred's West Saxon Version of Gregory's Pastoral Care*, London Early EnglishText Society 45, 1871

Tainter, J. 'Mortuary Practices and the Study of Prehistoric Social Systems', in M. Schiffer (ed.), *Advances in Archaeological Method and Theory*, Vol. 1, London, Academic Press (1978), pp. 106–43

Talbot, C.H. *The Anglo-Saxon Missionaries in Germany, Being the Lives of SS Willibrord, Boniface, Sturm, Leoba and Lebuin, Together with the Hodoeporicon of St Willibald and a Selection From the Correspondence of St Boniface*, London, Sheed and Ward, 1954

Thorpe, B. *Penitential of Theodore*, London, 1840

———. *The Homilies of the Anglo-Saxon Church: The Homilies of Aelfric Vol. II*, London, printed for the Aelfric Society, 1846

Thrupp, J. *The Anglo-Saxon Home: a History of the Domestic Insitiutions and Customs of England, from the 5th to the 11th Century*, London, 1862

Timby, J.R. *The Anglo-Saxon Cemetery at Empingham II, Rutland: Excavations carried out between 1974 and 1975*, Oxford, Oxbow Books, 1996

Trease, G.E. and Evans, W.C. *Pharmacognosy*, 11th edn, London, Balliere Tindall, 1978

Turner, T. 'The Social Skin: Interface with the World', *New Scientist* 82 (1979), 821–3

Ullrich, H. 'Estimation of Fertility by Means of Pregnancy and Childbirth Alteration at the Pubis, the Illium and the Sacrum', *Ossa* pt 1 (1975), 23–39

van Es, W.A. *Wijster, a Native Village Beyond the Imperial Frontier, 150–425 AD*, Groningen, J.B. Wolters, 1967

Van Gennep, A. *The Rites of Passage* (first published as *Les Rites de Passage*, 1932), Chicago, Phoenix Books, University of Chicago Press, 1960

Venezky, R. and Healey, A. de P. *A Microfiche Concordance to Old English*, Newark, Delaware, University of Delaware, 1980

Wade Martins, P. *Swaffham, the Anglo-Saxon Cemetery*, East Anglian Archaeology 2, Gressenhall, Norfolk Archaeological Unit, Norfolk Museums Service, 1976

Waldron, T. *Counting the Dead: the Epidemiology of Skeletal Populations*, Chichester, Wiley, 1994

Wall, R. 'Mean Household Size in England from Printed Sources', in P. Laslett (ed.), *Household and Family in Past Time*, pp. 159–294

Waterbolk, H.T. 'Odoorn im fruhen Mittelalter. Bericht der Grabung 1966', *Neue Ausgraben und Funde in Niedersachsen* 8 (1973), 25–90

Watts, D. 'Infant Burials and Romano-British Christianity', *Archaeological Journal* 146 (1989), 372–83

Wedlake, W.J. 'Excavations at Camerton, Somerset; a Record of Thirty Year's Excavation Covering the Period from Neolithic to Saxon Times 1926–56', Camerton Excavation Club, 1958

Wells, C. 'The Human Bones', in P. Wade Martins (ed.), 'Excavations in North Elmham Park 1967–1972', Vol. II, *East Anglian Archaeology* 9 (1980), Gressenhall, Norfolk Archaeological Unit, Norfolk Museums Service, 247–374

West, S. *West Stow: the Anglo-Saxon Village, East Anglian Archaeology* 24, 1985

——. *Westgarth Gardens Anglo-Saxon Cemetery, Suffolk Catalogue, East Anglian Archaeology* 38, 1988

White, R. 'Roman and Celtic Objects from Anglo-Saxon Graves', British Archaeological Reports British Series 191, Oxford (1988)

Whitelock, D. (ed.). *Anglo-Saxon Wills*, Cambridge, Cambridge University Press, 1930

——. (ed.). *Sweet's Anglo-Saxon Reader in Verse and Prose*, Oxford, Oxford University Press, 1967

——. (ed.). *Sermo Lupi Ad Anglos Exeter Medieval English Texts*, Exeter, University of Exeter, 1976

——. (ed.). *English Historical Documents I c500–1042*, 2nd edn, London, Eyre Methuen, 1979

Wiedemann, T. *Adults and Children in the Roman Empire*, London, Routledge, 1989

Wilkinson, L. 'Problems of Analysis and Interpretation of Skeletal Remains', in P. Rahtz, T. Dickinson and L. Watts (eds), *Anglo-Saxon Cemeteries 1979: the Fourth Anglo-Saxon Symposium at Oxford*, pp. 221–31

Wilson, D. *Anglo-Saxon Paganism*, London, Routledge, 1992

Woodward, M. (ed.). *Gerard's Herball*, London, The Minerva Press, 1971

Index

Numbers in *italics* refer to illustrations